LIFE OF THE TRAIL 5 HISTORIC HIKES AROUND MOUNT ASSINIBOINE & IN KANANASKIS COUNTRY

LIFE OF THE TRAIL 5 HISTORIC HIKES AROUND MOUNT ASSINIBOINE & IN KANANASKIS COUNTRY

Emerson Sanford & Janice Sanford Beck

Victoria Vancouver Calgary

Rocky Mountain Books
#108 – 17665 66A Avenue
Surrey, BC V3S 2A7
www.rmbooks.com

Library and Archives Canada Cataloguing in Publication

Sanford, Emerson
Historic hikes around Mount Assiniboine & in Kananaskis Country / Emerson Sanford & Janice Sanford Beck.

(Life of the trail ; 5)
Includes bibliographical references and index.
ISBN 978-1-897522-80-6

1. Hiking—Assiniboine, Mount (Alta. and B.C.)—Guidebooks. 2. Trails—Assiniboine, Mount (Alta. and B.C.)—Guidebooks. 3. Hiking—Assiniboine, Mount (Alta. and B.C.)—History. 4. Assiniboine, Mount (Alta. and B.C.)—Guidebooks. 5. Hiking—Alberta—Kananaskis Country—Guidebooks. 6. Trails—Alberta—Kananaskis Country—Guidebooks. 7. Hiking—Alberta—Kananaskis Country—History. 8. Kananaskis Country (Alta.)—Guidebooks.
I. Beck, Janice Sanford, 1975- II. Title. III. Series: Life of the trail 5

GV199.44.C22A4582 2010 796.51097123'32 C2009-907202-5

Front cover photo: Mount Assiniboine. Photo by Robert William Sandford
Back cover photo: Whyte Museum of the Canadian Rockies, NA- 66-2402

Printed in Canada

Rocky Mountain Books acknowledges the financial support for its publishing program from the Government of Canada through the Canada Book Fund (CBF), Canada Council for the Arts, and the province of British Columbia through the British Columbia Arts Council and the Book Publishing Tax Credit.

This book has been printed with FSC-certified, acid-free papers, processed chlorine free and printed with vegetable based inks.

Disclaimer

The actions described in this book may be considered inherently dangerous activities. Individuals undertake these activities at their own risk. The information put forth in this guide has been collected from a variety of sources and is not guaranteed to be completely accurate or reliable. Many conditions and some information may change owing to weather and numerous other factors beyond the control of the authors and publishers. Individual climbers and/or hikers must determine the risks, use their own judgment, and take full responsibility for their actions. Do not depend on any information found in this book for your own personal safety. Your safety depends on your own good judgment based on your skills, education, and experience.

It is up to the users of this guidebook to acquire the necessary skills for safe experiences and to exercise caution in potentially hazardous areas. The authors and publishers of this guide accept no responsibility for your actions or the results that occur from another's actions, choices, or judgments. If you have any doubt as to your safety or your ability to attempt anything described in this guidebook, do not attempt it.

Library and Archives Canada Cataloguing in Publication

The survival of adventurers and those who desired to know the land beyond, travelling for months away from civilization into rough, barren country, depended on carefully prepared outfits. The lowly packhorse has assured the success of many expeditions, and he is too rarely given credit for his accomplishments.

—F.O. (Pat) Brewster, *They Came West: Pat's Tales of the Early Days* [1]

Contents

Acknowledgements 11

Introduction 13

Route I
Site of the Cross: Duncan McGillivray's Route from the Bow River to the Kootenay River over White Man Pass 23
- Chronology 25
- History
  - Fur Traders, Missionaries and Spies 27
  - East–West Travellers 39
  - Mountaineers and Grizzlies 40
- The Trail Today 44
- Trail Guide
  - Old Bow Fort to the Cross River along the Spray Lakes and over White Man Pass 47
  - Devil's Gap to Canmore over Carrot Creek Summit 51

Route II
Reclusive Hideout: Sir George Simpson's Route from Devil's Gap (Lake Minnewanka) to the Kootenay River over Simpson Pass 57
- Chronology 59
- History
  - Banff's First Tourist 61
  - Roads, Prospectors and Campers 67
  - Lake Minnewanka 73
- The Trail Today 78
- Trail Guide
  - Devil's Gap to the Vermilion River over Simpson Pass 81

Route III
Lost on High Passes: James Sinclair's Route from Old Bow Fort to the Kootenay River over North Kananaskis Pass 89

Chronology		91
History	Following the Compass	92
	Exploring the Pass	96
	Overlanders	98
	Pleasure Seekers	101
The Trail Today		103
Trail Guide	Old Bow Fort to the Palliser River over North Kananaskis Pass	106

Route IV
Outfitting the Mountaineers: Tom Wilson's Route from the Simpson River to Mount Assiniboine over Ferro Pass 113

Chronology		115
History	First Visit	116
	Alternate Route	122
	Early Explorers	127
	A Cut Trail	130
The Trail Today		131
Trail Guide	Simpson River to Lake Magog (Mount Assiniboine) over Ferro Pass	133

Route V
Fast Lane: Tom Wilson's Route from Simpson Pass to Mount Assiniboine over Citadel Pass. 137

Chronology		139
History	Lost on the Trail	140
	First Ascents	143
	Non-climbers	149
The Trail Today		154
Trail Guide	Simpson Pass to Lake Magog (Mount Assiniboine) over Citadel Pass	159

Route VI
Walking Tour: Walter Wilcox's Route along the Spray River to Assiniboine Pass and Palliser Pass 163
Chronology 165
History
Bryant Creek 167
A Night in the Woods 168
The Business of Tourism 170
All in a Day's Work 172
Mountaineering at Palliser Pass 173
The Trail Today 180
Trail Guide
Mount Shark Parking Area to Trail Centre Junction 182
Trail Centre Junction to Mount Assiniboine Lodge over Assiniboine Pass 183
Trail Centre Junction to Banff along the Spray Lakes, Goat Creek and the Spray River 185
Trail Centre Junction to Leroy Creek along the Spray River and over Palliser Pass 187

Route VII
Talc Trail: Redearth Creek Route to Ball Pass, Redearth Pass and Gibbon Pass 191
Chronology 194
History
Scouting out the Area 196
Seeds of a Trail 199
The Cutting Begins 205
The Trail Today 210
Trail Guide
Bow River to Vermilion River up Redearth Creek and over Ball Pass 214
Healy Creek to Highway 93 over Healy, Whistling and Gibbon Passes 216
Redearth Creek to Natalko Lake along Pharaoh Creek 220

Notes 223
Image Credits 228
Bibliography 231
Index 233
About the Authors 239

Acknowledgements

The preparation for a book of this type requires the perusal of many secondary sources; during our research we read hundreds of books. The authors of the books used are acknowledged in the Notes section at the end of this book. Many of the books are still in print and readily available. Others required much diligence on the part of reference librarians to obtain interlibrary loans, and we wish to thank the personnel at the Canmore Public Library, especially Michelle Preston and Helene Lafontaine, for their assistance. Other books and documents were available only through the Whyte Museum and Archives, and we appreciate the efforts of Lena Goon, Elizabeth Kundert-Cameron, D.L. Cameron and Ted Hart in steering us on the right track and obtaining materials for us.

The Alpine Club of Canada in Canmore kindly allowed us the use of their collection of the *Canadian Alpine Journal*. Others who provided useful discussion and/or materials during the course of the research were: Carol at the Bruce Peel Special Collections Library at the University of Alberta, who was diligent in her search for the J.N. Wallace Manuscript Collection; Ron Tozer, Algonquin Park archivist; Lorna Dishkin of the BC Central Coast Archives; Keith Cole; Rene Morton; Thomas Peterson; Jon

Whelan; I.S. MacLaren; Meghan Power, Jasper-Yellowhead Museum and Archives (JYMA); Melanie Gagnon, Library and Archives Canada; and Kelly-Ann Turkington, Royal British Columbia Museum (RBCM).

A large part of the effort in preparing these volumes was in hiking all of the trails and routes described in the history section. Emerson wishes to thank his wife, Cheryl, for the many hours she spent taking him to trailheads and picking him up several days later at a different location, sometimes on remote gravel roads that were not easily accessible. Cheryl always had in hand a copy of the itinerary for the hike in order to contact the Warden Service if the solo hiker did not emerge from the wilderness at the appointed time (he always did).

In addition, Emerson wishes to acknowledge the many hikers on remote backcountry trails who stopped to chat and made the solitary hikes more enjoyable. Many of these are mentioned in the text. Others who do not receive mention were on trails near Lake Minnewanka, Athabasca Pass, Wildflower Creek valley, the Jasper Park north and south boundaries, Job Pass, the Rockwall and undoubtedly others. There were also several wardens along the way who contributed to the enjoyment of the backcountry experience.

For Janice, this project has been a labour of love, squeezed in amongst various family, community and work responsibilities. She would like to thank her partner, Shawn, and children, Robin, Rowan and Christopher, for their willingness to accommodate the time required for a project of this magnitude. She would also like to thank her parents for sharing their love of history and introducing her to the trails these volumes bring to life. Finally, the authors would like to express their appreciation to Don Gorman, Meaghan Craven, Chyla Cardinal and others at Rocky Mountain Books for their efforts in bringing this work from manuscript to publication.

Introduction

Like the earliest travels through the Rockies, today's excursions most often take place on foot. Between the time of the earliest Aboriginal travellers and contemporary backpackers, however, pack horses played a key role in transporting adventurers through the Rockies. Whether searching for game, trade, passage to the West or simply adventure, these expeditions depended heavily on the strength and endurance of their pack horses. Though Aboriginal travels through the Rockies began long before the acquisition of horses, it stands to reason that the Native-bred cayuse, whose forbearers had been the earliest domesticated animals to travel through the Rocky Mountains, would be best adapted to the terrain of the Rockies. Indeed, though greenhorns were not always confident in the beasts, veteran travellers generally agreed that the cayuse was the animal of choice.

The history of exploration in the Canadian Rockies can be divided into four periods: Aboriginal travellers, fur-trade explorers, railway men and scientists, and tourist-explorers and mountaineers. The cayuse began gaining its experience during the first of these phases. Aboriginal peoples are documented to have travelled through the mountains for purposes of hunting and trade for over 11,000 years. They began using horses to

Pack trains like this one are seldom seen on backcountry trails in the Rocky Mountains. In the era of the pack train, horses were not tied together or to a saddle horse as these heavily laden creatures are – nor did the trails tend to be in such good condition.

facilitate their travels through the Rockies around 1730 and continued to do so through the remainder of the first period of exploration. Unfortunately, however, these travels were not documented; our knowledge of them is primarily based upon the evidence of what trails the people left, tent poles and fire rings in campsites and the knowledge Aboriginal guides were able to impart to travellers of subsequent eras.

Not surprisingly, horses also formed a cornerstone of non-Aboriginal exploration in the Rockies. Though canoes and snowshoes are more commonly considered the vehicles for fur-trade transportation, horses were equally essential, particularly in the exploratory phases. David Thompson used horses on his arduous trip from Rocky Mountain House to the Athabasca River in 1810; later, a large herd of horses was kept at Jasper House for the use of fur traders crossing Athabasca Pass. The horses transported goods from the Athabasca River toward the pass and, when conditions allowed, sometimes even across the pass to Boat Encampment.

By the time of the third period of exploration, that of the railway surveyors and scientists, pack horses were well entrenched in their role in alpine travel. Between the Palliser Expedition of 1858 and the 1885 completion of the Canadian Pacific Railway, scientific types keen to assess the Rockies' suitability for settlement, transport and mineral exploitation were travelling throughout the region – virtually always on horseback – gathering as much information as they could about its natural features.

Once the railway surveyors' efforts had culminated in the completion of the Canadian Pacific Railway, visitors from the East began flocking to the mountains. The more timid remained in the railway hotels that had been established along the route, but the adventurous brought the era of the tourist-explorers and mountaineers to the Canadian Rockies. Until the 1930s, when the invention of lightweight Egyptian cotton tents and sleeping bags, steel-framed backpacks and the Primus stove made backpacking possible, pack horses were essential to the exploits of these adventurers.

For centuries, travellers had known the challenges of getting horses through the alpine timber but relied on hired hands to cut only as much trail as absolutely essential for passage; in the era of the tourist-explorers and mountaineers, Canadian authorities decided it was worthwhile to begin a trail-cutting program. The Banff Hot Springs Reserve had been set aside as a national preserve in 1885 and expanded into Rocky Mountains Park (today's Banff National Park) two years later. In 1909 Fire and Game Guardians were hired to protect the park, and by 1914 some 60 trails had been cut through the park to facilitate their patrols. By 1920 the Fire and Game Guardian Service had become the Warden Service and was patrolling 1,400 miles (2250 kilometres) of trails through the park. Wardens curious about the surrounding areas often explored side valleys along their patrols, thus establishing at least some of the non-historic trails within the parks. All of these trails were cut with a view to allowing passage on horseback.

By the 1930s, when the era of the pack train had come to an end, the network of mountain trails had essentially attained its current status. Very few trails have been cut since then, mostly only realignment or replacement of existing trails to preserve or rehabilitate ecologically sensitive areas – or to divert hikers from river crossings suitable for horses but not pedestrians. With the motor car and lightweight camping equipment democratizing alpine travel, so many visitors were able to access and use this network of trails that telling their tales would be nigh impossible. For this reason, our narrative draws to an end as the pack train recedes from the forefront.

The Life of the Trail series narrates historic routes through the Rockies. The individual volumes each concentrate on specific regions, with those regions primarily defined by the geographical boundaries that influenced nineteenth-century travellers. The series presents volumes in order of entry by non-Aboriginal explorers, and routes within each volume are described in order of first use. Each book, designed to fit neatly into a pack, outlines the history of the routes in its region, giving modern-day travellers a feel for how they were established and who has used the trails since.

Life of the Trail 1 records historic routes and hikes in the area bounded by the North Saskatchewan River on the north and the Mistaya River, Bow River and Lake Minnewanka on the west and south. The most historically significant trip in this area was David Thompson's journey along the Red Deer River to meet the Kootenay people and take them back to Rocky Mountain House. Later, the Aboriginal route over Pipestone Pass to the Kootenay Plains was used extensively by tourist-explorers and mountaineers. Today this area is bounded by the David Thompson Highway (#11) in the north and the Icefields Parkway (#93), the Bow Valley Parkway (#1A) and Lake Minnewanka on the west and south.

The earliest fur-trade route across the Rockies was over Howse Pass. The trail is described in *Life of the Trail 2*, which presents the area bounded by the Kicking Horse River to the south; the Columbia Icefields to the north; and the Bow, Mistaya and North Saskatchewan rivers to the east. Later explorers created a popular return trip from the Kootenay Plains by adding an old Native trail down the Amiskwi River to the Howse Pass route. Also included in the volume are the Yoho Valley and the Castleguard Meadows. Today that area is bounded by the Trans-Canada Highway to the south and the Icefields Parkway to the east.

Life of the Trail 3 describes a single route. It follows the Bow River to Bow Pass, then the Mistaya, North Saskatchewan, Sunwapta and Athabasca rivers to the junction with the Miette. Today this is the route of the Trans-Canada Highway and Highway 1A to Lake Louise and the Icefields Parkway north to Jasper.

Life of the Trail 4 details the history of three nineteenth-century fur-trade routes and one twentieth-century trail through what is now the southeastern section of Jasper National Park. The area is bounded by the North Saskatchewan River on the south and west, and by the Sunwapta and Athabasca rivers on the west and north. The fur-trade routes of Duncan McGillivray along the Brazeau River and Poboktan Creek, Jacques Cardinal along the southern boundary of Jasper National Park and on into the Job and Coral Creek valleys, and Michael Klyne along Maligne Lake and on into the White Goat Wilderness form the backbone of the trails in the area today. In the 1930s, Fred Brewster developed the Skyline Trail. Today the area is bounded by the David Thompson Highway (#11) in the south, the Icefields Parkway (#93) to the west and the Yellowhead Highway (#16) in the north.

This book, *Life of the Trail 5*, details the early history of the large area bounded on the north by Lake Minnewanka and the Bow River and on the west by Altrude Creek and the Vermilion and Kootenay rivers. Today's boundaries are Lake Minnewanka and the Trans-Canada Highway in the north and Highway 93 on the west. The two main driving forces for excursions into the region were to use White Man, North Kananaskis and Simpson passes to cross the Continental Divide, as well as to find routes leading to Mount Assiniboine. Early use of all three passes was a direct result of the fur trade, with Duncan McGillivray leading the way over White Man Pass, followed by George Simpson over Simpson Pass and James Sinclair over North Kananaskis Pass. Following closely behind these early explorers were the Overlanders, who sought a route to the goldfields in central British Columbia. After the Canadian Pacific Railway ushered the era of the tourist-explorer into Banff, routes to Mount Assiniboine were established over Ferro and Citadel passes to the west and Assiniboine Pass to the east. The volume is rounded out with details of the talc mining activity in the Egypt Lakes area.

Unlike other books in the *Life of the Trail* series, *Life of the Trail 5* covers an area that is a maze of parks and trails today. It is made up of parts of Banff and Kootenay national parks, Mount Assiniboine and Height of the Rockies provincial parks in British Columbia, and Kananaskis Country in Alberta – which includes the established Peter Lougheed and Bow Valley provincial parks, as well as several new ones:

Canmore Nordic Centre, Spray Valley, Bow Valley Wildland, Don Getty and Sheep-Elbow Wildland provincial parks. The trails interconnect in such a manner that there is no simple way to present the history of the area. The early historic routes – routes I, II and III – are fairly straightforward. McGillivray, Simpson and Sinclair wanted only to get through the mountains by the shortest possible route. Route IV, the Ferro Pass route to Mount Assiniboine, is also straightforward in and of itself, but the route can be accessed from either Vermilion or Simpson passes. The route to Mount Assiniboine through the Valley of the Rocks becomes more complicated. It can be accessed over Simpson Pass, through Sunshine Meadows or along the Simpson River and Vermilion Pass. The exit from Mount Assiniboine becomes even more complicated; once travellers reached Bryant Creek's junction with the Spray River, they could choose to travel north along the Spray River or the Spray Lakes or use Goat Creek to traverse from one trail to the other. Alternatively, they could travel south over White Man Pass, Palliser Pass and North Kananaskis Pass, or east along the Watridge Lake route. The Redearth Creek area is also confusing, as travellers could choose to travel west over Gibbon Pass, south over Ball Pass, east along Pharaoh Creek or through Whistling Valley. We have tried to present the history of the trails in as meaningful a way as possible but suggest that extensive use of the route maps may help avoid confusion as you follow the exploits of the early travellers, who often crossed from one route to another.

With the help of these maps and a little imagination, you will be able to accompany army spies Warre and Vavasour on the top secret mission over White Man Pass or join Hudson's Bay Company Governor Sir George Simpson on the first non-Aboriginal passage over Simpson Pass. You can tag along with James Sinclair and the 123 Red River Métis he leads over North Kananaskis Pass toward their new home in the Oregon Territory. Or if pleasure travel is more your style, you can join Walter Wilcox as he struggles to find outfitter Tom Wilson's suggested route to Mount Assiniboine over Citadel Pass. Alternatively, you can travel with Bill Peyto as he successfully follows Wilson's suggested route with mountaineer James Outram. And you can wrap up your tour by visiting eccentric mountain man Bill Peyto's talc mines near the Egypt Lakes and accompanying the very first backpackers in the Rockies, honeymooners Andrew S. Sibbald and his wife, as they traverse the difficult terrain between Vermilion Pass and the Sunshine Meadows without the assistance of horses.

Reading this volume, you will also gain the information you need to follow in their footsteps. Over the years, the authors have hiked many of these trails together. In the early twenty-first century, Emerson re-hiked each and every one of them to ensure the most accurate trail information possible. When we use the first person "I" in descriptions of adventures along the trails, we refer to Emerson and his experiences. We provide a complete trail guide for all routes, including those that do not fall within park boundaries, and we have highlighted the trails on a topographic map. Each section begins with a brief overview of the history of that portion of the trail, followed by stories of the known travellers who helped make it what it is today. With this book in your pack, you will be able to recline by the evening's campfire and share kinship with those who have gone before, no doubt agreeing with Andrew S. Sibbald that:

> [Backpack] travel is too arduous to be undertaken unless in first class physical condition. Equipment must be exactly adapted to the party so as to maintain that physical condition without including an extra ounce of weight. The person in charge should know the general topography of the country and have something of the capacity to find one's way by salient peaks and watercourses. There must be a readiness at times to experience real fatigue. But, granted these things and a willingness to prepare thoroughly and, if need be, to endure greatly, I know of no better way to see the Rockies than to go as a pilgrim with staff in hand and bundle on shoulder. It is so, and probably only so, that one can learn to know intimately their greatness and beauty, their power and their peace.[2]

BANFF
NAT'L
PARK
KOOTENAY
NAT'L
Mt. Assiniboine
Prov. Park
BANFF
CANMORE
Moraine Lake Lodge
Castle Mtn. Village
Johnston Canyon
Storm Mtn. Lodge
Stewart Canyon
Mount Norquay Ski Area
Lake Minnewanka
Ghost Lake
Devils Gap
Mount Inglismaldie
Carrot Cr. Summit
Harvie Heights
Stoney I.R. 142 143 144
Old Bow Fort
Nakoda Lodge
Seebe
Bow Valley P.P.
Exshaw
Dead Man's Flats
The Three Sisters
Lac des Arcs
Cave & Basin
Canmore Nordic Centre
Mount Rundle
Sundance Range
Brewster Creek
Bourgeau Parking Lot
Sunshine Village Ski Area
Fatigue Mtn.
Fatigue Pass
Allenby Pass
Valley of the Rocks
Golden Valley
Og L.
Police Meadows
Continental Divide
Mt. Bourgeau
Healy Cr.
Egypt L.
Shadow Lake Lodge
Shadow Lake
Ball Pass
Gibbon Pass
Arnica L.
Vista L.
Twin Lks.
Copper Mtn.
Redearth Cr.
Altrude Lks.
Boom L.
Vermilion Pass
Marble Canyon
Mt. Ball
Tokumm Cr.
Vermilion R.
Hawk Cr.
Floe Lake Parking Lot
Kootenay Parkway
The Rockwall
Floe L.
Mummy L.
Natalko L.
Verdant
The Monarch
Kootenay Park Lodge
Simpson
Surprise Cr.
Ferro Pass
Cerulean L.
Assiniboine Pass
Mt. Assiniboine Lodge
Lake Magog
Mt. Assiniboine
Lake Gloria
Wonder Pass
Marvel Lake
Bryant Cr.
Mitchell
Split Pk.
Mt. Harkin
Brisco Range
Spray River
Goat Cr.
Spray Lakes Reservoir
Canyon Dam
Mt. Lougheed
Nakiska Ski Area
Kananaskis Village
Mt. Engadine Lodge
Karst Springs
Fortress Mtn. Ski Area
Watridge
Currie Cr.
White Man Cr.
Mt. Shark
Commonwealth Pk.
Smith-Dorrien
Spray R.
White Man Pass
Burstall Pass
Peter
Kananaskis
Thomas Cr.
Mt. Howard
Elbow R.
Ghost R.
South
Old Fort Cr.
Cascade River
Forty Mile Cr.
Bow River
Alberta
BC
C P R
1
1A
93
40

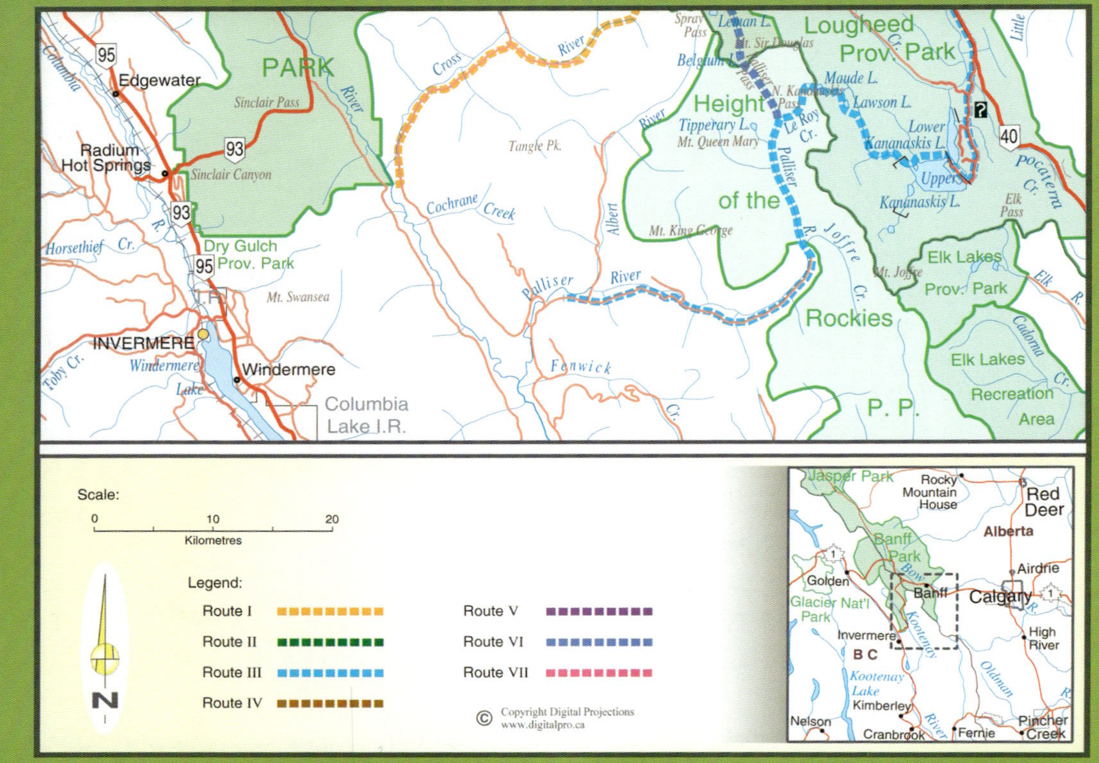
Edgewater
Radium Hot Springs
PARK
Sinclair Pass
Sinclair Canyon
Dry Gulch Prov. Park
Mt. Swansea
INVERMERE
Windermere Lake
Windermere
Columbia Lake I.R.
Horsethief Cr.
Toby Cr.
Columbia
Cross River
Tangle Pk.
Cochrane Creek
Albert River
Palliser River
Fenwick Cr.
Height of the Rockies P. P.
Tipperary L.
Mt. Queen Mary
Mt. King George
Joffre Cr.
Le Roy Cr.
Lougheed Prov. Park
Maude L.
Lawson L.
Lower Kananaskis L.
Upper Kananaskis L.
Elk Pass
Pocaterra Cr.
Elk Lakes Prov. Park
Elk Lakes Recreation Area
Cadorna Cr.
Elk R.
Scale:
0 10 20
Kilometres
Legend:
Route I
Route II
Route III
Route IV
Route V
Route VI
Route VII
N
© Copyright Digital Projections
www.digitalpro.ca
Jasper Park
Rocky Mountain House
Red Deer
Alberta
Banff Park
Airdrie
Golden
Banff
Calgary
Glacier Nat'l Park
Invermere
B C
High River
Kootenay Lake
Kimberley
Oldman
Nelson
Cranbrook
Fernie
Pincher Creek

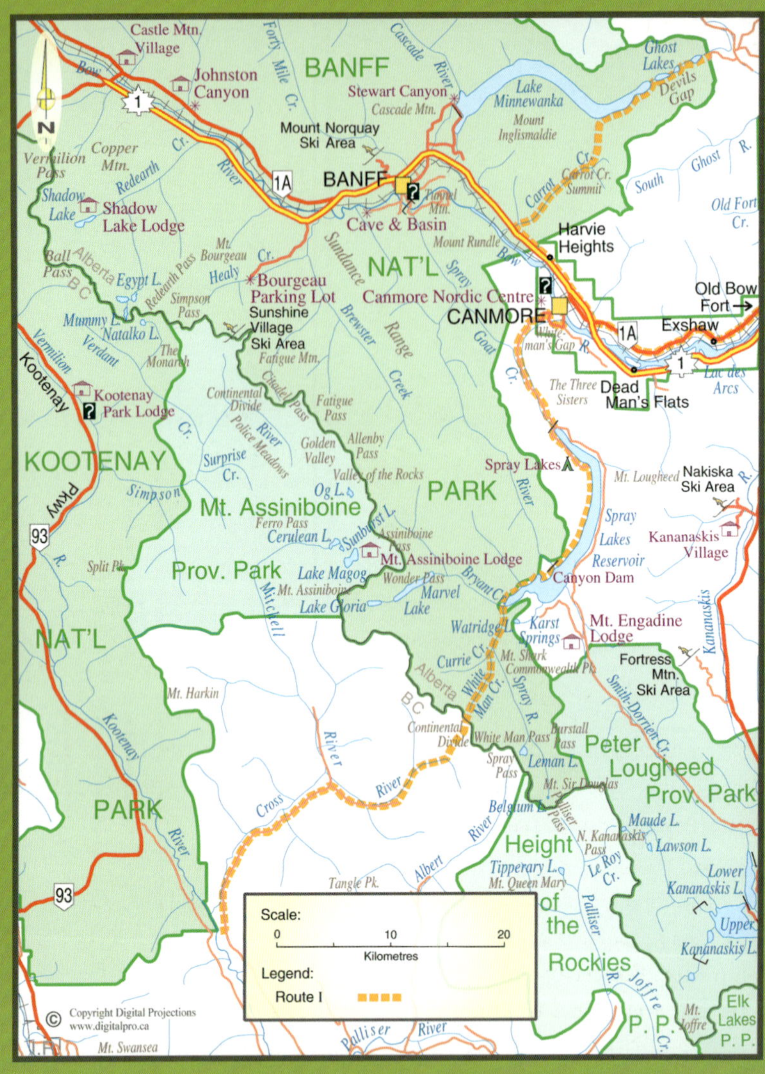

Duncan McGillivray's Route from the Bow River to the Kootenay River over White Man Pass

Route I

Site of the Cross: Duncan McGillivray's Route from the Bow River to the Kootenay River over White Man Pass

It had been a long hike to the campsite at the end of Lake Minnewanka. The trail I had been following was largely a new one, built after the Trans-Alta dam flooded the valley in 1940. My objectives were to explore the area at the head of the lake – the Ghost Lakes and Ghost River diversion – and, even more important, to investigate James Sinclair's route along the south shore of Lake Minnewanka to the Carrot Creek Summit trail.

The gravel flats of the Ghost River east of the Ghost Lakes had been greatly manipulated by heavy machinery and therefore held little interest for me. But the diversion of the Ghost River into Lake Minnewanka appears to have had little impact on the area immediately surrounding the Ghost Lakes. Following the trail along the Ghost Lakes and the south shore of Lake Minnewanka took me back nearly 170 years to James Sinclair and his incredible feat leading men, women, children, horses and cattle halfway across a continent.

The trail I trod upon appeared to be the same one Sinclair had used. Modern trails, cut after the lake was flooded, were laid out by surveyors and cut by contractors. They tend to be straight, except when major obstacles need to be circumnavigated. Aboriginal trails, developed centuries earlier during a period when saving time was less of an imperative and iron tools were not necessarily available, did not attempt to maintain a straight line but simply detoured around trees, stumps, rocks and wet spots. Trails of this type are very evident to the careful observer, and the trail on the south side of the lakes certainly fit this category. Slowly walking along this trail and allowing my mind to wander permitted me to briefly re-live some of the area's colourful past and renew my awe at how Sinclair managed to successfully execute his remarkable feat.

Two of the three Ghost Lakes are shown in this image, taken looking east toward Devil's Gap. The trail Simpson and Sinclair would have followed was to the right of the lakes.

Chronology

1801 Duncan McGillivray and David Thompson successfully use White Man Pass to cross the Rockies south of the Bow River. They follow the Columbia downstream to reach Athabasca Pass, which leads them back to the eastern side of the Rockies.

1841 James Sinclair leads a party of 23 Métis families – 123 people and two hundred head of cattle – over White Man Pass to the Oregon Territory.

An Irish-born American prospector, Joe Healy, claims to have arrived in the Bow Valley by travelling down the Spray River. If his claims are true, he most likely crossed White Man Pass.

1845 Father Jean de Smet decides to cross the Rockies on a peace mission to the Blackfoot. His party follows the Cross River to the summit of White Man Pass, where de Smet has a cross erected.

Lieutenants Henry James Warre and Mervin Vavasour, two army officers disguised as gentlemen of leisure, cross White Man Pass on their way to the Oregon Territory as part of a secret mission for the British government.

1850 At Simpson's request, James Sinclair and Chief Maskapetoon of the Wetaskiwin Cree cross White Man Pass to investigate the condition of Hudson's Bay Company (HBC) forts in the Oregon Territory.

1881 Major A.B. Rogers, engineer-in-charge of the mountain division of the Canadian Pacific Railway, makes his way through the Brisco Range and along Sinclair's route up the Cross River, over White Man Pass and along the Spray River and Lakes to the site of present-day Canmore.

1883 Geologist George Mercer Dawson crosses White Man Pass and names the Cross River, which flows down its western side. He translates the Aboriginal name, "tshakooap-te-ha-wapta," to White Man Pass.

PRIOR TO 1894 Colonel Robert O'Hara is one of the first non-Native people to attempt to reach Mount Assiniboine from the east. He travels though Canmore, crosses Whiteman's Gap and probably follows the west shore of the Spray Lakes before being turned back by forest fires.

1901 Tourist-explorers Walter Wilcox and Henry Bryant follow the Spray Lakes to their junction with the Spray River and Bryant Creek. Some of the party continues following the Spray River and crosses a pass, likely White Man Pass, into the Cross River valley.

1914 Oscar Lovgren, a young Swede pursuing a grizzly near White Man Pass, reports that he has killed the bear and returns to the site with two companions. As they approach, the wounded grizzly charges. Lovgren has no time to react, and the bruin crushes his skull with one mighty swing of its front paw.

Not far above the Grassi Lakes on a large rock in the canyon leading to the top of Whiteman's Gap, there are pictographs of a man and a caribou, thought to have been painted nearly 1000 years ago by ancestors of today's Kootenay people.

History

Fur Traders, Missionaries and Spies

Rocks and cliff faces in the upper canyon just before the top of Whiteman's Gap are adorned with pictographs believed to be more than 1000 years old – strong evidence that Aboriginal peoples (most recently Stoneys and Kootenays) have long used the route. The first "white men" to traverse White Man Pass (so named by George Mercer Dawson) were North West Company (NWC or Nor'wester) fur traders Duncan McGillivray and David Thompson. In 1800 Thompson, having been sent to Rocky Mountain House to help McGillivray find a route through the mountains, had distinguished himself as the first recorded non-Aboriginal person to enter the Canadian Rockies south of the Peace River. He and McGillivray conducted numerous exploratory journeys that winter,[1] but they were unable to find a route through the Rockies.

Thankfully, their fortunes improved later in the summer of 1801. McGillivray, Thompson and their men travelled southward to enter the Rocky Mountains via the Bow River (which McGillivray and Thompson had explored the previous year). They crossed the river then continued south through a remarkable notch in the mountains just south of today's town of Canmore. Today this notch is known as Whiteman's Gap. After passing through the gap, they followed an old Native trail along the Spray Lakes and River to White Man Pass.[2]

From the top of the pass, today's Cross River led the traders to the Kootenay River and south to Kootenay Lake. On his map of the Northwest, Thompson called the mountains they crossed Duncan's Mountains and the Kootenay River and Lake M'Gillivray's River and M'Gillivray's Lake, in accordance with the custom of the time of naming natural features after the first person of importance to see or use the feature. These names are taken as evidence that McGillivray and Thompson were actually in the area.[3] White Man Pass, as it was known to the Kootenays on its west side, was probably named for being the pass through which the first white man (Duncan McGillivray) entered the country.

Above: David Thompson and Duncan McGillivray are considered by some scholars to be the first white men to have crossed the Continental Divide over White Man Pass. They made the trek in 1801, and the name of the pass likely refers to them. This is an artist's depiction of what Thompson may have looked like, since no image exists.

Left: This break in the mountains, with Mount Rundle on the right and Ha Ling Peak on the left, is known today as Whiteman's Gap. It allowed early travellers access to a relatively easy pass over the Continental Divide (White Man Pass). As can be seen in this photo, today Whiteman's Gap contains the Spray Lakes Road on the right and the penstock feeding a power plant, in the centre.

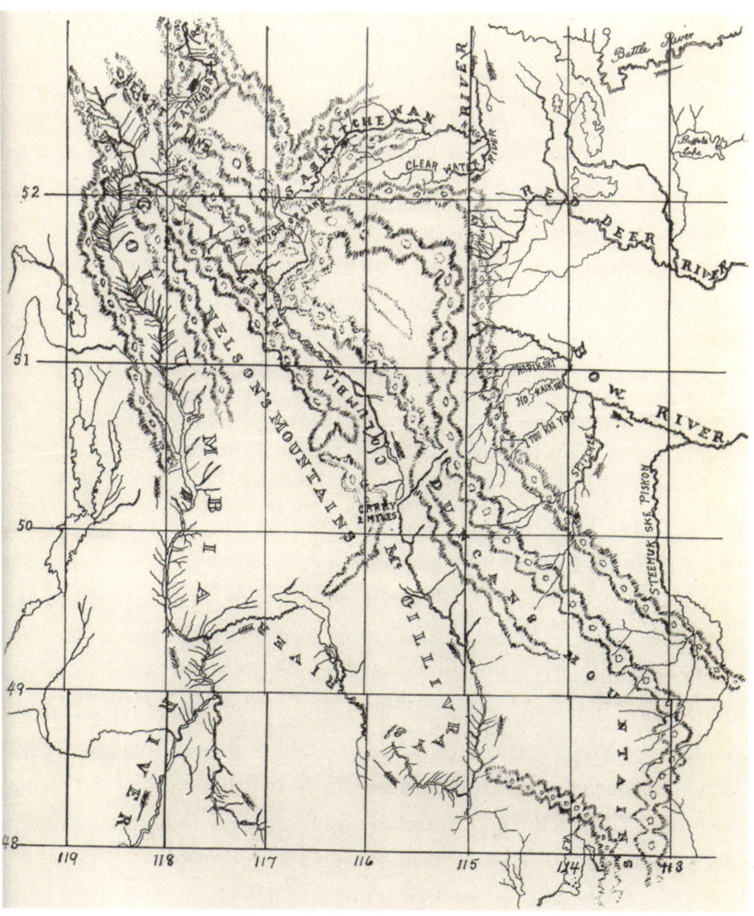

This portion of David Thompson's great map of the Northwest shows Duncan's Mountains and M'Gillivray's River. The names are both taken as evidence that McGillivray and Thompson crossed White Man Pass.

Despite being the first fur-trade route across the Rockies and a direct route from the Bow River to the Kootenay along the Spray Lakes and Cross River, the Nor'Westers did not use White Man Pass again, likely because it was too far south and had to be approached through Blackfoot country. Shifting priorities at Rocky Mountain House meant that it was

1806 before another attempt was made at crossing the Rockies – this time over the more northerly Howse Pass.[4]

Nevertheless, several other travellers did make use of the pass during the fur-trade era. In 1841 Sir George Simpson, governor of the merged Hudson's Bay Company and North West Company, recruited Fort Garry Métis James Sinclair to lead a party of 23 Métis families (123 people) with their two hundred head of cattle to the Oregon Territory to help reinforce British claim to the disputed area.[5] Most of the men were buffalo hunters who also knew about farming and stock raising. They understood what their westward journey would entail and were prepared to cope with whatever might occur on the trail. The party left Fort Garry on June 3, led by Sinclair with his mandated magnetic compass and spy-glass.

A rate of 20 miles per day put the travellers in Fort Edmonton in early August. Simpson's instructions were that Sinclair should proceed over Athabasca Pass, which had been the main fur-trade route across the Rockies since 1811. However, Simpson himself, in the midst of a round-the-world trip, had chosen a southerly route over today's Simpson Pass (see Route II below). Knowing this, Sinclair decided to defy instructions and follow Simpson's own southward route. The party engaged Maskapetoon, chief of the Wetaskiwin Cree, as guide and abandoned their Red River carts in favour of saddle horses. They left Fort Edmonton by the second week of August, following Simpson's route into the mountains through Devil's Gap, just north of the Bow River.

After a few days' rest on the shores of Lake Minnewanka, the party set off again, now deviating from Simpson's route along the north shore of Lake Minnewanka. At this point, Sinclair chose to travel along the east and south shores of Lake Minnewanka then climb Carrot Creek Summit to pass into the Bow River drainage. After crossing the Bow River near the site of present-day Canmore, Maskapetoon led the Métis through Whiteman's Gap and past the Spray Lakes to the Spray River. A branch of the Spray led them over White Man Pass to the Cross River. Following it to the Kootenay River, they rejoined Simpson's path along the river and passed through a narrow canyon – today's Sinclair Canyon, named after James Sinclair – to the site of present-day Radium and

Above: Devil's Gap, the break in the mountains between Phantom Crag and Orient Point, was an important entry point into the mountains for Aboriginal people and other nineteenth-century travellers. The third Ghost Lake is shown in the foreground of this photo. The trail, not visible here, follows along the right side of the lake.

Below: Sinclair chose the difficult route over Carrot Creek Summit and along Carrot Creek (shown here) to get his large party from Lake Minnewanka to the Bow Valley. The route is no longer maintained because it passes through a sensitive wildlife habitat.

the Columbia River. After a total of five months on the trail, the entire party – including the three children who were born en route – arrived safely in the Oregon Territory.

Four years later, another party crossed White Man Pass, this time from west to east. Since 1838 Father Pierre Jean de Smet had worked with Pacific Northwest Aboriginal peoples along the Columbia River. As time went on, he grew increasingly disturbed by the bloodshed resulting from Blackfoot incursions into his mission territory. By 1845 he had decided to cross the Rockies on a mission of peace to the Blackfoot. Accompanied by three Kootenays, who had bravely offered to lead him to the land of their enemies, hunt and interpret, Father de Smet followed the Columbia River to near the site of present-day Radium, passed through Sinclair Canyon and followed Simpson's route over Sinclair Pass to the Kootenay River.

From the Kootenay River, the party followed the Cross to the summit of White Man Pass, where they arrived on September 15. As the top of the pass marked the entry into Blackfoot territory, de Smet had a cross erected as "a sign of salvation and peace to all the scattered and itinerant tribes east and west of these gigantic and lurid mountains."[6] It is for this cross that Dr. George Dawson named the Cross River in 1883.

This small lake, very close to the Continental Divide at White Man Pass, is thought to be the original site of Father de Smet's cross, from which the Cross River takes its name.

Father Pierre Jean de Smet (1801–1873)

On January 30, 1801, Marie-Jeanne Buydens, the wife of wealthy ship outfitter Joost de Smet, gave birth to twins Peiter-Joannes and Colette-Aldegonde in Termonde, Belgium. Peiter-Joannes, also known as Pierre Jean, grew up to be a sturdy youngster with a yen for adventure and travel. He obtained his early education at Catholic boarding schools near Ghent and in 1819 studied at the Preparatory Seminary of Mechelen. Later that year his somewhat idyllic life was shattered by the death of his beloved mother.

In 1821 a sermon the Apostle of Kentucky delivered at the seminary inspired him to become a missionary to the United States. In the fall of 1821, de Smet arrived in Georgetown, Maryland, to begin his preparation for a lifetime of work among the Aboriginal peoples of the United States. He left Belgium without informing his father, who remained bitterly disappointed by this sudden departure and died in 1827 without seeing his beloved son again.

In the spring of 1823, de Smet volunteered to travel west to a new mission being established near St. Louis, at the mouth of the Missouri River. The difficult voyage to the mission field lasted two months, during which time the participants had to walk 400 miles (644 kilometres). Life on the frontier was demanding and funds were short, but de Smet persisted. On September 23, 1827, he was ordained a Jesuit priest and became Father Pierre Jean de Smet. Over the next several months he endured great difficulty travelling to surrounding communities to celebrate mass.

Later that year, the Jesuits of St. Louis established a new college and Father de Smet took a position teaching religion, English and agriculture. In 1832 the college was granted university status and de Smet became Professor of English. The following year, suffering from the ill health that resulted from ten years of hard life on the frontier, de Smet travelled to Europe for rest, to promote the cause of the Jesuit mission on the US frontier and to raise funds for its continuance.

Although still in poor health after his return to his mission on the Missouri in 1838, Father de Smet volunteered for a new mission being established farther west. He spent the next several years engaged in missionary work among the Potawatomis peoples of the Rocky Mountains, travelling back to St. Louis to report to his superiors and embarking on fundraising missions to Europe, all the while suffering from periodic bouts of poor health. In 1845, determined to pacify the Blackfoot enemies of his converts, de Smet set out overland from the Oregon Territory over White Man Pass on the Continental Divide and as far north as present-day Edmonton. He did not, however, manage to meet up with the northern Blackfoot peoples.

A year after this memorable trip to the north, de Smet's religious superiors in Rome decided to end his assignment among the Aboriginal peoples of the Rocky Mountains. He returned to St. Louis University, where he continued his work with the Jesuits and, through his writings and travels, became well-known on both sides of the Atlantic. As a missionary, he had a reputation for being able to exert an inexplicably positive influence on every band he met – a talent that led to work securing treaties between Aboriginal groups and the American government. He also continued to make trips up and down the Missouri, providing for the missions in the Rocky Mountains.

In 1871 de Smet made the last of at least 15 voyages to Europe. This time, poor health prevented him from returning to his adopted homeland until the following year, when he managed to return to St. Louis. In 1873 a new ship was christened *De Smet* in his honour, and on May 13 he baptized the vessel. It was his last public appearance. On May 23 the great Black Robe died and was buried at the nearby Jesuit mission in Florissant. He had travelled 180,000 miles (289,620 kilometres) over 30 years in support of his Native missions. On his death, America's First Peoples lost a good friend and genuine ally.

Father Pierre Jean de Smet was a Jesuit priest from the Oregon Territory who crossed White Man Pass on a mission of peace to the Blackfoot peoples. He failed to find the Blackfoot and today is best known in the region for the cross he erected near the top of the pass.

Even at that early date, the possible location and fate of Father de Smet's cross had become part of Rocky Mountain folklore. A Native guide's tale that a priest had erected a cross at the source of the river was enough to prompt Dawson to name the river, but James White, former topographic assistant to Dawson, was unable to find any trace of it in 1914. White was sceptical that any traces remained, reasoning that "our Indian knew exactly where it had been erected and it is very doubtful if any wood native to that region would last nearly 70 years."[7]

Nevertheless, in 1926, famed surveyor and Alpine Club of Canada co-founder Arthur Wheeler reported that "the well known guide and explorer of early days of Canadian Pacific Railway construction, Tom Wilson of Banff, stated to the writer that he had found at the summit of the pass [White Man Pass] what seemed to him to be relics of [de Smet's] cross."[8] Possible further insight into the fate of Father de Smet's cross has recently been revealed by Peter Ross, editor and publisher of *Mountain Heritage Magazine*, who explains that (likely in the 1880s):

> Wilson wanted to go prospecting and enlisted the partnership of a man named Ed Barrett. They worked their way down the Kootenay [River until] they came to this river. They went up the river and it was a very, very wet day in July. When they reached the summit, everything was soaking wet. They managed to get a little dry kindling, and then they found a pole in the bush. They pulled it along to where it was dry, and all that night they took turns sleeping and keeping the fire going. As the log burned, they pulled it down to a new part. In the morning, they found at the end of it a cross-bar. That was Father de Smet's cross. Now that is the first time the story has been told.[9]

Tom Wilson was a well-known storyteller, who developed a reputation for embellishing his stories to increase their entertainment value. However, if the events described above did take place in the 1880s, when Wilson was prospecting regularly, the tree would have only been around 40 years old.

At the top of a pass, where even summer temperatures are cool, the cross could conceivably have lasted that long.

We will likely never know the true fate of de Smet's cross. What we do know is that after erecting it, de Smet proceeded to the Bow River via the Spray Lakes, through the foothills to Rocky Mountain House and on to Fort Edmonton. Unsuccessful in his efforts to meet up with the Blackfoot, he used Athabasca Pass to return to his mission.

That same year, another group was on its way from Montreal to the Oregon Territory on an altogether different sort of mission. Great Britain and the United States were at odds regarding the boundary between their separate interests in the Pacific Northwest, and Hudson's Bay Company Governor George Simpson, who had a vested interest in the area, had suggested that the British authorities send army personnel to ascertain whether troops could be transported over the mountain passes. Two officers, Lieutenants Henry James Warre and Mervin Vavasour, were sent to the area disguised as gentlemen of leisure seeking to entertain themselves by hunting and fishing in the wilds of western North America.

On May 5, 1845, a party consisting of Governor Simpson, Warre, Vavasour, HBC Chief Factor Peter Skene Ogden, Secretary to the Governor Mr. Hopkins and Mr. Halket, a friend of the governor, left Montreal in two canoes. They arrived in Fort Garry on June 7, at which point Simpson left the party. On June 16 the remainder of the party departed for the West with a clerk named Lane, ten men and two carts. They reached the Bow River on July 23, at which point Ogden led them along Sinclair's route from the Bow over Whiteman's Gap and along the Spray Lakes. They crossed the Continental Divide at White Man Pass on July 27 and continued on to the headwaters of the Columbia.[10]

The hazardous journey saw Warre and Vavasour reach the Columbia with only 27 of the 60 horses they had brought from Fort Edmonton. They concluded that the passes through the Rockies were not suitable for troop transport and returned east via Athabasca Pass. There they met up with Father de Smet, whom they had also encountered on August 12, at Kalispell Lake, when he was heading east and they west.

Major A.B. Rogers, well-known for his picturesque profanity, traversed wild untravelled country through the Brisco Range to cross White Man Pass and meet up with his men on the Bow River.

East–West Travellers

No further use of the pass was recorded until 1850, when Sinclair and Maskapetoon returned to investigate the condition of HBC forts in the Oregon Territory. Governor George Simpson had asked Sinclair to evaluate the buildings, which had been left to deteriorate since the 1846 resolution of the border dispute with the United States. After their passage, the silence of the pass remained virtually unbroken by human sounds for 64 years. Through the era of exploration driven by scientists, railway surveys and railway construction (1850–1885), there are only three recorded uses of the pass.

An Irish-born American prospector by the name of Joe Healy claimed to have arrived in the Bow Valley in both 1863 and 1874 by travelling down the Spray River.[11] This path of approach would most likely have entailed crossing White Man Pass. Healy Creek, used by George Simpson in 1841, and Healy Pass are named in his honour.

In 1881 Major A.B. Rogers, engineer in charge of the mountain division of the Canadian Pacific Railway, arranged to meet a party of surveyors and packers at the junction of the Bow and Kananaskis rivers (at Padmore) in July. Rogers had been exploring the Selkirks in search of a pass through the range. He made his way through the Brisco Range, probably at present-day Radium, and followed Sinclair's route up the Cross River, over White Man Pass and along the Spray River and Lakes before crossing the Bow River near the site of present-day Canmore. According to historian Pierre Berton, the route "was wild, untravelled country, barren of human habitation, unmarked by trails or guideposts; but short of going back to San Francisco and across the American west by train, it was the best route available to Rogers if he was to link up with his men."[12] Rogers followed the Bow River downstream to Padmore, where he met his men on July 15.

Two years later, geologist George M. Dawson crossed the pass and translated the Aboriginal name for the pass, "tshakooap-te-ha-wapta" to White Man Pass.[13] Most writers believe that the name refers to Father de Smet's 1845 crossing, but it more likely refers to Duncan McGillivray.[14] Dawson also named the Cross River in honour of Father Pierre Jean de Smet.[15]

Mountaineers and Grizzlies

Until the early twentieth century, parties crossed White Man Pass with the objective of passing through the mountains. Many tourist-explorers and mountain climbers used trails leading to the Spray River (near the base of White Man Pass) as a route to Mount Assiniboine after 1899 and trails along the Spray River to Palliser Pass and River (described in Route VI below) were also popular among mountaineers, but White Man Pass itself saw little use. It was not a popular location for either exploration or recreation.

In the early twentieth century, however, the occasional exception to this rule began to emerge. Colonel Robert O'Hara, whose name is immortalized in one of the most beautiful areas in the Rockies, was one of the first non-Native people to try and reach Mount Assiniboine by travelling though Canmore, which would have meant crossing Whiteman's Gap and probably following the west shore of the Spray Lakes along Sinclair's route. The date of this attempt is not known, but it would have been prior to 1894. O'Hara was turned back by forest fires and did not succeed in his objective.[16]

1901 saw tourist-explorers and mountaineers Walter Wilcox and Henry Bryant exploring south of Canmore with Swiss guides Edouard Feuz and Friedrich Michel. Wilcox described Canmore as "a little village whose scenic charm grows with acquaintance, in a manner very surprising to those who only know it from a passing train. Broad, grassy meadows, and the swirling river, with many a pool and quiet back-water to reflect the green forests and grey mountain peaks, give a beauty, that with a little encouragement from the hand of man, would make a resort similar in many respects to Banff."[17]

Colonel Robert O'Hara (left), whose name is immortalized in one of the most beautiful areas of the Rockies, was a loner who passed through Whiteman's Gap in an attempt to reach Mount Assiniboine from the east. He is seen here with Tom Wilson, the man purported to have burned Father de Smet's cross near White Man Pass.

On July 23 they engaged a wagon in Canmore to take them to the base of Whiteman's Gap, "a wild pass, full of broken limestones, silent and mysteriously impressive, partly from a certain grandeur of cliffs rising above the narrow trail, and partly also from the abrupt change from the frame buildings and coal mines of Canmore, to the solitude of the untrammelled wilderness."[18] They crossed the gap carrying such items as a folding boat, rope, ice axes and a camera. After descending the valley of the Spray to White Man Pass on Sinclair's old route, they came upon the encampment of their men: guide Tom Lusk, axeman Ben Woodworth and wrangler Jim Wood, with 14 horses supplied by Tom Wilson. Wilcox was impressed:

> There is something peculiarly delightful in the first day's camp, but to come upon it suddenly, and find it all prepared, the tents and great tepee for the men set up, the fireplace in order, with a line of buckets each hanging from its hook, and sending clouds of steam and savoury odors into the forest air, the plates and dishes already set out on the canvas table giving promise of the coming meal, is indeed the height of wilderness luxury.[19]

The entire party continued along the lakes to the junction with the Spray River and Bryant Creek, where they set up a permanent camp. The following day some of the party continued up the Spray River and crossed a pass, likely White Man Pass, into the Cross River valley, from which they could approach Mount Assiniboine from the south. They were unsuccessful in climbing the mountain.

Thirteen years later, a young Swede met a tragic fate near White Man Pass. Twenty-four-year-old Oscar Lovgren had been in Canada 12 months and had just been hired by a sawmill operator near the Spray Lakes. While waiting to be put to work, he borrowed a rifle and set out in pursuit of a grizzly that had been frequenting the camp. Around noon, he returned to camp reporting that he had put five shots into the animal, killing the bear near White Man Pass.

That afternoon, he and two companions returned to the kill site to skin the bear and retrieve the meat. They found a great deal of blood but no bear. The young men followed the bloody trail with Lovgren, carrying the rifle, between and slightly behind his two companions. Suddenly, the wounded grizzly charged the men with a blood-curdling roar, making straight for the man with the gun. Before Lovgren had time to react, the bruin crushed his skull with one mighty swing of its front paw. The other two men immediately returned to camp to sound the alarm. Rescuers found a dead grizzly sow about three hundred yards (metres) from where Lovgren had been killed. She had five bullets in her carcass.[20]

Sid Marty, a southern Alberta writer, has immortalized the event in poetry:

The Silvertip (For Oldtime Guide Jim Boyce)

Up in Whiteman Pass
years ago
There were three men
following a wounded silvertip
up a darkening valley
under the lip of the sun

The man in the middle
with a pop gun 30.30, felt the warmth
fade from the back of his neck
He who had fired at Mustahyah
(seen rolling boulders
over the slides, feeding at peace
in his realm, the white jawed mountain)

He who had cancelled the distances
with five rounds of lead ball

Walking between his friends
carrying the smell of metal
Guilty, was singled out by the grizzly
who waited in the alder hells above

As he crept closer in the shadowland,
up reared King Grizzly and struck him dead
with one swipe of his paw

To illustrate with blood
the split between heart and mind
already opened, in the body of a fool
who would trifle with the god

of solitude[21]

Grizzly bears wander freely throughout the Canadian Rockies and are often seen by visitors on the trails and along the roads. Incidents such as that experienced by Oscar Lovgren have been rare since hunting was banned in the parks and a monumental effort made to keep human food away from omnivores.

The Trail Today

Duncan McGillivray's trip over White Man Pass began at the Bow River, which he had visited in the fall of 1800. He likely found an Aboriginal trail along the river between Old Fort Creek and the site of present-day Canmore. Though Old Bow Fort was not built until 1832, we use its site as the starting point for trips originating along the Bow River. For today's travellers, Highway 1A is probably a close approximation of McGillivray's route, except the section in the town of Canmore, where the original trail was likely closer to the river. Bicycling the route from Old Bow Fort to Canmore is the best way for today's travellers to get a feeling for McGillivray's route. Care is required, however, as Highway 1A can be heavily used by large trucks.[22]

James Sinclair used an entirely different, more difficult and much more interesting route to reach present-day Canmore. In 1841 the Devil's Gap route into the mountains was widely used by Aboriginal travellers, who followed the gravel flats of the Ghost River and the shores of three Ghost Lakes to Lake Minnewanka. At that time, the lake was much smaller, not yet having been dammed or having had the Ghost River diverted into it. The three Ghost Lakes, on the other hand, appear to be relatively unchanged and the trail along the lakes is likely the same one used by Sinclair and his large party.

Sinclair's route over Carrot Creek Summit was once heavily used by both equestrians and hikers, but it has been decommissioned by Parks Canada for environmental reasons. The scenery along the trail is not spectacular; the real loss for today's would-be hikers is missing the context for imagining how Sinclair managed to get his large and unwieldy party along what is now a narrow, heavily wooded and steep trail. Beyond the summit, a large number of creek crossings are required, which undoubtedly led to many wet feet for hikers but would not have affected equestrians – including Sinclair's party. Indeed, the route was generally wider, so the animals in Sinclair's party would likely have stayed in the creek much of the time. Once they reached the bottom of the pass, they would have easily followed the flat valley floor to the Bow River and present-day Canmore. They would have had to ford the river at some point, but the presence of several braided sections would have facilitated the task. Modern travellers wishing to retrace Sinclair's route from near the mouth of Carrot Creek to Canmore can either walk or cycle along the railway tracks and river into town or simply drive the route.

From present-day Canmore, both the McGillivray and Sinclair parties would have had a long and difficult climb from the Bow River to the top of Whiteman's Gap, at the base of the landmark Ha Ling Peak. The area from today's Quarry Lake to the beginning of the Grassi Lakes trail would have presented the easiest route for early travellers.

Early in the twentieth century, the portion of the trail between Canmore and the Spray Lakes was maintained by coal miners who enjoyed fishing in the lakes. Harry Musgrove, retired fireboss at the Canmore mines, reported: "As early as 1915, I started going to the Spray Lakes on fishing trips. You either walked or went horseback. We'd go every year, two or three times a year. Today when some of the boys and I talk about those fishing trips, I almost cry just thinking about it. Those were some of the most memorable days of all, outside of working in the mine."[23]

We describe a more direct and difficult route for hikers today, in order to avoid as many roads and residential areas as possible and to allow hikers to experience some of the difficulties of traversing from the Bow River to the pass.

Today's hikers can reach the Grassi Lakes by following a heavily used trail that is well worth hiking in its own right. The lakes provide a delightful oasis on the side of a steep mountain, and the canyon walls are a challenge for climbers. Both McGillivray and Sinclair likely stayed to the east (left) of the present-day penstock feeding the power plant below, and east of the gorge above the power plant. They would have reached the lakes and continued up the route of today's trail through the narrow and rocky canyon to the top. This last section would likely have been the most challenging, requiring the animals to pass single file. The fact that this was an Aboriginal route is attested to by the rock paintings still visible in the canyon on the large rocks that almost block the route. Other options for present-day travellers are to drive or cycle from the Bow River to

Whiteman's Gap or to cycle the road to the Grassi Lakes trail and the service road to the Grassi Lakes. From the lakes to the top of the pass would, however, require much carrying of the bicycle.

Hiking from the top of the pass to the Spray Lakes dam is straightforward, though wet and boggy in places. The route is fairly level and can either be hiked or cycled with mountain bikes. From the dam, the route follows a good gravel road along the west shore of the Spray Lakes Reservoir to the dam across the Spray River near the south end of the reservoir. Again, this route can be driven from the top of Whiteman's Gap to partway along the west side of the lake, where a gate blocks vehicle traffic.

From the south end of the Spray Lakes Reservoir, there is a good hiking trail to the top of White Man Pass. This trail can easily be accessed by hiking the six-kilometre trail to the Spray River from the Mount Shark parking area and another 11 kilometres to the top of the pass. Following a good trail another six kilometres takes hikers to the forestry road along the Cross River. The trail from the Mount Shark parking area to the Cross River is a good day hike for strong hikers or those who can arrange for a pickup at the south end.

This very historic trail is suitable for most hikers. The trail to the top of the pass is not particularly difficult. The scenery along the route is pleasant but not spectacular. The trail down the west side to the forestry road is steeper, sometimes with dramatic scenery. This, of course, makes the return journey more difficult for those choosing the round-trip option.

Trail Guide

Distances are adapted from existing trail guides: Patton and Robinson, Potter, Beers, and Eastcott, and from Gem-Trek maps. Distances intermediate from those given in the sources are estimated from topographical maps and from hiking times. All distances are given in kilometres.

Old Bow Fort to the Cross River along the Spray Lakes and over White Man Pass

Maps 82 O/3 Canmore

82 J/13 Mount Assiniboine

82 J/14 Spray Lakes Reservoir

Gem-Trek Banff and Mount Assiniboine

Gem-Trek Canmore and Kananaskis Village

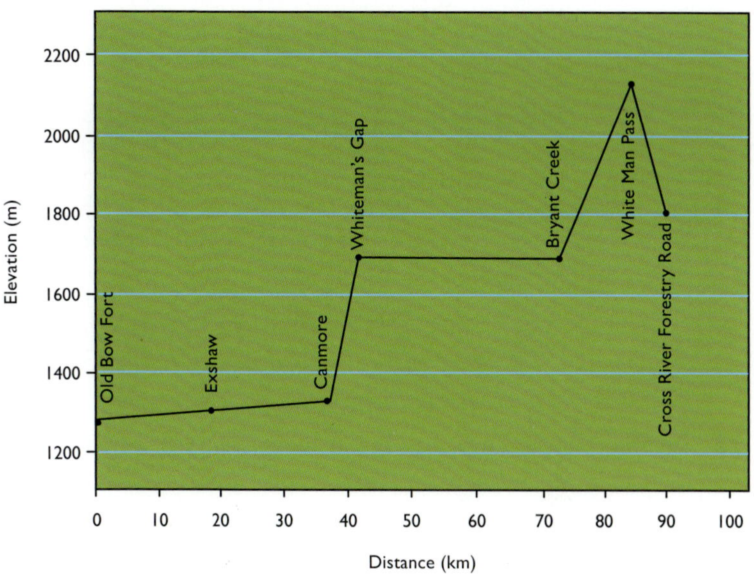

Trailhead

The remains of Old Bow Fort are located on the west end of the Stoney Indian Reserve, high on a plateau at the northeast junction of Old Fort Creek and the Bow River.[24] You will need permission from the Stoney Band to visit the site, but they were more than happy to extend this privilege to my wife, Cheryl, and me.

Unfortunately there are no trails remaining from Old Bow Fort to Canmore. These were almost entirely obliterated with the construction of first a wagon road and later Highway 1A. The highway approximately follows the route of the original trail. By bicycling along this road, modern travellers can appreciate the terrain McGillivray and his party traversed. To reach the trailhead, continue along Highway 1A into Canmore (where its name changes to Bow Valley Trail) as far as 17th Street. Turn left on 17th street, then right on 8th Avenue. Continue as far as the overhead power line near the golf course. The distance is approximately 36 km. The route continues at km 0.0 below.

0.0 Proceed southwest under the power line between the golf course and a soccer field. Cross a bridge, then a street, another bridge and another street.

0.8 A creek that is a branch of the Bow River. Turn left (southeast) on a well-made trail.

1.2 Trail junction. Turn right and cross the river on the old engine bridge. Continue straight ahead and cross the bridge over the power plant outflow.

1.8 Trail junction. Turn right and begin the long climb to Whiteman's Gap. Climb up the hill to the right of the stairs. At the break, turn left, then right, and continue climbing under the power line.

2.4 The Spray Lakes Road near the entrance to Nordic Centre Provincial Park. Stay on the right side of the road until the power line crosses the road again. Turn right under the power line. Continue uphill, cross the Spray Lakes Road again and continue under the power line.

3.6	Grassi Lakes parking lot. From here, follow the heavily used Grassi Lakes trail uphill.
5.0	Grassi Lakes. Continue uphill through the narrow rocky canyon to the top of the hill.
6.0	Spray Lakes Road and the top of Whiteman's Gap. Continue along the road that follows the reservoir's shore.
7.6	Goat Creek parking lot. Proceed west along the Goat Creek trail.
8.6	National park boundary. Turn left on a single track trail; continue through the woods to a clay berm and a small pond. Keep to the right of the pond, and then cross Goat Creek on the rocks or hike farther downstream to a bridge.
9.5	Goat Creek Pump House. Follow an old logging road south (right), parallel to the Spray Lakes Road. A power line comes in from the left (east). Continue under the power line.
15.7	Goat Pond dam. Continue to the right of the pond on the old logging road, which soon becomes rough and marshy. Pass through a gravel pit then continue under the power line.
18.8	Spray Lakes dam. Keep to the right of the reservoir, join a smooth gravel road (the West Side Road) and continue south east along the lake. There are campsites scattered all along the lake.
23.2	Spray Lakes West Campground and gate across the road. Pass through the gate and follow a good gravel road along the lake-shore in a southwesterly direction. It is very open with good views of the surrounding mountains and the lake.
34.1	Canyon Dam. Cross on top of the dam then over a spillway. The trail now climbs steeply away from the lake, crosses a headland and drops down again.
35.8	Trail junction. The Spray River Fire Road turns right (north). Continue ahead (southwest) along the fire road, parallel to the

lakeshore. Enter Banff National Park, with signs pointing northeast toward the Canyon Dam. Continue on the old road, just above the lake, with great views across the lake.

38.3 Turbulent Creek bridge. Just after the bridge is an old campsite. Continue southwest on the trail, sometimes adjacent to the national park boundary.

40.7 Trail junction. A trail leads off to the left. Keep right.

41.4 Trail Centre Junction. Trail to the right is the Bryant Creek trail. Keep left and cross Bryant Creek on a bridge.

41.9 Trail junction. The trail to the Mount Shark parking area is to the left. Continue ahead (south) on the Spray River trail. The trail is a well-beaten horse trail that initially passes through the woods along the river. It gradually opens up to provide views of the mountains to the south, then it reaches a small meadow.

44.5 At the end of the meadow, the trail splits, with the hiking trail going to the right.

45.1 Trail junction. The Palliser Pass trail goes to the left. Continue ahead (south) for White Man Pass. There is an old campsite just after the junction. The trail continues through the forest close to the river.

46.4 Curry Creek ford, knee deep.

46.7 White Man Creek. This creek can be crossed on an old log. Begin a gentle climb to a picturesque meadow with good views of the surrounding mountains.

49.0 Trail Junction at the end of the meadow. The trail to the left leads to the Palliser Pass trail. Continue ahead. The trail veers gently to the southwest and is more heavily used here as horses come in from the Spray River.

50.7 Begin the steep climb toward the pass. Cross a meadow at the base of an avalanche slope with good views of the mountains all around. After the meadow, cross a heavily forested ridge.

52.3 Meadow with a small unnamed lake. Go around the lake to the right and continue to climb.

52.8 White Man Pass and the national park boundary. The trees are very thin on top of the pass, with reasonable views to the south. A good trail continues steeply downhill to the southwest, entering a narrow, scenic, rugged valley. Keep left on a well-maintained trail with sheer rock cliffs at a sign pointing right to a scenic route. At the next trail split, keep right on the hiking trail. The trail continues along the creek between clear-cuts on either side. Before reaching the forestry road, the trail turns right (east) and crosses the creek.

58.8 Forestry road at the end of the trail.

Devil's Gap to Canmore over Carrot Creek Summit

Maps 82 O/3 Canmore

82 O/6 Lake Minnewanka

Gem-Trek Banff and Mount Assiniboine

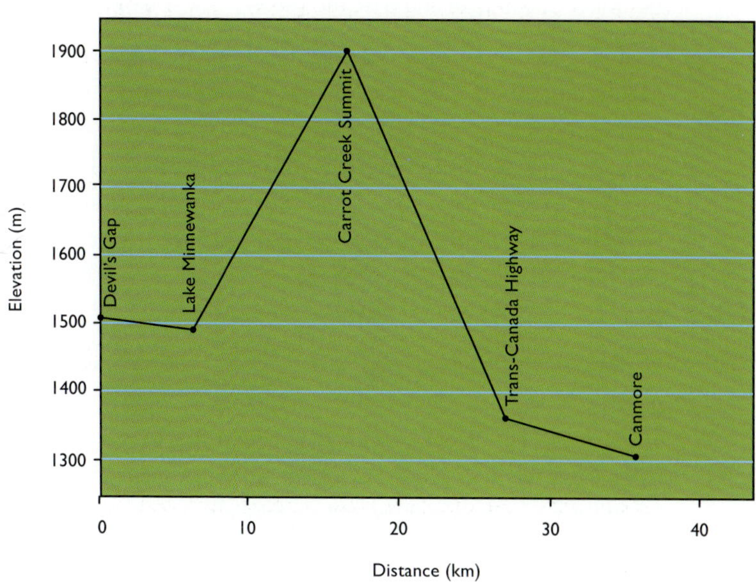

Trailhead

Most travellers will want to reach Devil's Gap by hiking or cycling the trail along the north shore of Lake Minnewanka past the three Ghost Lakes to the Banff National Park boundary at Devil's Gap. This route is described in Route II below. The other approach to Devil's Gap is from the east. Here, adventuresome travellers can drive north on Highway 40 from Highway 1A (a good backcountry road map is required) then head west on a rough secondary gravel road shortly after Highway 40 crosses the Ghost River. This road heads almost directly west to the gravel flats of the Ghost River and on to the national park boundary. Minor roads from the east are evident in the Devil's Gap area at the park boundary. A high-clearance vehicle is definitely an asset for those attempting this route. The authors have not braved it. The south end of the trail is at the west end of 8th Avenue in Canmore, under the power line in front of the golf course.

0.0 Devil's Gap and the Banff National Park boundary. From the park boundary, the well-worn horse trail twists and turns around natural contours. Proceed westward along the south shore of the third Ghost Lake and past the second Ghost Lake.

3.8 Trail junction. The trail to the right crosses the outflow from the second Ghost Lake and follows the north shore of Lake Minnewanka. Keep to the left for Carrot Creek. The trail follows the shore of the first Ghost Lake then parallel to the shore of Lake Minnewanka. The trail is quite straight and easy to follow. Most of it is treed, with views out over the lake. The trail is likely a new one cut after Lake Minnewanka was flooded in 1941.

12.8 National Parks Canada sign asking hikers not to enter this environmentally sensitive area. The trail is not closed, but the authors ask that hikers honour the request not to use the trail. I hiked this historically significant trail in the late fall, when any interference with animals would be minimized, and only to get a feeling for what Sinclair's large and cumbersome party would have experienced. From the sign, the trail proceeds through the trees with many deadfalls.

14.7 The trail starts to climb toward the summit, remaining in the forest. It crosses the creek many times; these are generally easy rock-hop crossings.

16.3 Carrot Creek Summit. This is a treed summit with no view of the lake. Continue downhill, always in the forest. The trail levels out.

18.8 Old campsite. Over the next 5 km, there are up to 24 creek crossings, some on old logs, but many requiring easy fords. By bushwhacking along the side of the creek when possible, I managed to keep to only 16 crossings. The trail was heavily used before its closure and remains easy to follow.

24.2 Mouth of Carrot Creek canyon. The next 2.6 km pass through a clearing that resulted from a forest fire and recent forest cutting, likely to provide a fire break. Most of the trail follows old logging roads. Keep to the right at junctions, heading parallel to Carrot Creek directly toward the Trans-Canada Highway to the southwest.

26.8 Fence along the highway. Since trail use is discouraged, there is no opening in the fence. Without scaling the fence, proceed a short distance west, parallel to the highway, to Carrot Creek. Cross the highway under the bridge, then follow the fence southeast until you reach an old road heading toward the railway, perpendicular to the highway. The fence has a gate at this point. Pass through the gate and turn right (southwest) along the dirt road.

27.8 Turn left at the railroad and proceed southeast on the dirt road, parallel to the railroad.

29.3 National park boundary. Continue ahead.

30.6 Harvey Heights ramp. Continue on an old road between the highway and the railroad.

32.0 Cross a small creek, then the railroad. Follow a trail leading off to the left. This very scenic trail follows close to the river, still heading southeast. Continue to the Canmore Golf Course, then turn left and continue following the road until it runs into 8th Avenue at the end of the golf course.

34.4 Overhead power line running southwest perpendicular to the road, and 8th Avenue running southeast. This is the end of this portion of the trail. The continuation of this trail is km 0.0 of the Old Bow Fort to the Cross River along the Spray Lakes and over White Man Pass trail above.

Carrot Creek flows through several narrow canyons on its way from Carrot Creek Summit to the Bow River. It is difficult to imagine James Sinclair leading 123 immigrants and 200 head of cattle through such narrow – though scenic – confines.

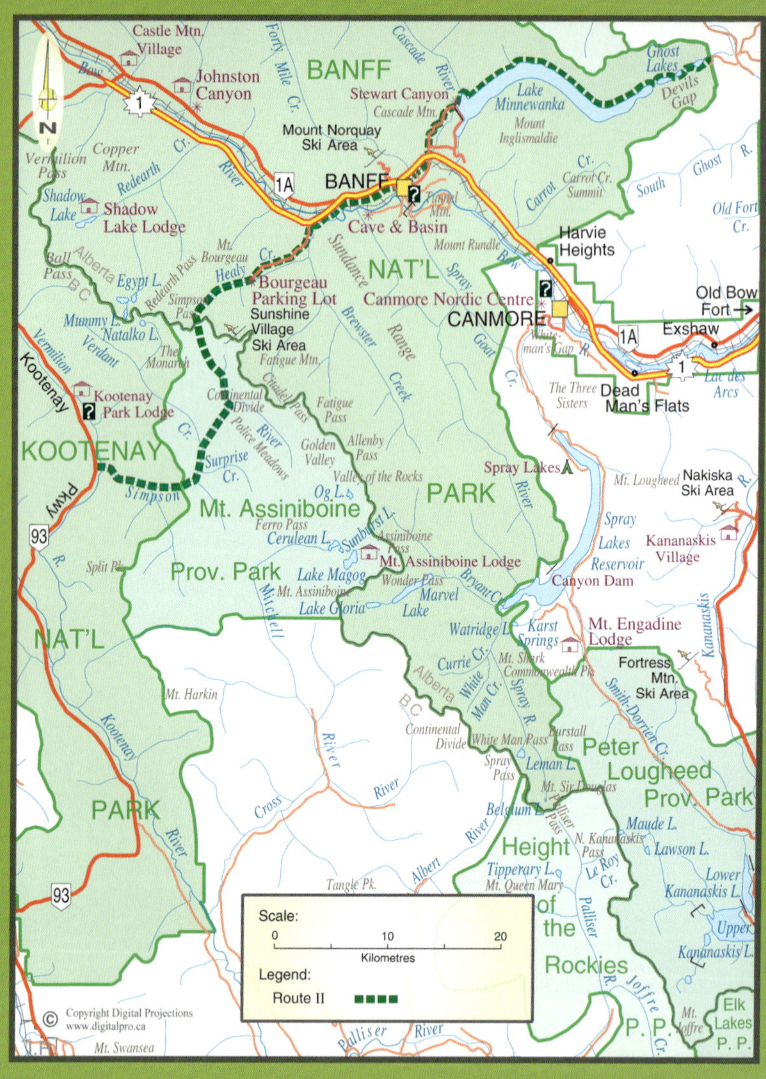

Sir George Simpson's Route from Devil's Gap (Lake Minnewanka) to the Kootenay River over Simpson Pass

Route II

Reclusive Hideout: Sir George Simpson's Route from Devil's Gap (Lake Minnewanka) to the Kootenay River over Simpson Pass

The western portion of today's Lake Minnewanka trail passes through meadows and grassy woodland en route to a lakeside campground (Lm8) – a very quiet and peaceful spot, save for the occasional motorboat passing by. It is a great location for wildlife lovers, with bighorn sheep, mule deer and the occasional hungry cougar frequenting the environs.

As I proceeded through this area deep in my own thoughts, with my backpack reaching high above my head shielding me from any noise from the rear, I suddenly heard a squealing sound immediately behind me. Startled, I jumped as high into the air as my heavy pack would allow. On retouching the ground, I quickly turned around, expecting to see a member of the cat family, the only animals that habitually approach people from behind.

Much to my chagrin, I found that the noise had come from a bicyclist applying his breaks to avoid running me down. I have had run-ins with cyclists on backcountry trails before and was prepared to forcefully give this person a piece of my mind. But before I could open my mouth, he began apologizing profusely in broken English with a definite East European accent. He did not realize that the combination of soft soil and grass on the trail meant that he had been travelling very quietly. Furthermore, the combination of my pack muffling the already-quiet bicycle and my mind in the clouds meant that I had not heard him coming. He was very sorry for having frightened me. My initial anger soon melted away, and I explained to him that he should speak, ring a bell or make some other noise when approaching hikers on any trail, as they often cannot hear cyclists coming. After getting over the apologies and explanations, we had a nice chat, and each continued on his way, grateful for the encounter.

Many parts of the trail along Lake Minnewanka are grass covered, as is this trail junction with the Aylmer Pass trail. Although the signs warn of bears in the area and cougars often hunt here, these deer are peacefully grazing, apparently oblivious to any danger.

Chronology

1841 Sir George Simpson, governor of the Hudson's Bay Company, enters the Rocky Mountains through Devil's Gap. He continues past Cascade Mountain and west along the Bow River, then along today's Brewster and Healy creeks to the Continental Divide.

1847 Reverend Robert Terrill Rundle visits Lake Minnewanka on June 28. He spends several days camped on the lakeshore, admiring the area's beauty.

1858 James Hector renames Shuswap Pass Simpson Pass in honour of Sir George Simpson and places it on his map.

1870s Donald McMillan, a surveyor for the Canadian Pacific Railway, runs a preliminary line from the Bow River to the top of Simpson Pass along Healy Creek. The route proves to be unsuitable for the railway and activity ceases.

1887 Construction begins on a wagon road from Banff to Lake Minnewanka. It is completed the following spring.

1895 A small wooden dam is built across Devil's Creek (which flows out of Lake Minnewanka) to control the water level at the Minnewanka Landing wharf.

Up to 1943. Legendary outfitter and park warden Bill Peyto uses the area near the top of Simpson Pass as his place of seclusion.

1896 Two prospectors, Smith and Temple, lose all their supplies when their raft upsets on the Vermilion River. Smith's failed attempt to retrace their steps over White Man Pass leads him up the North Simpson River and over Simpson Pass.

1899 Walter Wilcox travels along Simpson's old route from Banff to Lake Minnewanka on horseback. He follows an excellent trail on the north shore of the lake, passes the three Ghost Lakes and continues on to Devil's Gap and the valley of the Ghost River.

1909 The Warden Service contracts Jim Boyce to build a six-foot-wide (1.8-metre-wide) trail from Banff to the top of Simpson Pass, a distance of 19 miles (31 km).

1910 Park authorities consider the previously abandoned Canadian Pacific Railway route over Simpson Pass for a road link between the Bow Valley and the Columbia Valley. The Vermilion Pass route eventually wins out.

1912 The trail along the north side of Lake Minnewanka is extended to the Ghost River.

The federal government grants Calgary Power permission to build a storage dam on Lake Minnewanka. The structure raises the water level 12 feet (3.7 metres) and floods 1,000 acres (4047 square metres).

1917 Between July 13 and 31, the Alpine Club of Canada holds its eleventh annual camp on the meadow near Simpson Pass.

1919 Geologist and palaeontologist Dr. Charles Walcott searches for Upper Cambrian fossils around Lake Minnewanka while his wife, Mary, collects and paints wildflowers.

1920 The Walcotts spend a week camped at Lake Minnewanka, then continue past the lake to Devil's Gap and the Ghost River.

1940 Under the War Measures Act, Calgary Power is granted permission to build another dam on Lake Minnewanka and divert the Ghost River into the lake, raising the water level by a further 25 metres. The lake doubles in size and the valley is altered beyond recognition.

History

Banff's First Tourist

In July 1841, a pack train of 45 horses and 25 men entered the Rocky Mountains through Devil's Gap at the eastern end of Lake Minnewanka. Sir George Simpson, governor of the Hudson's Bay Company, was in the midst of an around-the-world tour, and this stage of the adventure entailed crossing the mountains by a route never before followed by non-Aboriginal travellers. Guiding him was Métis Alexis Piché, chief of the Mountain Cree.[1] Simpson explained that "the path which we had been following was a track of the Assiniboines [Stoneys], carried, for the sake of concealment, through the thickest forests. The Indians and Peechee [as he referred to Piché] were the only persons that had ever pursued this route; and we were the first whites that had attempted this pass of the mountains."[2]

Piché guided Simpson's party past the three Ghost Lakes, along the north and west shores of Lake Minnewanka and past Cascade Mountain, where "from the top of a peak, that rose perpendicularly at least two thousand feet, there fell a stream of water, which, though of very considerable volume, looked like a thread of silver on the gray rock. It was said to be known as the Spout, and to serve as a landmark in this wilderness of cliffs."[3] They continued west along the Bow River and on August 1 camped near what is today the town of Banff, making Simpson Banff's first tourist. The men built a raft to ferry men, horses and supplies across the river then spent the night on its south bank.

On his way from Lake Minnewanka to the Banff area, George Simpson commented on the mountain from which a spout of water emerged, which served as a landmark to Aboriginal travellers in the area. It was later named Cascade Mountain.

George Simpson (ca 1792–1860)

George Simpson was born in the tiny town of Dingwall, Scotland, around 1792. His father, George Simpson Sr., was the son of a Calvinist minister; his mother is unknown. As was the custom for children born out of wedlock at the time, the father took responsibility for raising the child. In this case, Simpson delegated the task to his sister, Mary. Young George was educated in the local parish school. Around 1808, he moved to London to train as a clerk in his uncle's sugar brokerage, Graham and Simpson, where he impressed his superiors with his quick and ordered mind. In 1812, the company was amalgamated with a Jamaican company controlled by Andrew Wedderburn, a dominant shareholder in the Hudson's Bay Company. This union would change George Simpson's life forever.

In 1820 Wedderburn, who had changed his name to Colville, recommended Simpson for the position of acting governor-in-chief of Rupert's Land for the Hudson's Bay Company. Simpson showed a remarkable ability both in managing men and in mastering the problems of the fur trade. When the Hudson's Bay Company merged with the North West Company in 1821, Simpson was appointed governor of the lucrative Northern Department. He immediately reorganized the department from top to bottom, and profits began to soar. In 1826 he was given the dual governorship of the northern and southern departments, and in 1839 he officially became governor-in-chief of Rupert's Land.

Simpson travelled widely throughout Rupert's Land, taking record-setting canoe trips, such as his 7,000-mile (11,260-kilometre) trip from York Factory on Hudson's Bay to Fort Vancouver (in present-day Washington State), considered the longest North American canoe trip ever taken in a single season. In 1841 he

Governor George Simpson of the Hudson's Bay Company was the first European to pass through Devil's Gap to the Ghost Lakes and Lake Minnewanka. As well, he went on to become the first European to pass through the present-day Banff area.

completed a trip around the world in 19 months and 19 days. That same year Queen Victoria knighted him in recognition of the Hudson's Bay Company's support for Arctic exploration.

Known to be ruthless and sometimes even cruel, Simpson ruled his empire with military-style despotism. He methodically catalogued the individual abilities of fur traders in his famous "Character Book" and did not hesitate to ruin the career of anyone who disagreed with him.

He also took a hard line with the Aboriginal people upon whom the success of the fur trade depended. He felt that an iron-fisted rule was needed to keep them in a proper state of subordination. He showed nothing but disdain for Aboriginal women, labelling them as "bits of brown" and regarding them largely as sex objects. In his early fur-trade years, he advised his "gentlemen" to form liaisons with local women as soon as they arrived in the West so as to procure the goodwill of their bands. He had several Native wives himself, abandoning them when he grew tired of them.

In 1830 Simpson married his cousin, Frances Simpson. Initially the family made their home in the Red River settlement, but Frances found herself unable to withstand the rigours of life in this frontier community and returned to England in 1833. She stayed five years then spent seven travelling back and forth between England and Lachine, Quebec. In 1845 she settled permanently in Lachine, where she died in 1853.

George and Frances Simpson had five children between 1831 and 1850. In addition to at least five Métis children he sired between 1820 and 1830, his descendents were rounded out by two illegitimate children he had fathered in England before 1820 and another in Lachine after his wife died. Though he was not proud of his own out-of-wedlock birth and tried to mask the details of his early life, his shame did not deter him from leaving a string of children in a similar fatherless state.

During his later years, Sir George Simpson invested in a variety of businesses. Land speculation, investments in two banks and shares in railway and shipping projects all contributed to generate sizeable wealth. During the summer of 1860, Simpson lavishly entertained the Prince of Wales (the future King Edward VII) at his estate near Lachine. Three days later, he suffered a stroke. He died on September 7 and was buried in Mount Royal Cemetery, Montreal, beside his wife, Frances. Known by some as "The Birchbark Emperor," Simpson had completely reorganized the fur trade, put it on a sound financial basis and expanded its business interests beyond trading in furs. Sir George Simpson left an indelible mark on the Hudson's Bay Company – and the future country of Canada.

Simpson recorded:

> Next morning, we began to ascend the mountains in right earnest, riding where we could, and walking where the horses found the road too steep to carry us, while by our side there rushed downwards one of the sources of the Bow River. We were surrounded by peaks and crags, on whose summits lay perpetual snow; and the only sounds that disturbed the solitude were the crackling of prostrate branches under the tread of our horses, and the roaring of the stream, as it leaped down its rocky course. One peak presented a very peculiar feature in an opening of about eighty feet by fifty, which, at a distance, might have been taken for a spot of snow, but which, as one advanced nearer, assumed the appearance of the gateway of a giant's fortress.

> About seven hours of hard work brought us to the height of land, the hinge, as it were, between the eastern and the western waters.... In addition to the physical magnificence of the scene, I here met an unexpected reminiscence of my own native hills in the shape of a plant, which appeared to me to be the very heather of the Highlands of Scotland.[4]

They had followed today's Brewster and Healy creeks to a pass across the Continental Divide that the Shuswap people used regularly to trade with the Bow Valley Stoneys. When the Palliser Expedition was passing through the Bow Valley in 1858, Dr. James Hector changed its name from Shuswap Pass to Simpson Pass and placed it on his map. Few non-Aboriginal travellers ever used the pass, however, and there is no longer a trail from its summit to the main branch of the Simpson River.

Near the top of the pass, Simpson and Hudson's Bay Company factor John Rowand carved their initials and the year on a tree. Lade Brewster found the fallen log with the "Simpson Register" in 1904 and gave it to her husband, Jim.[5] The register now resides in the Banff Park Museum.

From the top of the pass, the Simpson party made its way down the north branch of the Simpson River to the main river, which they followed to its junction with the Vermilion River and on to the Kootenay en route to the Columbia Valley and the Pacific Coast. Simpson never crossed the mountains again.

Right: At the top of Simpson Pass, George Simpson and John Rowand stopped to carve their initials and the year on a tree. The fallen tree containing the inscription was found 63 years later. The register now resides in the Banff Park Museum.

Opposite: George Simpson crossed the Continental Divide through a low pass (Shuswap Pass), the traditional route of Aboriginal peoples. Hector changed the name to Simpson Pass, but it was little used and there is no trail over the pass today.

Roads, Prospectors and Campers

During the era of railroad exploration (1850–1885), the tranquillity of Healy Creek and Simpson Pass was again disturbed. Canadian Pacific Railway surveyor Donald McMillan and his party crossed the Bow River west of Banff in the 1870s and ran a preliminary line along Healy Creek from the Bow to the top of Simpson Pass. The route proved to be unsuitable for the railway and activity ceased.

The next recorded use of the trail was in 1896, when the raft carrying prospectors Smith and Temple upset on the Vermilion River.[6] The men were on their way to the Kootenay country and by the time they reached the river, their horses were exhausted from being forced to march overly long days with excessive cargo. Hoping to salvage their mission, the men abandoned the horses, built a raft and proceeded down the river. Before long, rough water had destroyed the raft and scattered the men's precious supplies. With great difficulty, the men managed to get to shore – one on each side of the river.

After a considerable amount of shouting back and forth, neither managed to convince the other to cross the river. Temple ventured west while Smith set out to retrace their steps and find the horses. He became hopelessly lost, wandering for 11 days before desperately struggling up the North Simpson River and over Simpson Pass. On the verge of exhaustion and starvation, Smith lay down to die. The distant sound of a train whistle raised him from his despair, rallying his courage and giving him the strength he needed to continue. The sound guided him to the Bow River, where he managed to catch the attention of some trackmen working on the opposite side of the river. They promptly responded to his call, fetching him in a boat and taking him on to Banff.

When Smith told of his suffering and of his companion, Temple, who was still unaccounted for, the Reverend William Black of Banff and the great Stoney guide, William Twin, went looking for him.[7] Twin managed to retrace Smith's tracks up Healy Creek, over Simpson Pass and down to the Vermilion River, where the search party located the wrecked raft and one of the horses. After crossing the river, Twin then followed Temple's tracks for two days all the way to the Columbia River, where the would-be rescuers found that Temple had reached a stage road along the Columbia and had already been rescued. For some reason, Temple had mentioned neither his adventure nor his partner, Smith, who nearly died as a result of the ordeal, to his rescuers.

In the late nineteenth and early twentieth centuries, the area near the top of Simpson Pass became the hideout of legendary outfitter and park warden Bill Peyto. In 1977 Jim Deegan published a poem about Peyto, his cabin near Simpson Pass and his nearby talc mine.

Opposite above: Brothers Joshua (l) and William Twin were prominent figures in late-nineteenth- and early-twentieth-century Banff. William was a great tracker who managed to follow the path of a lost prospector for two days until his whereabouts were determined.

Opposite below: Bill Peyto was an eccentric but very competent guide and later park warden who built a cabin near Simpson Pass. He spent much of his life there as a recluse, prospecting and working his talc mine.

Prospector of Talc Mountain

On Simpson Pass, atop the Divide,
among the yellow tamarack
stands a cabin in a meadow,
a lone prospector's shack.

Weathering in the elements,
abandoned in the vale,
a sod-roofed fortress, built
beside an old packtrail.

The cabin tells a story
of a miner and his claim:
of a pioneer in the wilderness,
Bill Peyto was his name.

This log octagonal building,
its welcome mat of sharpened spikes
leaves a person with a feeling
old Bill had his dislikes.

Crowbars across the windows
to repel the grizzly bear,
nails driven through the outer door
make a person approach with care.

Six eight-lever locks secure the shack
from all inquisitive folk;
a bear-trap, set and oiled to spring
is enough to make you choke.

Mortared with clay, a floor of talc
runs the interior of that shack,

lots of canned provisions still
to lure the miner back.

The clanging ring of horse bells
echoed from Bourgeau
as Bill Peyto climbed the packtrail
from the town of Banff below.

He was heading for his talc mine,
the other side of Pharaoh Pass,
and his horses were right eager
to feed on alpine grass.

Down through the tangled forest
on mushy muskeg ground,
rode on toward his talc mine
which he, Bill Peyto, found.

His audience was the wildlife,
the cougar, wolf and bear;
who from a distance, safe and sure,
would watch this lone affair.

He abandoned his claim on the Great Divide,
his years spent alone left him reclusive and strange;
he traversed this land until he died,
as a Park Warden to patrol and to range.

This silent man of the Canadian Rockies,
whose companion was an old bloodhound
was as great a mountain traveler
as ever will be found.[8]

By the early twentieth century, leaders in Banff's growing tourism industry were catching on to the untapped potential of Simpson Pass and the adjacent Healy Pass and Meadows. In 1909 the Warden Service contracted Jim Boyce to build a six-foot-wide (1.8-metre-wide) trail from Banff to the top of the pass, a distance of 19 miles (31 kilometres). The following year, park authorities considered the previously abandoned Canadian Pacific Railway route as a potential road link between the Bow Valley and the Columbia Valley. The Vermilion Pass route won out, however, leaving the pass marked only by a permanent survey marker A.O. Wheeler placed in 1913 to mark the Continental Divide.

Pedestrians continued to use the pass, including the 82 diehard members of the Alpine Club of Canada who, in spite of the ongoing war in Europe, attended the club's eleventh annual camp from July 13 to 31, 1917, near Simpson Pass.[9] The alpinists began their excursion by taking a motor launch up the Bow River from Banff, almost to Brewster Creek. They then followed the well-cut trail to the Healy Creek valley. En route, they were treated to a glimpse of clouds scudding over the sky on the east side of the range through the great "hole in the wall" in the mountain opposite Mount Bourgeau, which Simpson had mentioned in his account of his

As George Simpson proceeded along Healy Creek toward Simpson Pass, he recorded seeing an opening in a mountain that took the appearance of the gateway to a giant's fortress. He named the mountain Hole-in-the-Wall Mountain. It is now known as The Goat's Eye.

around the world trip (see above). Enthusiastic climbers proceeded past the valley base camp to establish a subsidiary camp among the larches beside Bill Peyto's Lake (an unnamed lake near the remains of one of Peyto's cabins), higher up the mountain near the summit of Simpson Pass. Many of the most interesting climbing expeditions started from this camp, which commanded a fine view of The Monarch and other peaks.

Lake Minnewanka

In 1841 Alexis Piché had guided Sir George Simpson into "a defile between mountainous ridges ... [T]his valley, which was from two to three miles in width, contained four beautiful lakes, communicating with each other by small streams; and the fourth of the series, which was about fifteen miles by three, we named after Peechee, as being our guide's usual home."[10] Later in the nineteenth century, travellers knew Simpson's Peechee's Lake as Devil's Lake (from the Stoney *m'ne-sto*) and Devil's Head Lake. In 1888 the Department of the Interior officially recognized it as Lake Minnewanka, Stoney for "Lake of the Water Spirit." According to legend, "one of the first Indians who saw the lake, viewed it from the summit of one of the highest mountains which surround it. From this vantage point, he noticed a fish in the water which appeared to be as long as the lake, leading him to call the lake 'The lake of the Evil Water-Spirit.'"[11]

The area had an extensive history of Aboriginal use. Lake Minnewanka bears archaeological evidence of Clovis people living along its shoreline some ten thousand years ago; at the site where the Cascade River enters the lake at Stewart Canyon, archaeologists have found evidence of continuous occupation spanning one hundred centuries.[12] Nevertheless, prior to the 1885 completion of the Canadian Pacific Railway, few non-Aboriginal people recorded visits to the lake. George Simpson's 1841 sojourn was followed by the Reverend Robert Terrill Rundle's arrival on June 28, 1847.[13] Rundle spent several days camped on the lakeshore admiring its beauty. Before leaving for Devil's Gap, he carved his initials and the date on a tree. (Unfortunately, the marking has since disappeared.) Later, during the 1870s, Morley trader David McDougall regularly travelled through Devil's Gap to Lake Minnewanka.

After the railway went through the area, the number of visitors following Simpson's route from Banff to Lake Minnewanka increased dramatically; the trip was easy and the scenery magnificent. In the fall of 1887, George Stewart, superintendent of Rocky Mountains (Banff) National Park, initiated construction of a wagon road from Banff to the lake. Once completed the following spring, it enabled the lake to be reached by horse-drawn wagon rather than on horseback, greatly facilitating tourist travel. One of Banff's more famous visitors, glaciologist William Vaux, describes the "excursion of the day" during his stay in Banff in 1894:

> We had a three seated wagon, and Dr. McBride and wife went with us. I sat by the driver, a very intelligent Canadian who had been with the Mounted Police for six years, and seemed to be familiar with all the customs and traditions of the Indians, as well as to know the names of the principal mountain peaks. The drive of nine miles to the lake was over a good road, very level, and from which we had most superb views of the Cascade Mountains and Mount Inglismaldie.... Lake Minnewanka is beautifully situated among the mountains at about the same elevation as the hotel at Banff, i.e., 5000 feet.[14]

Five years later Walter Wilcox, a man who spent many summers exploring in the Rockies, travelled by horseback

> along its north shore to the chain of pools beyond.... An excellent trail, much favored by the Indians, follows the north shore. On the second day we passed the end of Devil's Lake and made camp finally by the borders of another small lake, in a place almost surrounded by mountains but commanding a view of the plains toward the east.... This is the valley of the Ghost River, a strange vale of limestone formation where no streams flow.... A few miles to the east, the mountains end abruptly, and the entrance upon the plains is called the Devil's Gap.[15]

Reverend Robert Rundle was a Methodist minister who spent eight years working with Aboriginal peoples on the plains south of Edmonton. He ventured into the mountains twice, and on one trip spent several days camped on the shores of Lake Minnewanka.

The area's popularity was such that a trail was built along the north side of the lake in 1910 and on to the Ghost River in 1912.

Unfortunately, most of the valley has since been dramatically altered. In 1895 a small wooden dam was built across the lake's outflow, Devil's Creek, to control the water level at the wharf at the tiny community of Minnewanka Landing. This structure did not alter the lake's water level, but in 1912 the federal government granted Calgary Power permission to build a storage dam on the lake to control flow into the Bow River and hence to its Seebe generating stations. This structure raised the water level 12 feet (3.7 metres), flooding 1,000 acres (4047 square metres). Much of the village had to be relocated from the lakeshore, and even the new trail along the north shore may have been wiped out.

When Charles and Mary Walcott, who travelled extensively throughout the Rocky Mountains, visited the lake on July 4, 1919, the view would have been significantly different from that which Mary's brother, George Vaux, had enjoyed in 1894. It is difficult to judge exactly how, as the couple was so busy searching for Upper Cambrian fossils (Charles) and painting and collecting wildflowers (Mary) during their five days at Lake Minnewanka that neither recorded their impressions of the scenery. Walcott's records were more along the lines of this July 6 diary entry: "All our party rode to head of lake and to Devil's Gap. Located next camp & place to try for Upper Cambrian fossils. A strong gale made everything difficult. Mary bro't in a number of wild flowers & some new to her."[16] Evidently the trip was sufficiently enjoyable that they returned to Devil's Gap the following year to spend a week studying geology, collecting fossils and photographing wildflowers and geological formations.

Twenty years later, the lakeshore was altered even more dramatically than it had been in 1912. Under the War Measures Act, in 1940 Calgary Power was granted permission to divert the Ghost River into Lake Minnewanka, raising the water level by 25 metres in order to supply electrical power.[17] The size of Lake Minnewanka doubled and the valley was altered beyond recognition. All trails along the shores were obliterated and had to be rebuilt at much higher levels.

Above: This dam, built on Devil's Creek in 1895, was intended to moderate the water level at the wharf at Minnewanka Landing. The original village on Lake Minnewanka was flooded by later dams.

Below: Lake Minnewanka is now a reservoir for TransAlta Utilities. The dam, seen in the front of this photo, was built in 1941 and raised the water level of the valley by 25 metres, totally submerging the original lakes and trail, as well as the village of Minnewanka Landing.

The Trail Today

The old Aboriginal trail George Simpson followed through Devil's Gap, along the south side of the second and third Ghost Lakes, and along the north side of the first Ghost Lake in 1841, is very likely the same one used by today's travellers. But once Simpson reached the east shore of Lake Minnewanka, he would have followed close to the lakeshore as it was then. That portion of Lake Minnewanka's valley is now entirely underwater. The modern trail, although still in the valley along much of the eastern half of the lake, rises high on the very steep side of the Palliser Range as it travels west. It then leaves the lakeshore to cross a forested headland before arriving at the western end of the lake. Observant hikers often see a herd of bighorn sheep grazing on the side of the trail, especially where the forest has been burned to allow revegetation.

In the summer of 2008, a group of vacationers in a small motorboat were treated to a very unusual display of the rules of nature at play. Along the shore, two bighorn sheep were grazing and perhaps taking a drink from the lake. Appearing to sense danger, one of the sheep left the area. Much to his peril, the second either did not notice or ignored the signs. A cougar (mountain lion) that had been carefully stalking the two concentrated on the remaining sheep. The observant boaters had a ringside seat as the cat pounced on his prey, and their photographs of the sequence of events appeared in the next issue of the local papers. It is extremely unusual for anyone to observe a predator taking down its prey and even more unusual to be able to photograph the event. These visitors left the lake with a most unique story for the folks back home.

Predators take advantage of the fact that the shore of Lake Minnewanka is often visited by bighorn sheep. Tourists in a small boat were able to capture this remarkable image of a cougar taking down a bighorn sheep on the lakeshore.

The west end of Lake Minnewanka is accessible by road, enabling today's hikers to break the route into sections. Travelling from the east, George Simpson and his party would have made their way along the eastern side of Cascade Mountain, likely along the Cascade River as far as Cascade Pond, then south to the Bow River and into what is today the town of Banff. Somewhere along the way they would have forded the Bow River and made their way south of the Vermilion Lakes, perhaps close to today's Healy Creek trail. The trail guide describes a route from Lake Minnewanka to Healy Creek that approximates the route Simpson might have taken, staying on existing trails and avoiding roadways as much as possible.

For those wishing to experience something close to Simpson's path, the route described from Devil's Gap to the Bourgeau Parking Lot at the Sunshine gondola station can be covered on foot or by bicycle, though the Tunnel Mountain Road section and the Sunshine access road are best done by cycle or automobile. Because there are so many roads in the area, the hikes can easily be split up into day hikes and are suitable for hikers of all ages. These are not wilderness hikes, as you are never far from motorized vehicles, but most sections make very pleasant family outings and are well worth doing.

From today's Bourgeau Parking Lot, modern hikers can retrace Simpson's route up Healy Creek and on to Simpson Pass. Driving to the parking lot shortens the trip sufficiently to make Simpson Pass and Healy Pass a very popular day hike for people of all ages. Simpson Pass is a low pass, below the treeline, and the scenery is not dramatic, but the meadow that marks the top of the pass and the Continental Divide makes a pleasant lunch spot. Other than the marker and the junction of two trails leading east to Sunshine Meadows and west to Healy Meadows and Pass, the pass looks much as it did when Sir George carved his initials on a tree in 1841.

In 2005 the authors took Janice's son, Christopher, to the campground just before the junction with the trail leading to Simpson Pass. At age five, his first backpacking trip was a real treat, and his own backpack carried the necessities for a five-year-old on his first major trip: boxes of Smarties.

Necessary supplies for legendary outfitter and guide Bill Peyto[18] would have been quite different when he established his cabin near Simpson Pass in the early twentieth century. Peyto spent much of the next 40 years in the area as a prospector, miner and park warden. The remains of the cabin are still there. Nature has taken its toll, but even with collapsed roof and walls, the cabin draws the imagination to the lifestyle of this reclusive and often lonely man.

From the top of Simpson Pass, the trip down the North Simpson River to the Simpson River is a rugged bushwhack. Only a few people have used the route since Simpson's time, and a trail was never cut to make the route more passable, perhaps because of the difficulty. Nicky Brink and Stephen Bown describe the route as it was in 2007 in *Forgotten Highways*.[19] This is a trip for the brave of heart (who are also experienced travellers). The authors do not recommend it.

The trip along the Simpson River, on the other hand, is straightforward river-valley hiking on a reasonably good trail. The section between Surprise Creek and Scout Camp is not heavily used by hikers and no longer maintained to the standards it once was, although it is still in good condition, with deadfalls. Most will want to access this section from the Vermilion River, which makes a suitable day hike for all ages.

From the junction of the Simpson and Vermilion rivers, Simpson's party would have followed the Vermilion to the Kootenay River. They then followed the Kootenay downstream to Swede Creek, which led them to Sinclair Pass, Creek and Canyon, and on to the Columbia River. This route can only be traversed today by road.

Bill Peyto built this cabin near Simpson Pass as a reclusive hideout. The cabin seems to have been built in stages, with both horizontal and vertical logs. Although in disrepair, it gives a good indication of Peyto's lifestyle early in the twentieth century.

Trail Guide

Distances are adapted from existing trail guides: Patton and Robinson, Potter, Beers, and Eastcott, and from Gem-Trek maps. Distances intermediate from those given in the sources are estimated from topographical maps and from hiking times. All distances are given in kilometres.

Devil's Gap to the Vermilion River over Simpson Pass

Maps 82 O/3 Canmore

82 O/4 Banff

82 O/6 Lake Minnewanka

82 J/13 Mount Assiniboine

Gem-Trek Banff and Mount Assiniboine

Gem-Trek Banff Up-Close

Gem-Trek Kootenay National Park

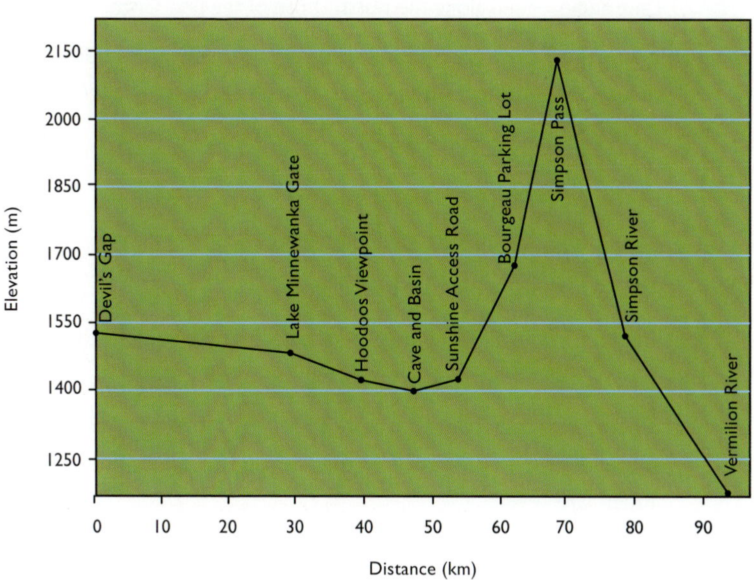

Trailhead

The trailhead at Devil's Gap is described above in Route I, Devil's Gap to Canmore over Carrot Creek Summit (page 52). Because the trailhead is difficult to access through the foothills to the east, the best way to reach Devil's Gap is to hike or cycle along the north shore of Lake Minnewanka as described below, km 0.0 to km 29.5, only in reverse. However, this does entail hiking or cycling this portion of the trail both ways. For instruction on accessing Devil's Gap by road, see Route I, Devil's Gap to Canmore over Carrot Creek Summit (page 52). The south end of the trail is at the Simpson River trail parking area on the east side of Highway 93, 5.9 km south of the Vermilion Crossing Visitor Centre. The site is well marked, and there is a bridge across the Vermilion River at the parking lot.

0.0 Devil's Gap and the Banff National Park boundary. From the park boundary, the well-worn horse trail twists and turns around natural contours. Proceed westward along the south shore of the third Ghost Lake then continue past the second Ghost Lake.

3.8 Trail junction. The trail to the left goes to Carrot Creek. Keep to the right (northwest), cross the shallow outflow from the second Ghost Lake and proceed along the north shore of the first Ghost Lake.

6.7 East end of Lake Minnewanka. The trail passes through light forest along the lakeshore with good views across the lake.

8.9 Narrows Campground (Lm22).

10.7 Mount Costigan Campground (Lm20).

18.4 Mount Inglismaldie Campground (Lm11).

20.2 Aylmer Canyon Campground (Lm9).

21.7 Junction. The trail to Aylmer Pass and Lookout goes to the right (north). Continue southwest along the lakeshore.

24.9 Before the trail starts to climb high above the lakeshore, a subterranean stream pours from the side of the mountain just above lake level.

26.5 At the top of the rise, a viewpoint looks out over the lake and surrounding mountains.

27.9 Junction. The trail to Stewart Canyon goes to the right. Continue ahead (west and south) and cross the Stewart Canyon bridge.

28.9 A Parks trail sign indicates the beginning of the trail along the north shore of Lake Minnewanka.

29.5 Access gate near the tour boat concession. Continue southwest along the access road leading to the lake.

30.5 Enter a field on the right and follow its southwest edge to an old road. Turn left (southwest) on the old road, circle to the right around an outfitter's cabin and corral and continue through the woods.

31.5 Trailhead for the Cascade Valley Trail (Cascade Fire Road). The C-Level Cirque trail goes to the right (northwest) from this parking lot. Exit the parking lot to the road and travel a short distance southwest along the road to the parking area for lower Bankhead. From the viewpoint, take the trail down over the side to the artefacts display area, continue south to the junction then turn right and follow a trail south.

34.6 Road to Cascade Ponds. Cross this road and follow a short trail to the main Lake Minnewanka access road. Turn left (south) and follow the road under the Trans-Canada Highway.

36.7 Junction. Turn left (east) on the Tunnel Mountain Road. Continue along this road, travelling east, then south, until the road turns west.

39.8 Hoodoos Viewpoint. Follow the trail on top of the escarpment west to the Tunnel Mountain Viewpoint. Continue west and south through the woods with some steep downhill sections. Soon after a field in the gap between Tunnel and Rundle mountains, start a steep uphill climb to the top of a ridge. Keep left at a trail junction then start downhill. At a Parks Canada sign turn right, climb the stairs to the road and follow Buffalo Street down to a trail on the left that follows the Bow River. Throughout this section, you are always heading south and west.

45.2 Bow River bridge. Cross the river on the bridge and turn right (west) on a gravel trail parallel to the road.

46.7 Cave and Basin parking lot. Continue west on the asphalt trail toward Sundance Canyon.

49.0 Junction. The trail to Sundance Canyon continues ahead and curves south. Turn right (west) on the Brewster Creek trail. Follow an old road parallel to the meandering Bow River.

51.8 Junction. The Brewster Creek Trail veers left and curves to the south. Continue to the right (west) on the Healy Creek trail, cross Healy Creek on a bridge and come to a parking lot.

53.6 Sunshine ski area access road. To continue along George Simpson's route, there is no alternative but to follow the Sunshine road to the gondola station.

62.6 Bourgeau Parking Lot. Proceed to the southwest end of the parking lot then continue past the gondola station to the trailhead signboard for the Healy Pass–Simpson Pass trail. Cross Healy Creek on a bridge and start uphill (southwest) on an old road.

63.4 Junction. The road continues ahead. Turn right (southwest) on the Healy Pass trail. Continue uphill through the forest on a good trail. Cross a bridge across a small creek.

65.7 Cross Healy Creek on a bridge and continue gently uphill through the forest, parallel to the creek. The trail crosses three avalanche paths that provide good views of the surrounding mountains.

67.8 At the end of the third avalanche path there is the foundation of an old log cabin off to the left, visible from the trail.

68.1 Healy Creek Campground (E5).

68.5 Junction. The Healy Pass trail continues to the right (west). Turn left (south), cross Healy Creek on a bridge and start to climb a rough rocky trail. The route is mainly through the trees but does include several meadows.

69.8 Open meadow with trail junctions and markers signifying the Alberta–British Columbia provincial boundary and the Continental Divide. The trail to the left goes to Sunshine Meadows. The Healy Pass–Egypt Lakes trail goes to the right. Straight ahead is the valley of the North Simpson River. This is the route Simpson took, but there is no trail there today. Proceeding ahead, hikers are faced with approximately 7 km of very tough bushwhacking before reaching the Simpson River. The authors do not recommend this route. Instead, we propose either hiking km 76.8 to 94.3 in reverse, starting at the Vermilion River and following the Simpson River to Scout Camp, or hiking from Simpson Pass to Citadel Pass and on to the junction with the Porcupine Camp trail (Route V below, Simpson Pass to Lake Magog (Mount Assiniboine) over Citadel Pass, km 0.0 to 18.1, pages 159–61). Turn right (south) and hike the 0.5 km toward Porcupine Camp, turning right (west) at the Simpson River and following the north side of the river 7.9 km to Scout Camp.

76.8 Simpson River at Scout Camp. Turn right on the Simpson River trail, heading slightly west of south. Immediately downstream, the North Simpson River joins the main river. I managed to cross this river on a log jam; there may be a footbridge upstream. A horse trail follows the river but is sometimes hard to locate. A better foot path climbs high above the river on solid ground and continues through the forest.

81.3 Verdant Creek. Cross the creek on a footbridge, continue through the trees and cross several small creeks and wetlands. The trail was once well maintained with split log walkways over wet areas, but it is no longer kept up and now has a lot of deadfalls.

83.4 Trail Junction. The trail up Surprise Creek to Ferro Pass branches to the left (east). Continue ahead along the Simpson River on the trail that veers southwest.

85.5 Kootenay National Park boundary. Continue heading west toward the Vermilion River. A good trail follows a fairly narrow valley quite close to the river, mainly through a burned out area. For the most part, hikers get good views of the surrounding mountains.

89.6 Cross a major stream on a footbridge. The trail is relatively flat and easy going along the river, mainly through a burned out area (2004).

93.4 The trail leaves the river and heads north.

94.1 Trail junction. The trail to the Mount Shanks lookout continues ahead. Turn left (west) for the Vermilion River footbridge.

94.3 Vermilion River and trailhead parking area. This river flows into the Kootenay approximately 25 km downstream.

When George Simpson crossed Simpson Pass and followed the Simpson River to the Vermillion, he would have continued south to the Kootenay River and on to the Columbia. Today travellers along the Vermillion River are often treated with a view of mountain goats such as these at a mineral lick on the side of the road.

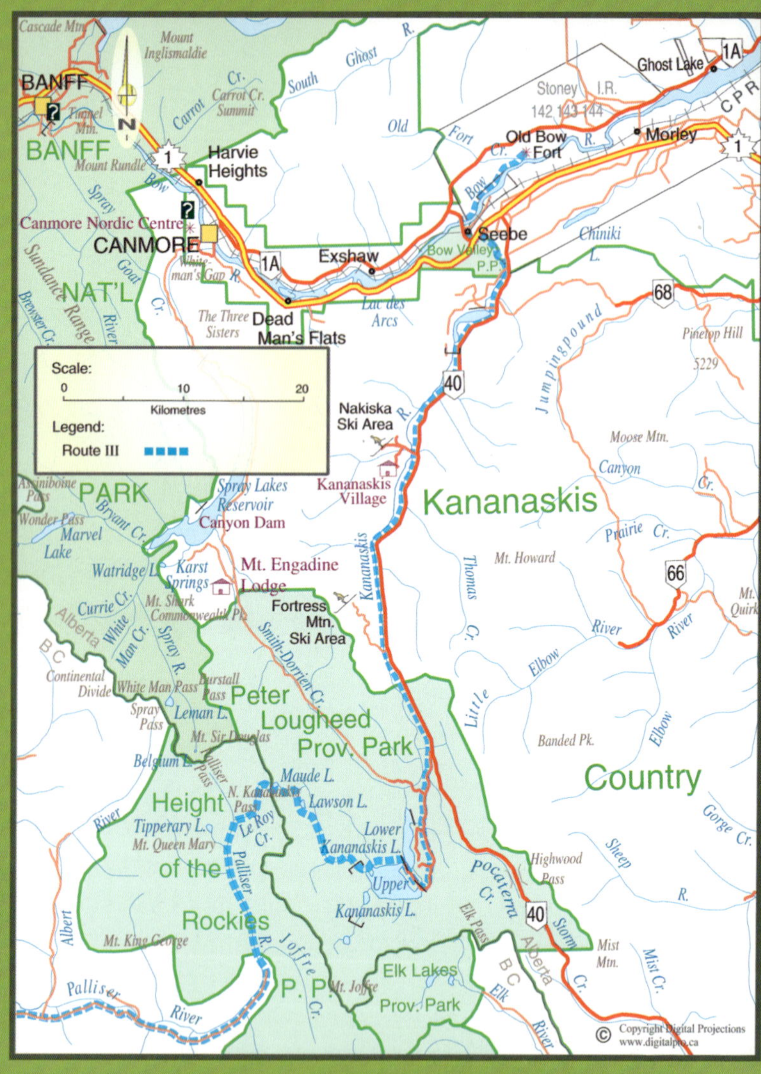

James Sinclair's Route from Old Bow Fort to the Kootenay River over North Kananaskis Pass

Route III

Lost on High Passes: James Sinclair's Route from Old Bow Fort to the Kootenay River over North Kananaskis Pass

My first trip over North Kananaskis Pass was with Janice and a group of her teenaged friends. We were nearing the end of a 13-day hike that followed the Continental Divide from the Ottertail River in Yoho National Park to the Kananaskis Lakes, crossing the divide six times. As we left the Palliser River to head up Leroy Creek, the well-defined trail we had been following came to an end. Fortunately – or so we thought at the time – there had been recent trail cutting, and the route was marked by a single strand of white thread. As unusual as it seemed for a trail to be marked with a strand of thread, the direction seemed right, so we followed it. The newly cut area and the strand of thread continued to climb steeply up the side of the mountain, veering a little to the left of where we thought we should be, but as no other route was visible, we continued along this path.

Eventually we realized that we were heading toward a dead-end valley, blocked by a glacier. Our only option was to turn right and make our way along the side of the mountain until we intercepted the trail going over the pass. After several hours fighting our way through shin-tangle and other vegetation, sustained only by glimpses of the pass far ahead, we made it to the drainage of Leroy Creek and the correct trail. By the time we reached the pass, we were exhausted, darkness was falling, the next campground was still some distance away and we had not yet eaten our evening meal.

When we reached Maude Lake, located a short distance past the top of the pass on a grassy plateau high above treeline, we decided to stop for the night. We knew there was no safe place to store our food, but we had lost the final rays of sunshine and few of the weary travellers had the energy to push on. I tried to console the group of young people – whom I had been conscientiously warning about the danger of bears – by insisting that bears did not normally frequent such high elevations nor such open plateaus. We set up our tents, ate and dove into our sleeping bags as quickly as possible. By breakfast the next morning, spirits had been restored, our gear was packed up and we proceeded on our way – only to find fresh grizzly diggings metres from our campsite! So much for my reassuring comments ...

This small lake, high above the treeline, is near the Continental Divide at North Kananaskis Pass. The trail to the pass can be seen on the right of the photo.

Chronology

1854 James Sinclair leads a party of one hundred people and their 250 cattle from Fort Garry to Kananaskis Country. When it becomes obvious that their guide, Maskapetoon, no longer knows the way, Sinclair takes over leading the large and unwieldy group and eventually finds North Kananaskis Pass.

1857 Captain John Palliser and four men set out to investigate North Kananaskis Pass, beginning at Old Bow Fort. They follow a fairly easy track from the Kananaskis Lakes to a height of land then descend to the river below, which they name the Palliser River.

1858–59 The Overlanders use North Kananaskis Pass to cross the Divide in their attempt to reach the goldfields of the Caribou via an overland route.

1881 A Canadian Pacific Railway survey crew runs a line from the Bow River to the summit of North Kananaskis Pass, demonstrating that the route is unsatisfactory for a railway.

1901 Walter Wilcox and Henry G. Bryant explore the Kananaskis Valley. They reach Lawson Lake, which Wilcox names before continuing on alone to Maude Lake. He does not continue down the west side of North Kananaskis Pass.

1923 A wagon road is built from the Bow River to the Kananaskis Lakes, a distance of 48 miles (77 kilometres).

1926 Caroline Hinman's Off the Beaten Track tour uses the new wagon road then continues across North Kananaskis Pass and down Leroy Creek to the Palliser River.

History

Following the Compass

In 1841 James Sinclair led a group of Métis immigrants from Fort Garry (Winnipeg) to the Oregon Territory over White Man Pass.[1] At the time, local Aboriginal people told him about another pass (North Kananaskis Pass) farther to the south. The Kootenay people regularly used both it and its sister pass to the south, South Kananaskis Pass, to provide a direct route from west of the mountains to a favourite hunting ground at the Kananaskis Lakes.

When Simpson asked him to repeat the trek in 1854, Sinclair was eager to explore the new route. He left Fort Garry on May 26 with one hundred adventurers: 28 men together with their wives and children – including Sinclair's own family – and 250 cattle. They headed directly west toward Fort Edmonton, meeting up with Sinclair's former guide, Chief Maskapetoon, along the way. The chief agreed to lead them over Sinclair's new pass.

The Métis settlers left Edmonton House in mid-August. This time, they proceeded directly south from Fort Edmonton, the women and children in ox-drawn carts and the men driving the cattle. They did not enter the mountains at Devil's Gap but continued on to the Bow River, which they followed west to the mouth of the Kananaskis River. They broke up their Red River carts at Old Bow Fort then proceeded south over very difficult terrain along the Kananaskis.

It soon became obvious that they were lost; Maskapetoon did not know the way over the Kootenays' pass. Determined to salvage the expedition, Sinclair took over leading the large and unwieldy group. Strong compass work eventually led him to North Kananaskis Pass, but the slow and tortuous route meant it would take them 30 days to cross the Divide, as opposed to the ten it had previously taken to cross White Man Pass. By the time they reached the pass in mid-October, the snow was already deep on the ground. They laboriously broke a trail over the pass then followed the Palliser River from its base to familiar ground

James Sinclair (1805–1854)

James Sinclair was born at Oxford House, an HBC post on the Hayes River north of Lake Winnipeg, en route to York Factory on Hudson's Bay. His father, William Sinclair, chief factor of the post, was originally from the Orkney Islands. His mother, whose name is unknown, was a Cree from the Nahovway band. As a boy, Sinclair was educated in the language and ways of his mother's people, learning the skills necessary for survival: hunting, trapping, canoeing, dog sledding and snowshoeing. When the elder Sinclair died in 1819, his wishes were fulfilled and fourteen-year-old James was sent to school in Orkney. At age 17 young Sinclair attended Edinburgh University, where he studied the arts and law. In spite of his father's hopes that he would stay in Britain following his formal education, James chose to return to Canada.

Sinclair apprenticed with the Hudson's Bay Company at Moose Factory on James Bay for a year then began to work for free-trader Andrew McDermot around 1827. Sinclair became well acquainted with the Aboriginal people at Red River and travelled widely with the Métis as far south as St. Louis, Missouri.

In 1829 he married Elizabeth Bird, daughter of HBC Chief Factor James Bird. The Sinclairs had nine children, several of whom died young. Their eldest daughter, Elizabeth, and only son, Alexander, died in an 1834 dysentery epidemic, and younger daughters Emma and Louise in a 1843 epidemic. Another son may have died during this period.

By the 1830s, both the United States and Great Britain had turned their attention to the Oregon Territory west of the Rockies. American settlers were rapidly occupying the area and Hudson's Bay Company Governor George Simpson was anxious to counteract this flow with settlers loyal to Britain. He arranged for James Sinclair to lead a group of Métis across the Rockies in

1841. Sinclair was considered a firm but fair leader who laid down the rules for the trip at the beginning and expected everyone to do his or her share. The large and cumbersome group arrived safely at Fort Vancouver in present-day Washington State on October 13.

Sinclair left Fort Vancouver in December but it was the following summer before he was able to reach Fort Garry. He resumed his work with McDermot, again travelling widely. In February 1845, Elizabeth Sinclair died, forcing James to close his house and send his three oldest children to boarding school while relatives looked after the youngest. Meanwhile, deteriorating relations between the Red River Métis and the HBC led to a request that Sinclair travel to London to plead the Métis case. He obliged, but to no avail.

When he returned to Red River in the spring of 1847, Sinclair married Mary Campbell, the daughter of Chief Trader Colin Campbell. Tension between his daughters and his new wife led him to send the girls, Harriet and Maria, to boarding school in Illinois. He spent the year of 1849 away from Red River, during which time he decided to move his family to Oregon and begin taking steps toward becoming an American citizen. In the meantime, George Simpson asked him to return to Oregon to investigate the condition of the HBC forts there. He returned to Red River in 1852 then headed back to the Oregon Territory the following year with another group of Métis settlers – including his own family. They left on May 24, 1854, and after a difficult crossing of the mountains by a new route, reached Walla Walla, Washington, in December. Sinclair left his family there while he escorted most of the group to Fort Vancouver, then he returned to Walla Walla to settle.

It was not long before Aboriginal uprisings began all along the Columbia, leading Sinclair to evacuate his family to Dalles on the Columbia River. On an 1856 journey back to Walla Walla to salvage what he could of the HBC property, Sinclair became embroiled in the conflict. He and 40 residents of the Cascades were hurriedly shepherded into the village store – the only defensible building in the vicinity. Sinclair took charge of their protection, opening the door when two more people were seen running toward the store for safety. This compassionate gesture ended his life. As the door swung open, a bullet struck Sinclair, killing him instantly. His body was hidden inside the building to prevent mutilation by the marauding band, and a day or two later the US Cavalry rescued the remaining occupants.

HBC Chief Factor MacTavish had Sinclair's body moved to Fort Vancouver, where he was given a full Masonic funeral. His wife, who was left with a step-son, three daughters and another son on the way, was compensated for her losses by the US government with a large land grant in the Walla Walla valley. When Governor George Simpson heard of Sinclair's death, he declared that the Hudson's Bay Company had lost one of its best men and ablest officers.

James Sinclair was a Métis born north of Fort Garry and educated in Scotland. He led two large groups of Red River settlers across the mountains to the Oregon Territory. The second trip involved a very difficult crossing of North Kananaskis Pass.

This image of North Kananaskis Pass looking south toward the Palliser River belies the difficulty of taking a large number of people and animals down this very steep and gravelly ravine. Sinclair's exploits continue to astound those who pause to ponder them.

at the Kootenay River. The one hundred immigrants and most of the cattle arrived safely at Walla Walla, Washington, on December 16, approximately three months behind schedule.[2]

Exploring the Pass

Captain John Palliser first heard of North Kananaskis Pass in 1848 when he happened to meet up with James Sinclair on a private hunting trip in Montana. Although Sinclair had not yet crossed the pass himself, he passed on the information he had received from Aboriginal people on his 1841 journey. Palliser obtained further information a number of years later in 1857, when a group of Sinclair's 1854 immigrants decided to return to Red River. Guided by a Métis named Whitford, the seven men, three women and their children spent three and a half months retracing their steps from the Columbia over North Kananaskis Pass and across the prairies. At Fort Ellis (in present-day Saskatchewan), they crossed paths with Captain Palliser, giving him the opportunity to interview them about North Kananaskis Pass.

One of the Palliser Expedition's mandates was to explore all the passes across the Rockies south of Athabasca Pass. Palliser was determined to investigate North Kananaskis Pass in 1858, starting from Old Bow Fort. His main problem was that none of the local men seemed to know where the pass was located. From his conversations with Sinclair and the returning Métis, he knew that the entrance to thc pass was up a tributary of the Bow River. He, four men and nine horses left old Bow Fort on August 18, forded the Bow River upstream of the fort and started up the Kananaskis River valley.

As they made their way up the valley, they could see traces of old Native trails and tepee poles still standing, but they saw no indication that Sinclair's party – or the herd of cattle – had passed through. Their progress was hindered by masses of fallen timber, mostly the result of earlier forest fires. Palliser had difficulty finding feed for his horses and must have wondered how Sinclair managed to feed his large number of horses and cattle.

They passed the waterfall that today houses an electricity generating plant then, farther up the valley, the glacial source of the Kananaskis River. They proceeded past Lower Kananaskis Lake and Upper Kananaskis Lake, spotting elk in the surrounding woods. "While going round the edge of this sheet of water, where the fallen timber greatly embarrassed us," Palliser reported, "one of our horses, strangely enough, adopted the other alternative of swimming across the lake. This effort of intelligence caused us serious misfortune and dismay, as his pack contained our only luxuries, our tea, our sugar, and our bedding."[3] The party continued on over a fairly easy track. Palliser explained:

> Our journey across the Kananaskis pass, although arduous, was not formidable, on account of the abrupt ascents and descents on the eastern slope of the mountains, and the principal difficulty to be overcome was the amount of timber to be cut in order to allow the horses to force their way through.[4]

Captain John Palliser of the Palliser Expedition first heard of North Kananaskis Pass from James Sinclair. Following a difficult crossing of the pass, his men named the river at its southern base after their leader.

They reached the height of land that marks the summit of North Kananaskis Pass on August 22 and camped in a small meadow containing a lake (Maude Lake).[5] The next day they began the steep descent to the river below. The going was not easy. "On the western slope," Palliser explained, "we found the descent very steep, and the obstructions from fallen timber so thick and so severe that on the 24th of August we were occupied 14 hours in accomplishing six miles, and hard work it was."[6] The men named the river after Palliser then followed it to the Kootenay. They returned to Old Bow Fort over the more southerly North Kootenay Pass.

Overlanders

Like White Man Pass and Simpson Pass (Routes I and II above), North Kananaskis Pass never became a popular route across the Continental Divide. It was, however, used in 1858 and 1859 by easterners headed for the goldfields of the Fraser River. Known as the Overlanders, most of these goldseekers travelled to Fort Edmonton then headed west through the mountains, crossing Yellowhead Pass to reach the source of the Fraser River. A smaller number crossed the mountains to the south, using Old Bow Fort to transition from the foothills to the mountains.

The first group to head south from Fort Edmonton was known as the Faribault men. Under the leadership of John Jones, the 12 men were guided by a Métis named Rossette.[7] They left very late in the season, not departing from Edmonton until October 20, 1858. At Fort Edmonton, Captain Palliser, Dr. Hector and Captain Blakiston of the Palliser Expedition had tried to discourage the Faribault party from trying to make the trip across the mountains so late in the season. Three of the men took their advice, opting to winter at the settlement of Lac Ste. Anne, west of Fort Edmonton. The remainder continued on, intent on crossing North Kootenay Pass.

They reached Old Bow Fort on November 2. Having decided to redirect their travels over Captain Palliser's North Kananaskis Pass, they began to retrace his route through the Kananaskis valley. Although only three months had passed since Palliser's men spent so much time chopping fallen timber, Jones made no mention of seeing any evidence of previous travel. By November 6, it was obvious that the guide did not know the way and was lost. Veering south, the party eventually managed to make their way through the deep snow blanketing North Kootenay Pass – the route they had originally intended. After a hard struggle, they reached Kootenay Fort on December 1. It took them another four and a half months of struggle and hardship to reach Fort Colville on the Columbia River – still a long distance from the goldfields of the Fraser.

June 9, 1859, saw another small group of Overlanders head out from Fort Edmonton. The self-guided Goodrich–Hastings party consisted of nine Americans intending to access the goldfields via Palliser's North Kananaskis Pass. En route from Fort Edmonton to Old Bow Fort, they were fortunate to meet up with Dr. James Hector and his party, who gave them a map of North Kananaskis Pass and travelled across the prairie with them long enough to set them on the right track.

The Goodrich–Hastings party arrived at Old Bow Fort on July 1, where they met up with four more Overlanders who had wintered at Red River. Continuing up the Kananaskis River, they found that travel "was very difficult and wearisome, the trail being covered with fallen timber, and numerous small streams being very high. Our provisions had given out soon after entering the Mountains and we suffered a great deal from hunger, our principal diet of more than twenty days being such berries and dried fish as we could obtain from the straggling Indians we met."[8] Nevertheless, thanks to Hector's guidance, they managed to successfully cross North Kananaskis Pass and arrived at Fort Colville on the Columbia River on August 10, 1859.

Another party of Overlanders, known as the New Brunswick party, left Fort Garry in early June and Fort Edmonton on August 3. Its 45 members were also headed for North Kananaskis Pass and they, too, met up with Hector on their way to Old Bow Fort. Their guide, a Métis named Whitford whom they had engaged at the Red River settlement, had earlier escorted a group of immigrants returning home from the Oregon Territory over North Kananaskis Pass. Under his expert leadership, the party made excellent time and crossed the pass with no trouble, arriving at Fort Colville on September 17.

Later that same year, a party of seven men left Fort Edmonton on September 20. Unable to find a guide, they decided to attempt to locate North Kananaskis Pass on their own. On October 4, they met the Earl of Southesk near Old Bow Fort, on his way out of the mountains.[9] The Overlanders were able to exchange salt, flour, rice and dried apples for tobacco, fresh meat, a moose skin and a shoeing hammer. Even more significant to the success of their expedition was the fact that they were able to obtain the services of one of Southesk's Stoney guides. Lacking an interpreter and unfamiliar with any Native language, they would not have been able to arrange this without Southesk's help – even if they had managed to meet up with a potential guide. The guide ably led them across the pass without incident, and they arrived safely at Kootenay Post on October 30.

This flurry of goldseeking activity marked the last widespread use of North Kananaskis Pass as an east–west route through the mountains. The only recorded visitors prior to the era of the tourist-explorer were David McDougall, a trader from Morley who travelled up the Kananaskis Valley and over the pass with Native bands in the 1870s,[10] and an 1881 CPR survey crew that ran a line from the Bow River to the summit of North Kananaskis Pass and concluded that the route was unsatisfactory for a railway.

Pleasure Seekers

Even after 1885, when the railway began ushering tourists and explorers to the Bow Valley, very few ventured as far east and south as North Kananaskis Pass. Walter Wilcox, who spent most of his summers in the Rocky Mountains, was one of the few who did. In 1901 outfitter Tom Wilson supplied Wilcox and Henry G. Bryant with 14 horses, guide Tom Lusk, wrangler Jim Wood and assistant Ben Woodworth. They travelled to the Kananaskis Lakes along a circuitous route over Elk Pass.[11] As part of their explorations in the area, Wilcox and Wood decided to seek out North Kananaskis Pass on foot. On reaching Lawson Lake, Wilcox named it and continued alone toward the pass. After some effort, he passed Maude Lake to arrive at the pass at four in the afternoon, but he did not continue down the west side. After three weeks on the trail, the group left the lakes on August 24 to follow Sinclair's old route down the

Henry G. Bryant explored with his friend Walter Wilcox in the Mount Assiniboine and Kananaskis Lakes region. The stream leading from Assiniboine Pass to the Spray River was named Bryant Creek in his honour.

Walter Wilcox explored extensively in the Rocky Mountains, pioneering the route east from Mount Assiniboine along Bryant Creek to the Spray River. He later explored the Kananaskis Lakes region to the south, making it as far as the top of North Kananaskis Pass.

Kananaskis River to the Bow and the railroad. An abandoned logging road facilitated the final stage of their journey.[12]

The only pleasure group to cross the pass during the era of the tourist-explorers and mountaineers was Caroline Hinman's 1926 Off the Beaten Track tour. Jim Boyce outfitted the excursion, with help from Charlie Hunter, Bert Mickel, Lew Blow, Slim and Max. Hinman's 11 guests – including four men and Hinman's friend and frequent travelling companion, Lillian Gest – followed Sinclair and Palliser's route along the Kananaskis River, undoubtedly over the 77-kilometre wagon road that had been built from the Bow River to the Kananaskis Lakes in 1923. They spent their second night, July 3, camped on Porcupine Creek near the Lower Kananaskis Lake, taking day trips to Elk Pass and Highwood Pass. On July 12 they proceeded toward North Kananaskis Pass, camping near the site of today's Turbine Canyon Campground. After a three-day layover, they crossed the pass and made their way down Leroy Creek to the Palliser River. They then made their way north over Palliser Pass and Wonder Pass to Mount Assiniboine.[13]

Right: Lillian Gest spent most summers of her adult life in the Canadian Rockies, often accompanying her friend Caroline Hinman on her Off the Beaten Track tours. Gest enjoyed hunting and fishing and is seen here with the spoils of one of her fishing adventures.

Below: In the first two decades of the twentieth century, Caroline Hinman led her Off the Beaten Track tours throughout the Canadian Rocky Mountains. Her 1926 tour took a group from the Kananaskis Lakes over North Kananaskis Pass to the Palliser River.

The Trail Today

Sinclair, Palliser and the Overlanders likely forded the Bow River somewhere near the mouth of the Kananaskis River then followed the latter almost to the top of North Kananaskis Pass. The route described here follows that route as closely as possible, although much of it is now highway rather than trail.

Starting at Old Bow Fort, follow highways 1A and 1X to the south side of the Trans-Canada Highway. This makes a pleasant cycling trip, although the shoulders are narrow. From a gate just east of the Trans-Canada to the Nakiska access road, there is a reasonably good horse trail, suitable for bicycles, hikers and equestrians, though it is rough and muddy in places and often passes through forested areas with no views of the surrounding countryside. This valley-bottom trail will appeal to cyclists more than to hikers.

The well-maintained trails around Kananaskis Village are suitable for both hikers and cyclists. Often located near the escarpment, they provide excellent views over the Kananaskis River valley. Deer are often seen in the area; I was fortunate enough to view a doe and two spotted fawns near the village a few years ago. The Terrace Trail leading to the Galatea Day Use Area is a pleasant cycle or hike, and because it stays high on the side of the mountain it offers good views of the golf course and river valley. Early travellers, however, probably remained down in the valley.

From the Galatea Day Use Area, follow Highway 40 to the entrance to Peter Lougheed Provincial Park and the park road to the North Interlakes Day Use Area. Sinclair and later travellers likely stayed close to the lakeshore, but the lakes have been dammed for power generation and look quite different today than they did more than 150 years ago.

Although there are trails that can be followed most of the way from Old Bow Fort to the Kananaskis Lakes (see Trail Guide below), most visitors will use the roads; the area is geared to picnicking and camping from automobiles. There are complete facilities for both in Bow Valley Provincial Park and numerous day use facilities along Highway 40 between Bow Valley and Peter Lougheed Provincial Parks. Within the latter, there are numerous camping and day use facilities. In addition, Kananaskis Village provides complete hotel and dining facilities.

The trail from the lakes to the top of North Kananaskis Pass is a true backcountry hiking and cycling trail, and the first section makes a good day hike. It is a well-maintained trail, though cyclists are only allowed as far as Invincible Creek. All of the major streams are bridged, and the amazing scenery of river, lakes, glaciers, a canyon, avalanche slopes and towering mountains continues all the way to the top. The trail is suitable for all hikers, though it is often steep between the Forks and Turbine Canyon. There are two backcountry campgrounds along the route, the largest being at Turbine Canyon.

Once at the top of the pass, the trail drops very steeply down toward the Palliser River valley. This part of the trail should only be attempted by strong hikers. The well-used horse trail is easy to follow along Leroy Creek, although some route-finding skills are required along the Palliser River. The south part of the route is largely a matter of following gravel flats along the river. Early travellers would have followed the Palliser River to the Kootenay and on to the Columbia. There are no designated camping spots along this route, but good random camping spots are available; the sites of old outfitters' camps are indicated in the trail guide.

Several years ago, the authors hiked over North Kananaskis Pass from the west with a group of five of Janice's teenaged friends. The trip down from Maude Lake to the Interlakes Day Use Area was the final day of a 13-day hike along the Continental Divide and everyone was looking forward to fresh fruit, "real food," hot showers and soft beds. As we approached the Turbine Canyon Campground for a morning break, I noticed a note protruding from a box near the entrance to the camp. Upon investigation, I found that it was addressed to Jo, one of the members of the party. I called out, "Hey, Jo, there is some mail for you!" Thinking that it was just a joke, she largely ignored the comment but was soon convinced that there was indeed a letter for her. Her letter contained instructions on how to find other notes, beginning an entertaining treasure hunt that provided a degree of levity for a tired group. But our best surprise was yet to come. As we proceeded down the trail, we met a group of friends

Deer are often spotted in the vicinity of Kananaskis Village. Fawns such as these, with white spots indicating their young age, are a delight to locals and tourists alike.

who, after all the hugs and joyous greetings, presented us with the luxury of fresh apples! It is hard to describe how the common apple could be such a treat for a group who had been sustained by dried foods for nearly two weeks. As it turned out, these young people had hiked the route the previous day, leaving the notes in the campground for us to discover.

Trail Guide

Distances are adapted from existing trail guides: Patton and Robinson, Potter, Beers, and Eastcott, and from Gem-Trek maps. Distances intermediate from those given in the sources are estimated from topographical maps and from hiking times. All distances are given in kilometres.

Old Bow Fort to the Palliser River over North Kananaskis Pass

Maps 82 J/11 Kananaskis Lakes

82 J/14 Spray Lakes Reservoir

82 O/3 Canmore

Gem-Trek Canmore and Kananaskis Village

Gem-Trek Kananaskis Lakes

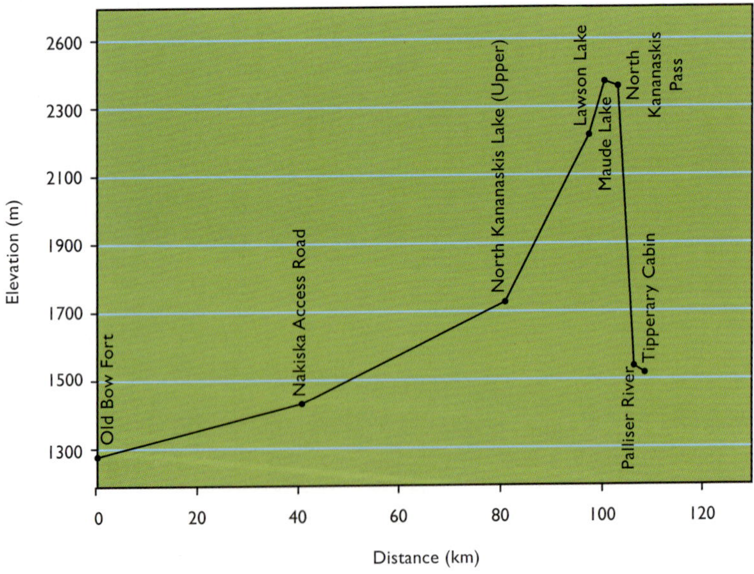

Trailhead

The remains of Old Bow Fort[14] are located on the west end of the Stoney Indian Reserve, high on a plateau at the northeast junction of Old Fort Creek and the Bow River. You will need permission from the Stoney Band to visit the site, but they were more than happy to extend this privilege to me and my wife, Cheryl. The south end of the trail can be approached from the forestry road along the Kootenay and Palliser rivers. Information and maps should be obtained from the British Columbia Forest Service. The authors have not travelled this route.

0.0	Old Bow Fort. Follow the road north from the remains of the fort.
2.4	Junction with Highway 1A. Turn left (southwest) and follow the highway.
8.6	Junction with Highway 1X. Turn left (east) on Highway 1X. Pass the Kananaskis Guest Ranch and cross the Bow River on the highway bridge, and then cross the railway on an overpass and enter Bow Valley Provincial Park.
12.9	Cross the Trans-Canada Highway on an overpass. From here, use the Gem-Trek Canmore map. At the cross-roads, Rafter Six Ranch is on the left, the YMCA on the right. Take the gravel road leading straight ahead (south, then curving east). Pass through a gate, past the site of *Ti-jurahi-chubi* (sacred lodge dance) and through another gate.
16.8	Kananaskis River. Turn right on a dirt road running south and east along the river. Keep right when a branch road goes down to the river. Come to picnic tables and a fire circle at Broken Bridges. A rough single-track horse trail now heads inland to the southwest. It passes through two steep gullies then reaches the top of a ridge, offering good views across the valley. Continue along the top of the ridge, keeping left at an old road junction and again when the single track joins an old road at a hairpin turn. Just downhill from the junction is another trail off to the left; keep ahead.

21.2 Trail junction. The trail to Camp Chief Hector goes to the right (north). Keep left (south) on an old road: the Stoney Trail.

23.3 Trail junction. The Prairie View Trail crosses perpendicular to the Stoney Trail. Turn left (south) on the Prairie View Trail to travel steeply downhill toward Barrier Lake. Follow along the lakeshore then under a power line.

25.3 Trail Junction with the Stoney Trail. Turn right (southwest) on this gravel road.

26.7 Trail junction. The Jewel Pass Trail goes to the right. Keep ahead on the Stoney Trail, which is also the service road for the power line. The road follows under the power line, curving left to avoid a steep bank then right around a marsh and past the Mount Allen substation.

39.0 Nakiska ski area access road and parking lot. From the parking area, head north and west, then turn left on the Troll Falls trail. All trails in this area have government maps posted and should be checked at each intersection. Climb to the top of a small hill, turn left again and cross the Nakiska road.

39.6 Ribbon Creek Day Use Area. Turn left along Ribbon Creek, cross the creek on a bridge then turn left on Terrace Trail. The trail map is posted at the end of the parking area. Continue uphill on Terrace Trail, a good double-track trail. The Kovach Link goes to the right. Keep left. The Terrace Link goes to the right; keep ahead on the Terrace Trail, pass a parking lot and continue on a smooth gravel trail.

41.8 The Kovach Trail goes to the right (west). Continue ahead (south) on the Terrace Trail. The trail splits, with the trail on the left curving back toward the village. Continue ahead (south) on a good single-track trail that climbs to a high ridge overlooking the golf course, enters the woods, crosses a gravel flat of a shallow creek then follows the river and turns left to cross a bridged creek. Turn left at the Galatea Creek Trail, cross the Kananaskis River on a suspension bridge and climb a hill to the parking lot.

49.4 Galatea Day Use Area. From here there is no trail heading south. Continue on Highway 40.

66.7 Road junction. Turn right into Peter Lougheed Provincial Park. Follow this road south through the park.

82.0 North Interlakes Day Use Area. Cross the causeway from the parking area, heading northwest.

82.3 Trail junction. The trail to Mount Indefatigable goes to the right. Keep ahead (west), parallel to the lakeshore.

82.9 Trail junction. The trail going around the lake branches off to the left. Keep right (west) on the Three Isle Lake Trail. The trail leaves the lakeshore and starts a steady climb on an old road.

84.2 Cross a large alluvial fan rock fall. At the end of the rock fall, follow the trail to the left that joins the lakeshore trail. The open area around the rock fall provides great views of the surrounding mountains.

86.0 Bridge across Invincible Creek and the end of the cycling trail. The trail is now a single track.

87.8 Cross the Kananaskis River on a substantial bridge. The trail follows the river through fairly open woods, crossing several bridged side streams.

90.0 Trail junction and Forks Campground. The trail to South Kananaskis Pass goes to the left (west). Keep right, veering northward, for the Maude–Lawson Trail leading to North Kananaskis Pass. The trail soon starts climbing steeply up the side of an avalanche path.

93.5 Cross a rapidly rushing bridged stream. There is a magnificent towering mountain on the left. The trail continues to climb, but more gradually.

94.4 Meadow with a small pond. The trail runs along the side of the meadow, crosses a ridge then heads downhill.

96.3 Beautiful spot on the shore of Lawson Lake. The trail passes through a meadow-like area, goes around the left (west) side of the lake then continues to the northwest. It crosses a bridge over Maude Brook.

98.2 Turbine Canyon Campground. After the campground, the trail swings sharply to the west. Remaining in a meadow between two high mountain ranges, it starts a steady climb toward the pass with views of Beatty Glacier on the left before it begins to drop.

99.0 Trail summit and Maude Lake. The trail goes around the lake on the left (west) side, now above treeline.

100.3 North Kananaskis Pass. Start an extremely steep downhill on a challenging open gravel trail. The well-beaten and easy-to-follow trail gradually enters the trees and flattens out somewhat.

102.0 Valley floor. The easy-to-follow trail meanders back and forth through the valley.

102.5 Leroy Creek. Cross the creek by rock-hopping, then continue south steadily downhill on a good trail along the northwest side of the creek. The trail swings to the southwest into the Palliser River valley, continuing along Leroy Creek.

105.4 Palliser River ford. This is a thigh-deep ford. On the west side of the river, the trail splits, with branches running both north and south. Do not mistake the old camping spot on the left (south) for the trail. Turn north at the junction, following the trail left (west) through a meadow skirting north of some wetlands. After a short distance, the trail swings south away from the river on a well-beaten horse trail through the trees. Continuing south, cross two creeks by rock-hopping before reaching a large creek coming in from the right (west).

107.9 Tipperary Creek. This is a knee-deep ford. A short distance beyond is Tipperary Cabin, an outfitter's backcountry cabin. This is the end of the defined trail. The horse trail continues south from the cabin along the river, but after about 1 km, any defined trail disappears. The horses likely follow the gravel flats of the river, crossing the river and side streams at will. The Palliser River Forest Service Road is approximately 15 km south of the cabin, but I did not attempt to travel down the Palliser River much beyond the cabin as there was no obvious trail. The forestry road leads to the Kootenay River and on to the Columbia.

The very steep descent of the west side of North Kananaskis Pass offers this spectacular view of the Leroy Creek valley. From the creek, the trail continues its steep descent to the Palliser River valley, visible in the background of this image.

Tom Wilson's Route from the Simpson River to Mount Assiniboine over Ferro Pass

Route IV

Outfitting the Mountaineers: Tom Wilson's Route from the Simpson River to Mount Assiniboine over Ferro Pass

Solo backpacking in the Canadian Rockies usually affords the traveller little or no human contact either on the trail or in the campgrounds. On such trips I normally spend my time observing the trail and surroundings, constantly watching and listening for indications from Mother Nature about what is happening in the vicinity and sometimes using trail-finding skills to determine the route. Other than spotting animals from time to time, hikes are normally peaceful and uneventful, with nothing exciting to report when I return home. On one trip, however, I met up with a couple of young New Englanders in the midst of a highly eventful first backpacking trip in the Canadian Rockies.

While quietly walking along the trail, many kilometres from any other known person, they were spontaneously compelled to climb a small rocky outcrop. They were startled to spy, immediately ahead of them and just off the trail, a grizzly bear feeding on a carcass – potentially the most dangerous situation a person could encounter in the mountains. Grizzlies will ferociously defend a food source, especially a high-protein source like a carcass. They have been known to attack without warning any intruder they perceive to threaten their food supply.

Realizing that they were extremely lucky to have been able to observe this situation from a safe vantage point, the young couple quietly retraced their steps along the trail without alerting the bear to their presence. They reported their finding to the authorities as soon as they were able, and trained park personnel removed the remainder of the carcass and cleaned up the area, thus preventing any injuries or frightening experiences for other hikers.

The couple's story was a poignant reminder of the importance of remaining keenly aware of one's surroundings in the backcountry. Even without climbing to the viewpoint, some hikers would have detected the situation in time to retreat to safety. But I shudder to think of those who would have stumbled across the bear at his dinner table. Careful observation of the trail ahead will always stand hikers in good stead.

When Tom Wilson and Robert Barrett set out to find a route to Mount Assiniboine in 1893, they began by taking the old Native trail up Healy Creek to Simpson Pass. Today this trail (shown here) is heavily used by both backpackers and day hikers to access the campground on the Healy Pass trail and the scenic wonders of Healy Pass.

Chronology

1845 Father Jean de Smet includes Pyramid Mountain on his map. This is believed to be the first recorded reference to Mount Assiniboine.

1883 Dr. George M. Dawson of the Geological Survey of Canada definitely reports on Mount Assiniboine after viewing it from Copper Mountain, west of Redearth Creek.

1893 Banff outfitter Tom Wilson leads the R.L. Barrett party over Ferro Pass to record the first visit to Mount Assiniboine. Wilson had heard of the mountain from Dr. Dawson and viewed it in 1889 from near Simpson Pass.

1894 Samuel E.S. Allen and Yule Carryer plan a self-guided trip to Mount Assiniboine. Colonel Robert O'Hara recommends Vermilion Pass as the best access to the Simpson River. This route leads them to Ferro Pass and the mountain.

1895 Samuel Allen and Dr. Howard Smith hire a guide and packer from outfitter Tom Wilson to travel over Simpson Pass and Ferro Pass to reach the Mitchell River valley, near Mount Assiniboine.

Walter Wilcox makes his first trip to Mount Assiniboine. He and companions J.F. Porter and R.L. Barrett meet up with Samuel Allen and Howard Smith in the Mitchell River valley.

1909 The National Park service has a six-foot-wide (1.8-metre-wide) trail suitable for pack horses cut westward from Banff and up Healy Creek to the top of Simpson Pass, a distance of 19 miles (31 kilometres).

1910 Alpinists Tom Longstaff and his sister, Katherine Longstaff, use the new trail to Simpson Pass to reach Mount Assiniboine. Tom successfully reaches the summit.

History

First Visit

After the coming of the railway to Banff in 1885, the era of the tourist-explorers and mountaineers swung into full force. A key feature of interest in the area south of Banff was Mount Assiniboine. This giant pyramid-shaped mountain sits west of the Continental Divide, approximately halfway between the region's two known passes: Simpson Pass (see Route II above) to the northwest and White Man Pass (see Route I above) to the southeast. Although the latter pass did not provide a direct route to Mount Assiniboine, following a tributary of the Spray River just south of the Spray Lakes near the base of White Man Pass allowed for easy access.

The first recorded reference believed to be of Mount Assiniboine was Jesuit Father Jean de Smet's note that "the monuments of Cheops and Cephren dwindle into nought before this great architectural cliff of nature,"[1] which he named Pyramid and placed on his map. However, Mount Assiniboine cannot be viewed from the trail de Smet was following over White Man Pass. There is, none-the-less, another pyramidal peak on the Continental Divide just west of the pass. Although it is not massive in size and generally has no snow on its peak during the summer, this may be the mountain the inexperienced alpine traveller was referring to.[2] In 1883, however, Dr. George M. Dawson of the Geological Survey of Canada definitely viewed Mount Assiniboine from Copper Mountain, west of Redearth Creek.During their 1886–1894 topographic survey south of the railway, J.J. McArthur and other surveyors determined its exact location.

Mount Assiniboine (top, left of centre) can be seen from a high ridge on the Continental Divide east of White Man Pass. This vantage point also gives a view of the small lake and meadow just below the pass (on the right).

George Mercer Dawson (1849–1901)

George Mercer Dawson was born in Pictou, Nova Scotia, on August 1, 1849, to Margaret A.Y. Mercer and Nova Scotia Superintendent of Education James William Dawson. In 1855 the family moved to Montreal, where James Dawson took up an appointment as principal of McGill College (later McGill University). At the age of nine, George Dawson was stricken with Pott's Disease, a rare and serious form of tuberculosis that affects the spinal vertebrae. The disease left him with a deformed back and the physical stature of a 12-year-old. Being bedridden for several years, he was educated at home by tutors and his father. He entered McGill on a part-time basis in 1868. A year later, he moved to London to study three years at the Royal School of Mines. He graduated at the top of his class, returning to Canada in 1872 to pursue a career in geology.

Dawson's first position was a temporary one, assaying some iron ore deposits near Pictou, Nova Scotia, for the Albion Mines Company. His heart, however, was set on investigating the largely unexplored Canadian West. The opportunity to head west arose the following year when he joined the British North America Boundary Commission as geologist and botanist. Dawson was assigned to report on the natural history of the international boundary region from western Ontario to southern British Columbia. His report, published two years later, is considered a classic in Canadian geology.

Dawson joined the Geological Survey of Canada in 1875, spending the next 20 years exploring parts of Alberta, British Columbia and Yukon. His work required him to cover thousands of kilometres of uncharted wilderness on foot and by horseback, canoe, steamboat, wagon train and railroad. He spent the summers of 1883 and 1884 in the Rockies, the first travelling through largely untracked territory in southern Alberta and British Columbia and the second in the area between Mount Assiniboine and Kicking Horse Pass.

Dawson was elected to the Royal Society of London in 1891. That same year, the Geological Society of London awarded him the Bigsby Medal, and Queen Victoria named him a Companion of the Order of St. Michael and St. George. Two years later he was elected president of the Royal Society of Canada. Over the course of his career he was awarded many honorary doctorates from leading Canadian and American universities.

In 1895 Dawson was named director of the Geological Survey of Canada. For the next six years he diligently administered a department badly strapped for funds. Throughout this difficult period, he maintained his contact with the scientific community. In 1900 he served as the president of the Geological Society of America, and in December he delivered the President's Address: The Geological Record of the Rocky Mountain Region in Canada. Three months later, on March 2, 1901, Dawson died suddenly of acute bronchitis at home in Ottawa. He is buried in the family plot in Mount Royal Cemetery in Montreal.

Dawson has been described as vibrant and full of energy, able to combine brilliance with self-discipline. He strove to achieve excellence in his own work and that of others. He was highly respected by his countrymen and the international scientific community. He demonstrated an aptitude for hard work in his physically demanding career and never allowed the effects of his early illness to hold him back. His ability to observe and draw conclusions in the fields of geography, geology, ethnology and history soon established his reputation, and his studies made a significant contribution to the scientific knowledge of the West. His name lives on in Dawson City and the Dawson mountain range in Yukon, Dawson Creek and Glacier in British Columbia, and in the name of a tiny mouse, whose descendants still scamper across the far northern tundra.

George Dawson was a brilliant scholar and skilled surveyor. Few could match his physical endurance despite the fact that a childhood illness left him with a hunchback and the stature of a young boy. This image of him (standing, centre) with fellow surveyors and helpers gives an indication of his size but not his ability.

Early mountaineers used three main routes to reach Mount Assiniboine. Two originated in the west, using Simpson's route over Simpson Pass and along the Simpson River to access either Ferro Pass or, later, Citadel Pass. The other began with Sinclair's approach to White Man Pass but turned west before reaching the pass to follow Bryant Creek to Assiniboine Pass.

The first recorded visit to Mount Assiniboine took place in 1893. Banff outfitter Tom Wilson had heard George Dawson's tales of the mountain to the south and had seen it from near Simpson Pass while working with W.S. Drewry's survey party in 1889. In the fall of 1893, Chicago businessman Robert L. Barrett approached him intent on climbing a mountain. Wilson suggested Mount Assiniboine, and his client readily agreed.[3]

With Wilson's former partner in the retail business, George Fear, as cook, the threesome left Banff on September 1 and followed old Native trails up Healy Creek and over Simpson Pass to the Simpson River, then they followed the river south to where a tributary (Surprise Creek) joined the main river. Having reached the end of existing trails, Barrett and Wilson could see no obvious route to the mountain. The pair managed to attain the top of a ridge (probably Simpson Ridge), where their first close-up view of Mount Assiniboine was spread before them. Barrett, who later climbed in the Himalayas, wrote to Wilson in 1924: "I don't think even old K2, the 28,000, looked to me as high and imposing, and as terrible as old Assiniboine when you and I finally won through to where we could have a good look at him."[4]

The next day, with considerable chopping, the men were able to force their way to the top of Ferro Pass. After descending into the valley below, they followed the Mitchell River to its headwaters near the base of Mount Assiniboine. Pioneering the approach route was the most noteworthy aspect of the expedition; the lateness of the season and corresponding unfavourable weather prevented Barrett from even attempting to climb Mount Assiniboine. The party retraced their steps to the Simpson River, which they followed south to the Vermilion River, then north over Vermilion Pass: the route of today's Highway 93.

Tom Wilson did not leave any records of his travels, but his route over Ferro Pass likely resulted from having been in the vicinity with surveyors. His knowledge of the mountains, which was second to none during the late 1880s, was a boon to his successful outfitting business.

Alternate Route

A year later, Philadelphian Samuel E.S. Allen, a Yale University student and ardent explorer of the Rocky Mountains, and Yule Carryer, an Aboriginal student at the University of Toronto, planned a trip to Mount Assiniboine. They decided to forego the services of an outfitter or guide – a bold move given the state of the trails at the time. As mountaineer Lillian Gest explained, "there were no trails except those made by animals which Indians used for their hunting trips. Following these trails through brush and fire-devastated areas, and finding good fords for crossing even the tributaries of the streams, was difficult. [Following these trails] ... is an art both difficult to acquire and delightful to practice."[5]

Allen had met Colonel Robert O'Hara in Lake Louise in the summer of 1894, and the Colonel recommended Vermilion Pass as the best way to access the Simpson River. Allen and Carryer left the Bow River on September 5, 1894. With Dr. Dawson's map as a guide, they and their single horse struggled to follow the old Native trails. They forded the Simpson River then followed it upstream along Wilson's old route to the third stream on the right (Surprise Creek), which they ascended. As was his custom, Allen chose a Stoney word to name the stream they were following: Walandoo (Deception) Creek. After successfully crossing the pass (Ferro), he and Carryer spied a beautiful lake (Cerulean Lake) some distance ahead. When the clouds separated, they caught their first glimpse of magnificent Mount Assiniboine, which Carryer declared to be "the most awful mountain"[6] he had ever seen. By the time they reached its base, they had run out of time to explore. To return to town, they reversed the approach of Wilson's earlier party, returning to the Bow River over Simpson Pass and Healy Creek.

Colonel Robert O'Hara explored the Vermilion Pass area and recommended it over Simpson Pass as the best way to access the Simpson River. In spite of its greater length, the Vermilion Pass route continues to be used to reach Ferro Pass.

Samuel E.S. Allen (1874–1945)

Samuel Evans Stokes Allen was born in 1874 in Philadelphia, Pennsylvania, to parents of British ancestry. Allen was a very intelligent child, active and alert, and his parents' financial status allowed him to attend the best private schools. After passing the entrance exams for Yale University at the age of 16, he proceeded to pursue the study of languages. He was a brilliant student and graduated Phi Beta Kappa (an academic honour society) in 1894. He obtained his M.A. in 1897, then, following his religious convictions, he enrolled in a Ph.D. program intending to become a minister of the Protestant Episcopal (Anglican) Church.

Allen first visited the Canadian Rockies on a circuitous route home from the California Sierras in 1891. Though he made only four visits, Samuel Allen left an unmatched legacy of exploration in the Lake Louise–Mount Assiniboine area. His academic study of languages prompted a keen interest in the Stoney language. Allen spent much of his time in the West trying to learn that language's complexities and used his gained knowledge to name many peaks and features in the areas he explored.

On his first visit, 17-year-old Allen disembarked the train in Field. He explored around Emerald Lake[7] before walking from Field to Laggan and briefly visiting Lake Louise. Captivated by the magnificence of the Lake Louise area, he vowed to return. He spent the following summer honing his mountaineering skills in the Alps, climbing the Matterhorn and several other peaks before returning to the Rockies in 1893. He and his friend Walter Wilcox, another Yale student with similar interests, devoted the bulk of the summer to a serious exploration of the Lake Louise area.

Samuel Allen conducted most of his explorations in the Rockies in the Lake Louise–Lake O'Hara areas but made two trips to Mount Assiniboine, one over Vermilion Pass and the other over Simpson Pass.

The two returned to Laggan in the summer of 1894 with three other Yale students: Yandell Henderson, Louis Frissell and George Warrington. Brashly labelling themselves The Lake Louise Club, they set about climbing, mapping and exploring the area. That fall, Allen made one of the most impressive solo trips in the Canadian Rockies, demonstrating his legendary stamina and endurance by travelling on foot from his camp in Paradise Valley over Wasatch, Wenkchemna and Opabin passes and back in one day. Along the way, he named many features and landmarks, including the ten mountains surrounding Moraine Lake, which he identified with the Stoney numerals from one to ten: Heejee, Nom, Yamnee, Tonsa, Sapta, Shappee, Sagowa, Saknowa, Neptuak and Wenkchemna. Unfortunately, all but two of these peaks were later renamed – one of them, Mount Allen, in his honour. Later that year, Allen visited and explored the Lake O'Hara area, again bringing the Stoney names for many landmarks into common use.

Allen's final visit to the Canadian Rockies consisted of his 1895 explorations in the Mount Assiniboine area with Dr. Howard Smith. Sadly, Allen did not complete his written account of this final adventure, and his father ordered him not to undertake any further trips to the mountains. Shortly after receiving his M.A. in 1897, Allen was diagnosed with dementia praecox, a form of schizophrenia. One result of his illness was an obsession with climbing mountains, including Mount Everest; however, he was confined to an insane asylum for more than 40 years. He died in 1945 of pneumonia complicated by kidney failure, with the beloved mountains of his youth his only remaining memories.

Above: The Simpson River arises in a valley north of Mount Assiniboine then flows west into the Vermilion River, below Vermilion Pass. This route was not regularly used to access Mount Assiniboine.

Below: Although Ferro Pass was the first route used to get to the Mount Assiniboine area, it was only used a few times before a better route was developed. In this image, taken at the top of the pass, Mount Assiniboine and Wedgwood Lake are clearly visible.

Early Explorers

Allen returned the following year, this time with Dr. Howard Smith. With the guide, packer and six horses they hired from outfitter Tom Wilson, they opted to use the short route over Simpson Pass and Ferro Pass to reach the Mitchell River valley. They set up camp near the base of Mount Assiniboine and spent the next several days exploring the area, photographing, mapping and making notes.[8]

At about the same time, Wilson was also outfitting a larger party headed for the same destination. Walter Wilcox, who had been travelling extensively in the Rocky Mountains since 1893, was making his first trip to Mount Assiniboine. Mountaineers J.F. Porter and R.L. Barrett rounded out the party, along with Ralph Edwards as guide, packers Bill Peyto and Harry Lang, and a cook.[9] The paying customers chose to walk, as was quite common in the early days of mountaineering. Wilcox explained:

> Our journey began on the sixth of July, though the day was wet and showery. Our four men with nine horses started before noon for our first camp at Healy's Creek, about six miles from Banff. Barrett, Porter, and I came later, on foot, and after a mile or so of good road, plunged into the difficulties of a bad trail in a burnt timber country, and left the last sign of civilization behind. We came at length to Healy's Creek, a large stream that comes roaring out of the mountains from the west and drains the Simpson Pass to swell the Bow River. We shouted across and soon saw Peyto, one of our packers, coming at a gallop through the brush. Chiniquay, an Indian Cayuse which he rode, had to carry us one by one across the creek, which was rather deep and swift.[10]

On reaching Simpson Pass, they found it still covered in six feet of snow. The men had to pack a trail to get the horses through. At this time, Edwards had to retrace his steps to retrieve a forgotten axe, and Peyto took over as guide.

Once across the Divide, Wilcox reported that "an Indian trail led us down by a stream [North Simpson River] which, at first a mere rivulet

Left: This September image looking toward Simpson Pass and showing the Alberta–BC boundary marker at the Continental Divide gives an indication of how early winter comes to high passes. The six feet (two metres) of snow the Wilcox party found in July would not have been unexpected.

Opposite: Cerulean Lake is the first major lake encountered when descending from Ferro Pass toward Lake Magog. The trail skirts the lake on its west and north shores for a significant distance.

from melting snow, had now become a brawling torrent.... The day's march ended at the Simpson River, where we camped in a level place beside many Indian teepee-poles."[11] The next day, July 9, they followed the Simpson River downstream for several hours then

> made a final crossing before we should ascend the opposite mountain side to a distant valley opening.... After we had been on the march for six hours we found ourselves entering a high valley much encumbered by rock-slides which, though easy enough for us to walk over, were very trying and dangerous to the horses. It was impossible to camp in this vicinity, and after an exhausting march of three hours more and an ascent of fully two thousand feet from the Simpson River, we made camp in a delightful place near a stream.... Filled with the hope of getting our first view of Mt. Assiniboine during the day, we were on the march at an early hour.... Finally a long bare ridge, well exposed to wind and sun, offered us a fine route through the unbroken snow fields and led us to the summit [of Ferro Pass].[12]

They descended into a valley and camped near a small stream in a burned out area. The following day they rested the horses and recovered from their journey. Then, on July 12, Peyto led them

> east for two hours, finding a route among the fallen timber as well as we could. At length a steep ascent brought us by a waterfall to a grove of larches beyond which a beautiful lake

[Cerulean] appeared.... A well-marked trail led around the winding shore on our left, and other side of the narrow lake being hemmed in by rock-slides and cliffs.... The trail led us by the lake for half a mile and then, leaving it, ascended a rocky ridge through a grass-lined opening. Another lake [Sunburst] was immediately disclosed, and beyond it mighty Assiniboine.... Continuing once more, we traversed some open places among low ridges covered with beautiful larches. We passed through a delightful region which descended gently for half a mile to a treeless moor, where we pitched camp. Behind us was a clump of trees, before us

> Mt. Assiniboine, and on our left a lake [Magog] of considerable size, which washed the very base of the mountain and extended northwards in the bottom of a broad valley.[13]

After Edwards left the party to retrieve the missing axe, a supply of provisions and details of the next day's route were left at each campsite for his instruction. Nevertheless, ten days passed without any sign of him. The party agreed that after a brief rest Peyto should retrace their route over Simpson Pass to find the missing guide. During Peyto's absence, the remainder of the party decided that they were ill-prepared to tackle Mount Assiniboine and instead contented themselves with climbing several lesser mountains. Peyto returned on July 26 with the news that their guide had gotten lost and returned to Banff. Wilcox and Barrett decided to set out on foot to accomplish the first circumnavigation of the huge mountain. En route, they met up with Allen and Smith at their camp near a fork of the Mitchell River. Two weeks later the Wilcox party followed Barrett's previous itinerary, returning to Banff over Vermilion Pass.

A Cut Trail

The trip to Mount Assiniboine was simplified in 1909, when the National Park Service had a six-foot-wide (1.8-metre-wide) trail suitable for pack horses cut westward from Banff and up Healy Creek to the top of Simpson Pass. By then, the trail over Citadel Pass (see Route V below) had become the favoured route from the west, but as the Ferro Pass route also started from the top of Simpson Pass, it, too, was facilitated by the new trail.

Mountaineer Tom Longstaff and his sister, Katherine Longstaff, made use of the trail the following year when they engaged Jimmy Simpson and helper James Brierly to help them reach Mount Assiniboine. They left Banff on July 1, reaching the base of the mountain in a mere three days, as opposed to the seven Peyto had spent leading his larger party 14 years earlier. CPR Swiss guide Rudolf Aemmer assisted with the climbing portion of the trip, successfully helping Longstaff climb Mount Assiniboine on July 4, while his sister stayed in camp. To exit the area, the party crossed Assiniboine Pass and followed Bryant Creek to the Spray River.[14]

The Trail Today

The Ferro Pass trail is the original historic route to the base of Mount Assiniboine. Most of today's hikers prefer the shorter routes from Mount Shark[15] or from the Sunshine Meadows over Citadel Pass.[16] My own trip along the Simpson River and over Ferro Pass took place on the July 1 long weekend, and I did not see anyone on the trail. My solitude gave me plenty of time to soak in the beauty of the mountains and reflect upon Tom Wilson leading the Barrett party over a pass that was entirely new to him. I continue to be amazed at how pioneers like Wilson could find their way through the mountains on untrodden trails. Even the tepee poles and other signs of Native use that travellers often mention do not seem to have been present along this route. Perhaps route-finding is easier from horseback, but I expect that it is the skills of the equestrian (and not the Equus) that play the most important role.

Those who wish to immerse themselves in the more historic route will find the trail along the Simpson River to Surprise Creek very pleasant river-valley hiking. The trail along Surprise Creek to the top of the pass works its way steadily uphill through a narrow valley. Rock slides have left numerous clearings that provide good views of the surrounding mountains.

The trail from the top of the pass down toward Lake Magog is much more heavily used due to people visiting the pass as a day hike from Mount Assiniboine Lodge, the Naiset Cabins and the campground. This is a very interesting hike, dropping down the side of a steep gully with good views. Farther along, the small lakes and views of towering Mount Assiniboine with its snow and glaciers are very scenic. Strong hikers can complete the entire distance from the Vermilion River to Lake Magog in one day, but most will want to stop at one of the three campgrounds along the way, using two days to allow a more leisurely hike.

As hikers pass Sunburst Lake, a small lakeside cabin is visible through the trees. In 1950, 53-year-old Lizzie Rummel purchased this dwelling from Pat Brewster to create the basis for her backcountry tourist business, along with four tent-frame cabins and another small cabin behind the main cabin, which was often given to honeymooners free of charge. She ran the business both summer and winter for the next 19 years.[17]

Above: After passing Cerulean Lake on the trail from Ferro Pass, hikers soon come to Sunburst Lake, shown here, and pass by the cabins on its shore, where Lizzie Rummel entertained guests for 19 years.

Right: The trail along the Simpson River toward Ferro Pass was heavily impacted by the fire that swept through the area in the summer of 2003. The many deadfalls that impeded my progress have likely long since been removed.

Trail Guide

Distances are adapted from existing trail guides: Patton and Robinson, Potter, Beers, and Eastcott, and from Gem-Trek maps. Distances intermediate from those given in the sources are estimated from topographical maps and from hiking times. All distances are given in kilometres.

Simpson River to Lake Magog (Mount Assiniboine) over Ferro Pass

Maps 82 J/13 Mount Assiniboine

Gem-Trek Banff and Mount Assiniboine

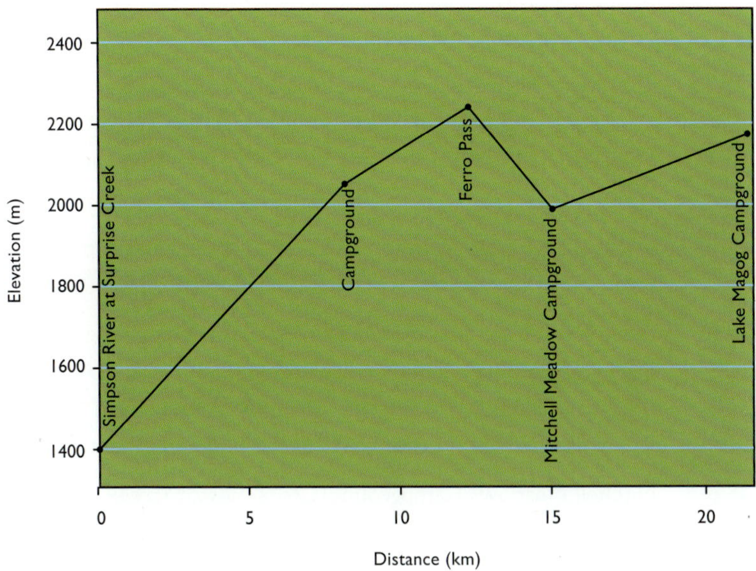

Trailhead

The junction of Surprise Creek and the Simpson River can be approached from two directions. Tom Wilson's original route over Simpson Pass and along the Simpson River is described in Route II above. Going from the Bourgeau Parking Lot (Sunshine gondola station) to the junction of Surprise Creek is km 62.5 to km 83.4 of the Devil's Gap to the Vermilion River over Simpson Pass route. Alternatively one can start at the Vermilion River and hike up the Simpson River to Surprise Creek; this is the route that most will want to take today and is km 94.3 to km 83.4, the reverse of the Devil's Gap to the Vermilion River over Simpson Pass Route.

0.0	Cross the Simpson River on a suspension bridge.
0.1	Surprise Creek Cabin and Campground. Begin a steady climb to the east along the bank above Surprise Creek. There are many rockslides, which provide good views of the surrounding mountains. As the trail approaches Simpson Ridge to the east, it swings around to the southeast then continues to climb close to the creek. The valley is quite narrow with rocky craggy peaks and a sheer rock wall on the right.
7.5	Trail junction. Rock Lake is on the right (west); the trail to Ferro Pass continues straight ahead (southeast). The trail stays high above the left (east) side of the lake, with a good view of the lake.
8.3	Campground. The trail continues to climb, crosses a bridged creek then enters a meadow-like area. The trail circumvents a rocky ridge on the left.
12.0	Ferro Pass. A signboard marks the top of the pass. Wedgwood Lake and Mount Assiniboine are visible from the top. A heavily used trail drops down the side of a deep gully. Though forested, it remains fairly open with views of the lake and mountain.
15.6	Mitchell Meadows Campground. Cross Nestor Creek on a split-log bridge. The trail goes south then turns east as it climbs the side of the valley.
17.0	Trail junction. The trail to the left (east) goes to Chuck's Ridge and Nub Ridge. Keep right (southeast) toward Cerulean Lake. The trail is initially level. Cross a creek on an old bridge then

climb another ridge close to a sheer rock wall before reaching a beautiful little lake nestled right up against the mountain.

18.7 Cerulean Lake and trail junction. The trail to Wedgwood Lake goes to the right (west); turn left for Lake Magog. The trail follows the shoreline of Cerulean Lake to the northwest.

19.9 Trail junction. The trail to the left goes to Elizabeth Lake. Keep right (southeast) to the shoreline of Sunburst Lake and then follow the northeastern shore of the lake.

20.4 Sunburst Ranger Cabin. The cabin faces the lake with a spectacular half-circle of mountains and glacier in the background.

20.9 Trail junction. The trail to the left goes toward the Naiset Cabins. Keep right (southeast) for the campground.

21.3 Lake Magog Campground. Mount Assiniboine is in full view across the lake to the south.

After crossing Ferro Pass and passing Sunburst Lake, hikers are treated to this view of Lake Magog and the cabins of Mount Assiniboine Lodge spread along the top of the ridge. The water level in Lake Magog was much lower than normal when this image was taken.

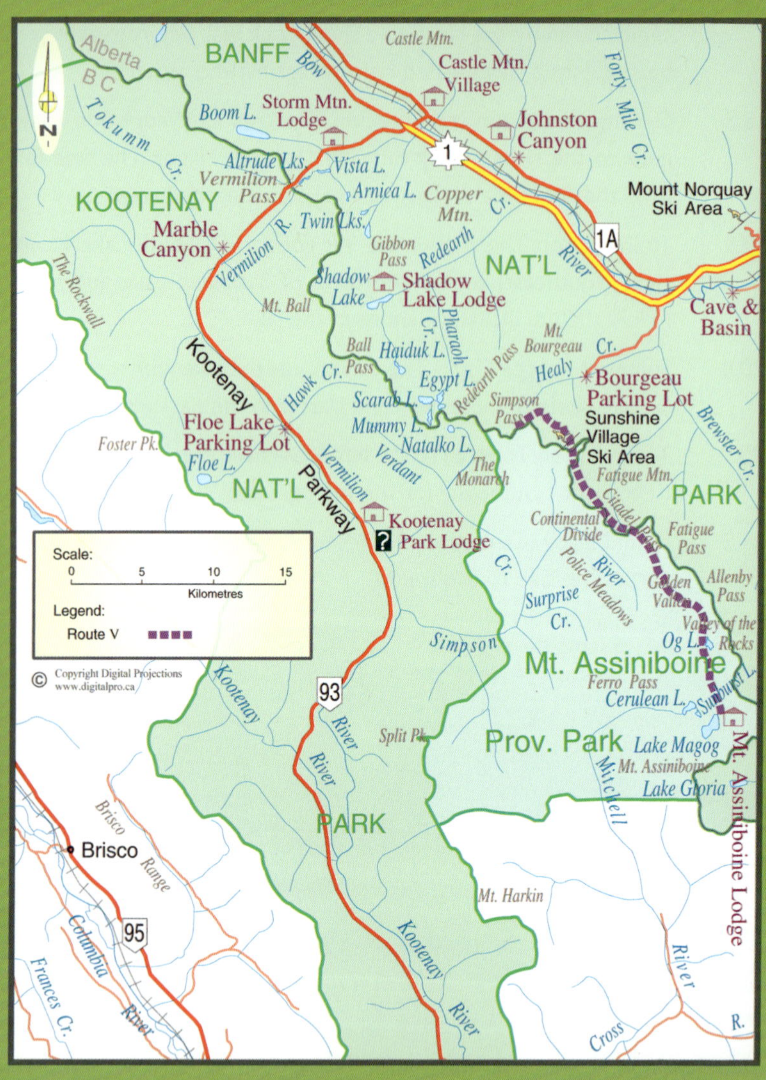

Tom Wilson's Route from Simpson Pass to Mount Assiniboine over Citadel Pass

Route V

Fast Lane: Tom Wilson's Route from Simpson Pass to Mount Assiniboine over Citadel Pass.

After a long and very dry (we ran out of water) hike from Howard Douglas Lake over Citadel Pass and through the Valley of the Rocks to Og Lake, we decided to call it a day. Partway through a 13-day hike, the six teenaged hikers and I felt that the remainder of the beautiful day offered a perfect opportunity to dry out damp clothing and bathe in the lake. Soon after the tents went up, clothes lines were strung between trees and the site truly looked like wash day in the country.

While wandering around the campsite, I befriended one of the only two other campers present. At one point in the conversation, the young man suggested that this would be a great place for a guy to propose to his girlfriend. Believing it was just a general comment, I agreed with him, and no more was said on the topic. About half an hour later, the man approached our tent site, where the seven of us were milling around, each involved in his or her own tasks. He asked if I would call our group together as he wanted to tell us something. When everyone was gathered, he announced that he had just proposed to his girlfriend and would like us to shout out congratulations. This we did, and his new fiancée smiled and waved her acknowledgement.

The man was a very outgoing friendly sort and was in no hurry to return to his own campsite. After some chatter, one of the girls observed, "I noticed that you have a very small tent. What were you going to do if your girlfriend said no to your proposal?" The man, being very quick witted, immediately replied, "Oh, I scouted around and noticed that you have a very large tent, and decided that I could probably join your group!"

Later on in the conversation, he revealed that he was from Oregon and someone asked what he did for a living. He replied that he was a sales rep for a company called Nike, then asked, in innocent sincerity, if we had heard of the company. The response was spontaneous and loud as each of the teenagers shouted out the name of their favourite model of Nike runners: "Nike Air Max, Nike Air Pegasus, Nike Air Equalon!" He got the picture and was suitably embarrassed.

A short while later, one of the girls, who was sitting with her back to the group finishing up drying some dishes, was referred to as Jo by one of her friends, short for Joanna. Without bothering to look at the person spoken to, the Nike rep made some comment about Joe, obviously referring to her as a male. This tall, slim, attractive young woman turned and rolled her big brown eyes toward the man, who simultaneously looked at her. This time he was truly embarrassed and shortly thereafter decided to take his leave before he could put his foot in his mouth again.

The abundant bushes at the Og Lake Campsite made excellent drying racks for backcountry laundry.

Chronology

1899 Tom Wilson suggests a new route to Mount Assiniboine. From the top of Simpson Pass travellers could turn east and follow the Continental Divide to today's Sunshine Meadows, then continue along the Divide to Citadel Pass and follow the Valley of the Rocks to Lake Magog, near the base of Mount Assiniboine.

Walter Wilcox returns to Mount Assiniboine with American alpinist H.G. Bryant and Englishman L.J. Steele. A snowstorm impedes this first attempt of Wilson's new route, but the men eventually locate the route to Lake Magog and the base of the mountain.

1901 Bill Peyto promises that he can escort Reverend James Outram from Banff to Mount Assiniboine in two days and bring him back in even less time. Peyto holds true to his promise, and his client makes the first ascent of Mount Assiniboine.

1904 Peyto once again travels to Mount Assiniboine over Citadel Pass, this time to escort famous mountaineer Gertrude E. Benham to the peak. Benham becomes the first woman to climb Mount Assiniboine.

1916 Dr. Charles Walcott and his wife, Mary Vaux Walcott, take the Citadel Pass route to Lake Magog, where Charles collects fossils and studies the geology and palaeontology of the region and Mary paints, photographs and collects wildflowers.

1920 The Alpine Club of Canada holds its annual camp near Lake Magog.

1927 The Trail Riders of the Canadian Rockies make their first trip to Mount Assiniboine.

1933 The Crosby family from Minneapolis cross Citadel Pass en route to the Mount Assiniboine area.

Cliff Kopas and his bride, Ruth, take the Crosbys' route in reverse from Mount Assiniboine over Citadel Pass and along Wilson's trail to Simpson Pass.

History

Lost on the Trail

In 1899 outfitter Tom Wilson, a seemingly never-ending source of knowledge about the mountains, suggested a new route to Mount Assiniboine. He proposed that after following Healy Creek to the top of Simpson Pass, travellers could turn east. Instead of crossing the pass, they could then follow the Continental Divide to today's Sunshine Meadows and continue along the Divide to Citadel Pass before dropping down into Golden Valley and following the Valley of the Rocks to Og Lake and Magog Lake near the base of Mount Assiniboine.

The first trip along the new route did not turn out to be as straightforward as Wilson made it sound. Eager to return to Mount Assiniboine, adventurer Walter Wilcox had ventured west with American alpinist H.G. Bryant and Englishman L.J. Steele. The outfit, supplied by Tom Wilson, was guided by Bob Campbell and equipped with a Topographical Survey of Canada contour map, as well as a compass and aneroid barometer for measuring elevations. Nevertheless, the party could not locate the trail amidst the deep snow on the Continental Divide, nor could they see the mountains and ridges through the fog and mist. Wilcox explained:

> Our route, according to the map, lay for several miles through an undulating country, which was, in fact, the very backbone of the continent. On one side was the deep valley of the Simpson, 3000 feet below, and on the other side, the streams which unite into Healy's Creek. It soon appeared that with every mountain concealed from view, and every high hill, even to the narrow circle of snow-covered ground near us, shrouded in mist and flying snow, the task of keeping a certain direction through the maze of ridges and impassable snowdrifts was not easy. Several times we found ourselves on the crest of a precipice, overlooking the blackness of unknown depths, or, still more disheartening, near a lake or a stream that looked remarkably like what we had passed long before.[1]

The trail east from the top of Simpson Pass proceeds along a high ridge to the top of Wawa Ridge, shown here. The trail then drops downhill (on the right of the image) to present-day Sunshine Village ski resort.

Using the map and compass, they were eventually able to locate the Simpson River and, by following it east, climb out of the Simpson River valley into the Valley of the Rocks. Wilcox described their passage through this unique valley as follows:

> Ascending the steep slopes of this abrupt hill, we entered a valley that is almost unique in these mountains. The whole place for three or four miles is a succession of weird hillocks of grey and whitish limestone of fantastic form and outline. No springs or streams water this 'valley of the gnomes,' as we called it ... The termination is at a small limestone-girt lake [Og Lake], which is about four miles from our old camp at Mt. Assiniboine.[2]

Wilcox and his companions were unsuccessful in climbing the mountain. They departed over Assiniboine Pass, following the creek that now bears Bryant's name to the Spray River.[3]

Above: From the top of Quartz Ridge, just east of Sunshine Meadows, the route Wilcox and his party would have taken past Howard Douglas Lake toward Citadel Pass can be seen along the lake's left shore and around the left of the mountain in the centre background.

Below: The unusual rock formations in the arid Valley of the Rocks make for interesting hiking. The trail can be seen in the foreground on the left of the image.

First Ascents

Two years later, the route led another mountaineering party to far greater success. Not only did guide Bill Peyto accurately navigate the route, but his client became the first climber to ascend Mount Assiniboine. During the summer of 1901, the Reverend James Outram was climbing with Edward Whymper and his party in the Yoho Valley.[4] Reasons for the failure of previous attempts to climb Mount Assiniboine were widely debated around Whymper's campfire. Outram longed to correct the errors – and overcome the bad luck – of his predecessors but had decided that the distance and expense put the entire enterprise beyond his reach. Then Peyto privately promised to take him from Banff to Mount Assiniboine in two days and bring him back in even less time. Outram did not believe that the trip had ever been made in less than three days, and Peyto's bold offer proved too much for him to resist.

On August 31, 1901, the secret expedition set out for Mount Assiniboine:

> First the cavalry; Bill Peyto, picturesque and workmanlike, led the way upon his trusty mare, then followed four pack horses, the fastest and most reliable of Peyto's bunch, laden with tents, provisions, and our miscellaneous impedimenta; and Jack Sinclair, our assistant packer, also mounted, brought up the rear, to stimulate laggards and maintain the pace. Then came the infantry, comprising the two Christians [Swiss guides Christian Häsler and Christian Bohren] and myself.... Soon we reached Healy Creek where it emerges from a narrow gorge, and crossed its double stream, the pedestrians having to clamber up behind the horsemen to make the passage dryshod. Leaving the broad, level valley of the Bow ... we plunged into the ravine beside the swift, translucent river, until we mounted a very steep trail through thick forest and emerged high above the creek in a fine valley ... Our path led through a tract of burned and fallen timber to more open ground, trending steadily towards Simpson Pass....[5]

The party camped the first night near Simpson Pass and in the morning diverged from the Simpson Pass trail to follow a steep, rocky and sometimes wooded route south to a beautiful open meadow: today's Sunshine Meadows. They continued along the Continental Divide. The trail was relatively easy to follow; Peyto set such a fast pace that the men on foot were hard pressed to keep up. Soon they encountered a new experience:

> a tremendous drop ... into an extraordinarily steep, weird valley, narrow and fire-swept ... the lower end an intricate maze of fallen logs ... through which Peyto steered the horses with marvellous skill and rapidity, until we gained the valley of the chief source of the Simpson River [Golden Valley] ... A zigzag track conducted us to the lowest point ... a fitting prelude to the long valley [Valley of the Rocks] on which we now entered.... Green-gray rocks and stones were strewn and piled in wild confusion amid sparse, stunted pines and firs.[6]

After several miles, conditions began to change. They passed a rocky lake, and the terrain became more park-like, rich and green with clumps of dark forest, with Mount Assiniboine in full view. By 7:20 that evening, they had reached their camping spot near the shore of Lake Magog. Although the light showers and distant thunder overnight did not bode well for climbing, the party set off by 6:00 the next morning, laden with two days' provisions. September 3 dawned brilliantly. Outram explained that at half-past 12, on their second attempt, "we stood as conquerors 11,860 feet above the sea ... on the loftiest spot in Canada on which a human foot had then been planted."[7]

The climbers not only made a successful first ascent of the mountain but also traversed it before turning on their heels to return to Banff along the same route. Outram had been extremely lucky to make his ascent when he did; after the climb, he reported, "we took a last look at the splendid obelisk above us, radiant in the moonlight against the dark star-strewn canopy of heaven. A last look it proved; for next morning we awoke to a white world, with nothing visible of Mt. Assiniboine but an occasional glimpse, through sweeping, leaden clouds, of its steep flanks deeply covered with the freshly fallen snow."[8]

The storm did not let up for the return trip. Outram described the struggle as follows:

> Next day we made a most tremendous march in the teeth of a driving snowstorm. The valley, [Valley of the Rocks] with its gaunt, spectral tree trunks, was drearier and more weird than ever, the blackened timber, outlined against the dazzling snow, showed in a mazy network; the bushes, with their load of fruit, peeped out forlornly amid their wintry environment, and every flower bore a tiny burden on its drooping head. The steep ascent of 1500 feet was made in ever deepening snow, and on the alp above we met the fierce blasts of the keen north wind, sweeping across the unprotected uplands. Wearied with our forced marches and two long days of arduous climbing, the tramping through soft, drifting snow, the steady upward trend of our advance and the hard conflict with the driving storm, it was with deep relief that we crossed the final ridge and could descend to calmer regions through the dark, snow-laden pines. Still on we went, down Healy Creek to the Bow Valley ... [9]

Even impeded by these challenging conditions, Peyto kept his promise to make the return trip in less than two days. The men arrived in Banff just five days and five hours after their departure.

Three years later, Peyto again made the trek to Mount Assiniboine, this time escorting the famous English mountaineer Gertrude E. Benham and her Swiss guides, brothers Christian and Hans Kaufmann, to the mountain. Packers Jimmy Wood and Jesse Trot assisted, and Benham succeeded in becoming the first woman to climb Mount Assiniboine on her first and only trip to Canada.[10]

James Outram (1864–1925)

James Outram was born on October 13, 1864, in London, England, the eldest son of Sir Francis Boyd Outram and Jane Anne Davidson. He was educated at Cambridge and ordained in the Church of England at the age of 25. Over the next 11 years he oversaw several parishes, his last being St. Peter's Anglican Church in Ipswich. The intensity with which he pursued this work, however, led to a nervous breakdown. In 1900 Outram and his brother, William, travelled to the Canadian Rockies in hopes of restoring his health.

Over the next three summers, the personality traits that had led to Outram's health problems did not soften. Having had some experience climbing in the Alps, Outram set his sights on first ascents. His unrelenting competitive urge brought him into conflict with other more experienced mountaineers, who referred to him as an interloper when he took advantage of their explorations to climb new mountains before they had the opportunity. Jimmy Simpson, the most famous and highly respected of the pioneer outfitters, declared that Outram "wanted all the glory himself" and treated his Swiss guides as "just help."[11]

During his first year in the Rockies, Outram made several climbs around Field and Lake Louise, as well as ascending Cascade Mountain near Banff and Sir Donald at Rogers Pass. From the summit of Cascade, Outram caught a glimpse of Mount Assiniboine and determined that he would climb it the following summer. When the time came, a shortage of funds threatened to keep him from hiring an outfit to take him to the more remote mountains. Fortunately, he was able to team up with Edward Whymper, the most famous mountaineer of the time, who was climbing in the Yoho Valley region. After Tom Wilson introduced the two mountaineers in Field, Outram was

Reverend James Outram (centre) and climbing guides Christian Häsler (left) and Christian Bohren, ready for an outing with their climbing paraphernalia ready. The three were the first to climb Mount Assiniboine.

invited to join Whymper's team, which turned out to be the ticket to fulfilling his mountaineering dreams.[12]

Bill Peyto, Whymper's former guide, promised to take Outram to Mount Assiniboine and back in less than four days' travel time, a promise that put the trip within Outram's means and led to what was perhaps his most notable climb. Outram's first ascent of Mount Assiniboine also alleviated his financial woes; the Canadian Pacific Railway put its full support behind his efforts.

Outram's driving ambition and incredible stamina were in full force during his final climbing season. During the summer of 1902, he managed to complete ten first ascents of peaks over 10,000 feet (3048 metres) for a grand total of 32 first ascents, many of them on the region's most difficult peaks, over the course of his three summers in the Rockies.

Outram subsequently chose to settle in Vermilion, Alberta, becoming involved in a land development company: The Northern and Vermilion Development Company. Like so many similar ventures, the company went bankrupt after the First World War. Fortunately, Outram had inherited his grandfather's baronetcy in 1912 and was able to retire to Calgary in 1920, where he lived the remainder of his life. While in Calgary, he married the daughter of an old family friend, Joseph Balfour of Athelstone House in Brighton, England.

Though he continued to visit the mountains and attended Alpine Club of Canada camps as a distinguished member, Outram disappeared from serious mountaineering as abruptly as he had entered it. He gave lectures on his climbs to both the Canadian and American Alpine Clubs, wrote articles on mountaineering and had a book, *In the Heart of the Canadian Rockies*, published in 1905, but he never again climbed aggressively. He died of a stroke in 1925, leaving a legacy of climbing matched by very few.

The area was again invaded by mountaineers when the Alpine Club of Canada held its annual camp near Lake Magog in 1920. Rather than taking the usual horse trail from Banff to Healy Creek, a motor boat transported the party up the Bow River to a landing opposite Mount Edith. There they met up with the pack train that helped them cross the marshes west of Vermilion Lakes and headed up Healy Creek to Simpson Pass. They turned east to follow the ridge along the Continental Divide to Sunshine Meadows and the Sunshine Camp, where they spent the night. The next day they continued parallel to the Divide, crossed Citadel Pass and descended into Golden Valley, where the second camp was set up. The third day saw them pass through the Valley of the Rocks, past Og Lake and on to the main camp on Lake Magog, near the base of Mount Assiniboine.[13]

Non-climbers

Dr. Charles and Mary Walcott formed the first of several non-mountaineering groups to visit Mount Assiniboine. Charles, whose family had discovered the now-famous Burgess Shale in Yoho Park, spent every summer between 1907 and 1925 collecting fossils and exploring the geology of the Canadian Rocky Mountains. In the summer of 1909, Walcott met Mary Vaux, a woman who had first come to the mountains with her parents and brothers in 1887 and had returned every year since 1894. Her initial interest was the glacier studies she and her brothers engaged in, but she later turned her attention to wildflowers. After their 1914 marriage, Mary accompanied Walcott, painting, collecting and photographing wildflowers while he studied geology.[14] Unlike most visitors, the Walcotts did not hire an outfitter for their travels, preferring to keep their own horses and hire their own help.

In July 1916, the Walcotts, their faithful cook and camp manager Arthur Brown, and packer Alex Mitton headed toward Simpson Pass with their pack train. After some delay due to deep snow on the pass, they proceeded east along the Continental Divide and made their way to the main branch of the Simpson River. Steady rain and fallen timber hampered progress as they headed southeast to Lake Magog, where Walcott collected fossils and studied the geology and palaeontology of the region. The men visited Wonder Pass and Assiniboine Pass as part of Walcott's studies; while they were gone, Mary remained around camp painting wildflowers. Still suffering from inclement weather, they retraced their steps along Wilson's route to the Simpson River then crossed Citadel Pass to Healy Creek.[15]

Charles Walcott, a workaholic who spent almost every summer of the last 20 years of his life studying geology and searching for fossils throughout the Canadian Rockies, is shown here pursuing a rare leisure activity.

Above: Mary Vaux first came to the Canadian Rockies in 1887 and returned seven years later. For the next 40 years, she spent nearly every summer in her favourite playground. In 1914 she married Charles Walcott and they travelled together, with Mary pursuing her main interest of painting and photographing wildflowers.

Below: Early Trail Riders of the Canadian Rockies outings tended to be very well attended. A large party, similar to this one photographed at the Lake of Hanging Glaciers, travelled to Mount Assiniboine in 1927.

Arthur Brown, long-time servant of the Walcott family, was treated like a family member. Reputed to be the best camp manager and cook in the Canadian Rockies, he sometimes caused a bit of a stir among locals as there were very few black people in the Rockies at the time.

A much larger group of adventurers used the Simpson Pass trail when the Trail Riders of the Canadian Rockies made their first trip to Mount Assiniboine in 1927. John Murray Gibbon, general publicity agent for the Canadian Pacific Railway, had founded the club three years earlier to provide the CPR's international membership with the opportunity to participate in organized trail rides. Its 1927 excursion followed a route up Brewster Creek and over Allenby Pass to Assiniboine Pass and Lake Magog, where participants enjoyed a one-day layover. From there, they followed Wilson's route through the Valley of the Rocks and over Citadel Pass to Sunshine Meadows. They spent the night in the meadows, and then they followed the Continental Divide to Simpson Pass, where they held their "Grand Powwow." On the sixth day, they returned to Banff along Healy Creek.[16]

After the stock market crash of 1929 and the Great Depression of the 1930s, major pack-train trips through the Rockies became a rarity. But in 1933 a unique 30-horse pack train travelled all the way from Banff to the international boundary at Waterton Lakes. The clients were nine members of the wealthy Crosby family from Minneapolis: the father, Mr. Crosby, his daughter, Margaret, and his two sons, Albert and Henry, with their wives and children. The trip was outfitted by George Harrison, with head guide Rudolph Aemmer, cook Mike Wassil and wrangler Harry Smith. Ken Jones, later to become the first Canadian licensed mountain guide, acted as packer on the trip, no doubt happy to obtain any work during this difficult period.[17]

Ken Jones, the first Canadian to become a licensed mountain guide, spent most of his life in the mountains, guiding on both mountaineer exploits and outfitted trips. He is shown here when he worked as a climbing guide at a 1936 Mount Assiniboine camp.

Early in the journey, the large pack train intersected Simpson's trail up Healy Creek by crossing from Redearth Creek through the Egypt Lakes area and over Healy Pass.[18] At Simpson Pass, the party turned east and continued over Wilson's Citadel Pass route, camping at Porcupine Camp near the upper reaches of the Simpson River. Ken Jones reported:

> It sounds routine, but it was the most miserable day I have ever spent on a pack trip. It was very hot and the ground was very dusty. The horses raised a continuous cloud of dust. George Harrison went at the head of the pack train. He was OK as he was out of the dust and could stop now and then for a drink out of a stream. Mike was at the end so he got a lot of dust, but he also could stop occasionally and get a drink. Harry Smith and I had the dubious honour of being in the middle of the string. When you are in the middle you can't get off and get a drink, you have to stay in the line and move with the horses.[19]

They passed Mount Assiniboine the following day but did not camp there; the riders proceeded across Wonder Pass to Marvel Lake. The pack train was taken across Assiniboine Pass and down to Bryant Creek, which was a gentler route but not as pretty. From Bryant Creek, the pack train moved up Marvel Creek to meet up with the remainder of the party at Marvel Lake. Together they continued along the Palliser Pass route to the south.[20]

That same year, honeymooners Cliff and Ruth Kopas took the Crosbys' route in reverse, following Wilson's trail from Mount Assiniboine to Simpson Pass and on to Redearth Creek. The Kopases were travelling from southern Alberta to the Pacific Ocean at Bella Coola with five horses and their life savings of $2.65.[21]

The Trail Today

Tom Wilson's original route from Simpson Pass is by far the most interesting approach to the Mount Assiniboine area. Today, most hikers will take the bus to Sunshine Village and start their hike from there, saving the one-hour hike from the Bourgeau Parking Lot to either Simpson Pass or Sunshine Village. The bus also gives hikers the option of doing both the route to Simpson Pass and the route to Citadel Pass as day hikes.

The trail from Sunshine Village to Simpson Pass begins by climbing to the top of a ski hill. After reaching a high ridge (Wawa Ridge), it proceeds through a very open area, then past scenic vistas along ridges and adjacent to cliffs, ending up in a small meadow where a group can eat lunch with one half in British Columbia and the other half in Alberta. From the rather uninspiring summit of Simpson Pass, the bushwhacking route to the North Simpson River is clearly visible. Though the trail from Sunshine Village drops two hundred metres from Wawa Summit to the top of Simpson Pass, the elevation change is gradual and the good trail can be enjoyed by all hikers.

From Simpson Pass, a trail leads west to connect with the trail to Healy Pass.[22] En route it passes through a meadow with a significant-sized lake. Near this lake is the backcountry cabin of legendary outfitter and park warden Bill Peyto. The cabin's remains are still standing, but it is not the cabin normally identified as Bill Peyto's cabin near Simpson Pass in the 1913 photo.[23] The most significant difference is that the cabin in the 1913 photo has its door in the side whereas the existing cabin has its door in the end.

In the fall of 2008, as I ate my lunch on the cabin's doorstep, surrounded by artefacts left by much earlier visitors, a very heavy piece of chain about 60 centimetres long hanging from a roof beam in what had been a porch began to gently sway in front of me, much like a hypnotist's pendulum. In this eerie context, it took little imagination to feel that the great man was standing there talking to me. I envisioned him explaining that he was not really a recluse, just a private man who, having lost his young wife and been estranged from his infant son, was unable to find another soulmate,[24] and that he preferred to spend his time alone rather than with others with whom he did not have a close bond. After our brief conversation, Peyto's image faded, and I was left with the chain still gently swinging, mirroring the surrounding treetops that swayed in a gentle breeze.

Starting at Sunshine Village and proceeding east toward Citadel Pass, hikers are treated to a wonderful trip across high alpine meadows and open mixed forests of larch and spruce, with the high peaks of the Continental Divide never very far from sight. In summer the meadows are covered with wildflowers, and a herd of bighorn sheep is often seen near the pass. In the autumn, the grasses turn a golden brown and a faint odour of decaying organic matter fills the air as the larch trees display their golden splendour in the distance. The elevation change to the top of the pass is only two hundred metres, spread over the entire distance (9.3 kilometres) so this makes a delightful hike for people of all ages.

Strong hikers wishing to continue to Lake Magog will be able to make the trip from Simpson Pass in one long day, but most will want to

Og Lake has no obvious inlet or outlet. It is a delight for parched hikers travelling east from the arid Valley of the Rocks.

Above: This view of Lake Magog was taken in front of Mount Assiniboine Lodge. The trail on the right leads to the campground; the Naiset Cabins are out of sight to the left. Mount Assiniboine is shrouded in clouds in the centre of the image.

Below: Mount Assiniboine Lodge was first built in 1928 by the CPR and was enlarged to its present size between 1958 and 1963. It is one of the best backcountry lodges in the Rockies; the view of Lake Magog and Mount Assiniboine from in front of the lodge is without comparison.

Trail Guide

Distances are adapted from existing trail guides: Patton and Robinson, Potter, Beers, and Eastcott, and from Gem-Trek maps. Distances intermediate from those given in the sources are estimated from topographical maps and from hiking times. All distances are given in kilometres.

Simpson Pass to Lake Magog (Mount Assiniboine) over Citadel Pass

Maps 82 O/4 Banff

82 J/13 Mount Assiniboine

Gem-Trek Banff and Mount Assiniboine

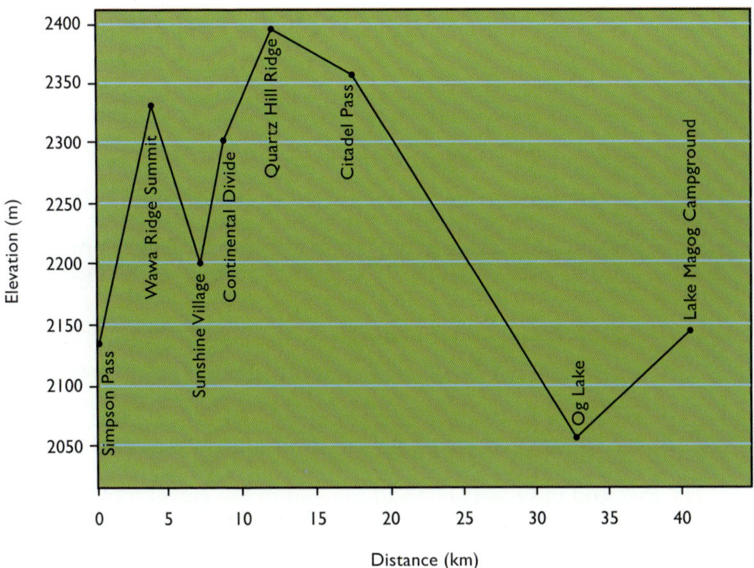

Trailhead

Simpson Pass can be accessed by taking the Healy Creek trail from the Bourgeau Parking Lot (Sunshine gondola station) to the pass. This trail is described in the Devil's Gap to the Vermilion River over Simpson Pass trail, Route II above, km 62.6 to 69.8 (km 69.8 of Route II is km 0.0 of this route).

0.0 In a small meadow with provincial boundary markers, turn to the left (east) and start climbing a trail through the trees to the left of a high ridge. The trail veers to the northeast and follows to the right of a cliff parallel to the Healy Creek valley, continuing to climb gently through mature forest as it curves to the southeast.

2.8 Top of a ridge. The trail climbs more steeply through an open area.

3.3 Monarch Viewpoint. This is a very open area on top of a ridge. Hikers can look out over broad meadows, with The Monarch to the southwest. Continue through an open area on a smooth, well-made, gravel trail.

3.7 Wawa Ridge summit.

4.0 Trail junction. The trail to the right goes to Rock Isle Lake. Continue ahead (east). The top of the Wawa Chair (ski lift) is to the right. The well-made trail continues along ski runs, turns south toward Sunshine Village and continues to drop downhill.

5.6 Sunshine Village. Continue uphill (southeast) on a gravel road.

5.8 Small log cabin. Keep right on a wide gravel path. Pass the top of the Strawberry Chair and the base of the Great Divide Chair (ski lifts).

6.8 Continental Divide and the Alberta–British Columbia provincial boundary.

6.9 Trail junction. The trail ahead (south) goes to Rock Isle Lake. Keep to the left (southeast) toward Citadel Pass. The smooth trail climbs through the meadows then enters a mixed spruce/larch forest as it starts to climb toward the top of the ridge.

10.8 East end of Quartz Hill and the end of the gravel trail. The dirt trail drops very steeply toward a lake.

11.4 Howard Douglas Lake and Campground. (Warning: hikers should fill their water bottles here as there is very little water over the next 15 km.) The trail continues through meadows and open forest, keeping to the left of Citadel Peak as it heads southeast, climbing around the mountain toward the pass.

14.9 Citadel Pass and trail junction. The trail to Fatigue Pass goes to the left. Continue ahead (south) for Mount Assiniboine. The trail initially curves to the east then heads south toward Golden Valley, switchbacking steeply downhill into a very impressive valley.

17.9 Viewpoint offering a fabulous vista of the Simpson River valley, with the Police Meadows shelter in the distance.

18.1 Trail junction. The trail to Porcupine Camp goes downhill to the right (south). Keep ahead (southeast) for Og Lake. The open trail stays high on the side of the valley, following along the base of Golden Mountain. It becomes very rocky as it begins to drop down into Golden Valley.

22.1 Trail junction. The trail to the right heads northwest through the Simpson River valley (a short distance along this trail there is a small lake, for those who are short of water). Continue ahead to the southeast, climbing out of Golden Valley on a steep, switch-backed trail through heavy forest into the very rugged Valley of the Rocks. The trail stays on the left side of the valley close to the mountains along the Continental Divide then drops down into a narrow rocky valley.

27.8 Og Lake and Campground. The trail continues due south, climbing out of a narrow rocky gully onto a highly scenic, broad, flat meadow.

30.5 Trail junction. The trail on the right heads toward the Nub Ridge trail. Continue ahead (southeast) through a meadow.

31.9 Trail junction. The trail to Og Pass goes to the left (north). Keep right (south).

32.1 Trail junction. The trail on the right goes toward the Nub Lake trail. Keep moving forward (south).

32.6 Trail junction. The trail to Assiniboine Pass goes to the left. Keep right (south).

32.9 Trail junction. Assiniboine Lodge left. Keep right for Lake Magog Campground.

33.1 Trail junction. The Nub Lake trail goes to the right. Keep left.

34.5 Lake Magog Campground.

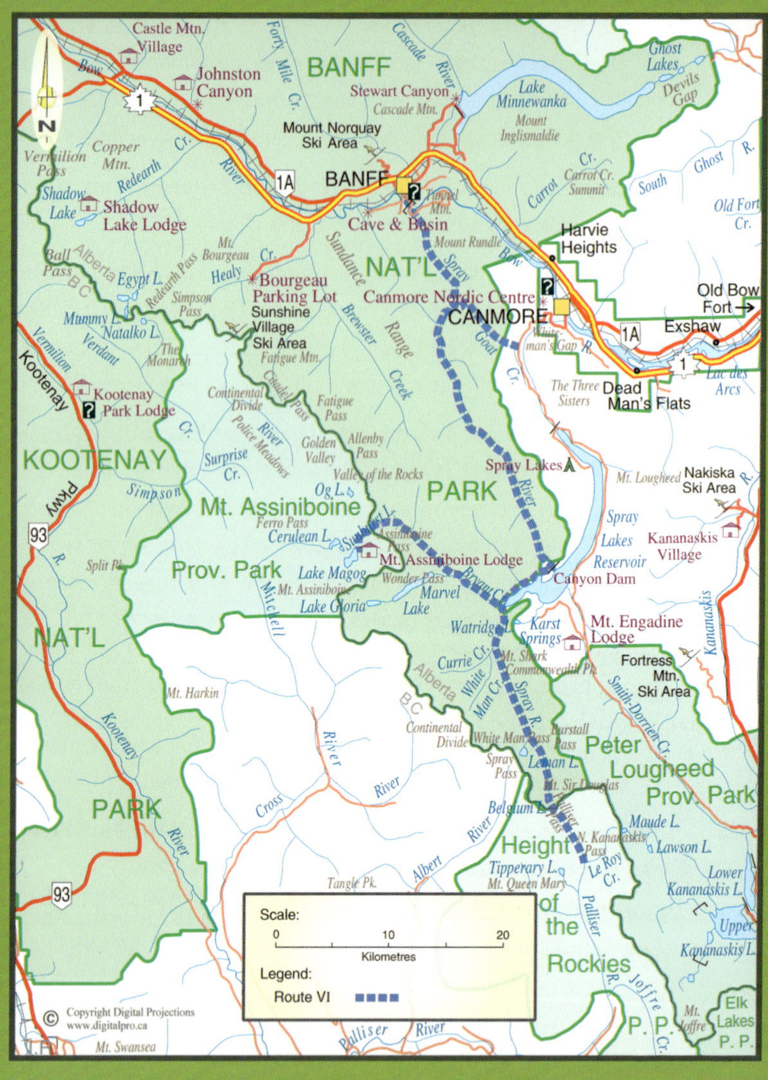

Walter Wilcox's Route along the Spray River to Assiniboine Pass and Palliser Pass

Route VI

Walking Tour: Walter Wilcox's Route along the Spray River to Assiniboine Pass and Palliser Pass

I first crossed North Kananaskis Pass with Janice and a group of her friends. We had been following the Spray and Palliser rivers from Mount Assiniboine area but turned east too soon and ended up climbing high on the side of Mount Leroy before managing to traverse to the actual trail. When I returned to gain information for this trail guide, I was determined to stay on the trail. I therefore started at Upper Kananaskis Lake, crossed the pass from the east and followed the trail down the west side of the Continental Divide. The trail connected with the Palliser River trail, which I followed south, hoping to retrace Sinclair's route as far as the logging road along the Palliser River.

Partway along the trail I came across an outfitter's cabin on a rather messy site. Tipperary Cabin is quite large: a two-storey log structure with a small open balcony on the front. There were signs of recent occupancy, but no one was around and the cabin was locked. I surmised that outfitters must bring visitors to the site for overnight accommodation and decided that I, too, would spend the night there. There was plenty of cleared ground upon which to set up a tent, but the second-floor balcony was just too appealing. Rather than troubling myself to set up my tent, I climbed the outside ladder to the railingless balcony and spread my sleeping bag and foam sleeping pad for a good night's sleep in the open air.

The next day I set out southward on the horse trail along the Palliser River, but the trail soon left the woods to follow the river's gravel flats, crossing the meandering streams at will. Following such a trail is easy work for horses, but slow and tedious for a hiker, and there was no visible trail on the gravel flats. Since my objective was to write a trail guide and not a bushwhacking guide, I abandoned the idea of reaching the logging road, retreated to Tipperary Cabin and continued north toward Palliser Pass.

Tipperary Cabin is on the Palliser River south of Palliser Pass. It appears to be well used and was an obvious stopping point for outfitters in the area.

Chronology

1899 Walter Wilcox and fellow mountaineers Henry Bryant and Louis Steele follow the creek that now bears Bryant's name from Assiniboine Pass to the Spray River, then retrace Sinclair's route along the Spray Lakes and through Whiteman's Gap to Canmore.

1900 The Chicago-based Walling brothers, Willoughby and English, and a Montreal artist by the name of Farrell return from Mount Assiniboine by crossing Assiniboine Pass and following Bryant Creek to its junction with the Spray River. The men separate from the pack train and get lost along the Spray River. They spend a night in the woods before being rescued.

1901 Walter Wilcox and Henry Bryant head south from Canmore over Whiteman's Gap and along the Spray Lakes to the junction of Bryant Creek and the Spray River, where they set up a base camp.

1904 Eight-year-old Pat Brewster of Banff successfully leads a group along the Spray River to the Spray Lakes.

1910 The Warden Service cuts a six-foot-wide (1.8-metre-wide) trail from Banff to the Spray Lakes along the Spray River, a distance of 24 miles (39 kilometres).

1912 The trail is continued along Bryant Creek to Mount Assiniboine, a distance of 18 miles (29 kilometres).

1917 Caroline Hinman conducts her Off the Beaten Track tour from Banff to Whiteman's Gap then along the Spray Lakes to Bryant Creek and over Assiniboine Pass to Mount Assiniboine.

1919 Mountaineer Val Fynn and his wife leave Banff on August 2 with another couple, the Eddys. They follow the Spray River–Goat Creek–Spray Lakes route to Bryant Creek then continue past the creek along the upper Spray River to set up base camp at the foot of Palliser Pass.

Mountaineers J.W.A. Hickson and A.C. Stead of Montreal use the route through Canmore and Whiteman's Gap and along the Spray River to reach the base of Palliser Pass.

1920 Arthur Wheeler decides to implement a walking tour from Banff to Mount Assiniboine along the Spray River to Goat Creek, up the creek to the Upper and Lower Spray Lakes, on to Bryant Creek and over Assiniboine Pass to Lake Magog.

1921 Henry Hall and his friend, Marcus Morton Jr., head out from Banff on Wheeler's walking tour route. At Bryant Creek they leave the route to follow the Spray River to the Hickson campsite just below Palliser Pass, then on to another Hickson campsite on Leroy Creek.

1922 The Alpine Club of Canada holds its annual camp at Belgium Lake, near the base of Palliser Pass, from July 29 to August 12. They use the Hall–Morton route for access.

1926 Caroline Hinman's Off the Beaten Track tour crosses North Kananaskis Pass then follows the Palliser Pass–Spray River route to Bryant Creek.

1927 Artist A.C. Leighton travels along Bryant Creek to Mount Assiniboine and finds the scenery to his liking.

1928 Mountaineer J.W.A. Hickson returns to the Palliser Pass area. This time he continues over Palliser Pass and down the Palliser River valley to Joffery Creek and Sylvan Pass.

History

Bryant Creek

In the early days of travel to Mount Assiniboine, many parties approached the peak via Citadel Pass, the Valley of the Rocks and Lake Magog, then they left by crossing Assiniboine Pass and following Bryant Creek to its junction with the Spray River. At this junction several route choices presented themselves. Often travellers followed the original trail along the west shore of the Spray Lakes to Whiteman's Gap and Canmore, from which point the Bow River could be followed to Banff.[1]

Another option was to follow the Spray River south to Palliser Pass then join the North Kananaskis Pass–Palliser River trail.[2] Alternately, travellers could follow the west shore of the Spray Lakes a short distance to the Spray River then follow it northwest to its junction with Goat Creek. From there, they could continue to follow the Spray to Banff or, as Walter Wilcox did in 1901, join a trail to the east along Goat Creek that led to Whiteman's Gap and on to Canmore and Banff. This route was also sometimes used in reverse to access Mount Assiniboine, or extended south along the Spray River to climb around Palliser Pass.

Walter Wilcox, H.G. Bryant and L.J. Steele were the first mountaineers to use the creek from Assiniboine Pass to the Spray River to exit the Mount Assiniboine area. The year was 1899 and the men had just attempted the first approach to the mountain via Citadel Pass.[3] After making a difficult trip through a snowstorm and failing to accomplish the peak's first ascent, the threesome was relieved to return to Banff without incident. As Wilcox later explained:

> Of the four routes to Assiniboine which are familiar to me, the one by which we returned to Banff in 1899 is the easiest, and at the same time most uninteresting. A gap in the mountains northeast of Mt. Assiniboine leads to the headwaters of the Spray River [where the river flows from the Spray Lakes], and a rapid descent from the elevated plain where

> our camp was to the bottom of the deep valley is the most attractive part of the journey. Part of our route was through the White Man Pass [Whiteman's Gap at Canmore], and the white men have burnt up all the woods. However the timber is all standing between Assiniboine and the Spray lakes, so that the traveling is excellent. From the Spray lakes to Canmore the miners have kept the trail in excellent condition for the sake of the fishing, and in proof of this we marched twenty miles on the last day of our journey.[4]

A Night in the Woods

The following year saw one of the most unusual trips in the history of the Bryant Creek trail. Brothers Willoughby and English Walling from Chicago hired Tom Wilson to outfit a trip to Mount Assiniboine and secure the services of three Swiss guides: Edouard Feuz and novices Henry Zurfluh and Charles Clarke. The brothers invited a Montreal artist by the name of Farrell to join them. Jimmy Simpson, the outfit's cook, later recounted that for unexplained reasons, as the Walling brothers neared Assiniboine's lofty peak, the guides decided to turn back.[5] Discouraged, the Wallings were keen to return to Banff as soon as possible. The guides led the pack train over Assiniboine Pass and down Bryant Creek to its junction with the Spray River.

Choosing the shortest and most direct route from there to Banff, they attempted to follow the Spray northward. Thwarted by fallen timber, the head guide had to turn back with the pack train and take the route along the Spray Lakes. The remaining six men took one horse and continued along the Spray River. At some point, they separated into two parties. The Swiss guides made it to their Banff hotel that night. The Wallings, on the other hand, lost their way and ended up killing the horse for meat and spending the night in the woods. The Swiss guides did not report the missing men until the next morning, at which point a rescue party set out immediately. The hapless travellers were found within 50 yards of a lumber road leading to Banff. Not surprisingly, there is no record of the Wallings ever returning to the Rockies.

Following his somewhat audacious start at the age of eight, Pat Brewster went on to become a well-known trail guide and citizen of Banff. This member of the famous Brewster family recorded many of his early exploits in three small books.

Four years later, Canada's youngest trail guide, eight-year-old Pat Brewster of Banff, successfully led a group along the same route the Wallings had attempted from the Spray Lakes. The party did not proceed to Mount Assiniboine. The self-confidant boy explained: "I had been there before, you see; I knew how to get there ... Of course there was a packer with me, a trail man, but I showed them the way."[6]

Other parties were also using the increasingly popular Spray River trail, and in 1910 the Warden Service had a six-foot-wide (1.8-metre-wide) trail suitable for pack horses cut from Banff to the Spray Lakes along the Spray River, a distance of 24 miles (39 kilometres). Two years later, the trail was continued a further 18 miles (29 kilometres) along Bryant Creek to Mount Assiniboine. Never again would a party suffer the Walling brothers' ordeal.

The Business of Tourism

A group intent only on enjoying the mountains headed for Mount Assiniboine along the new trail in 1917. Caroline Hinman was conducting the first of her Off the Beaten Track tours to take place entirely within Canada. Jimmy Simpson outfitted the party, assigning Ulysses LaCasse as head guide to the nine young ladies, assisted by Jim Boyce as cook and Max Brooks and Howard Deegan as packers. Simpson himself saw the pack train on its way by accompanying Himman's party from Banff to Whiteman's Gap, where he let LaCasse take over. Elizabeth Brown Robbins reported on her experience camping at the gap:

> I shall never forget that first night, as it was an absolutely new experience to sleep on the ground with the sky glistening with stars overhead. Slowly the northern lights appeared, first showing in dull rose streaks which broadened and deepened as the time flew toward midnight and finally developed into a glorious radiance transfiguring the entire sky, while directly overhead it was dazzlingly bright.[7]

The large party continued along Wilcox's route to Bryant Creek then over Assiniboine Pass to Lake Magog. After a four-day layover, they proceeded over Citadel Pass and on to Simpson Pass, Healy Creek and Banff.[8] Hinman returned to the area with her 1926 Off the Beaten Track tour, which crossed North Kananaskis Pass then followed the Palliser Pass–Spray River route to Bryant Creek.[9] They followed the creek to Marvel Lake then deviated from Wilcox's route by crossing Wonder Pass to Lake Magog.

In 1920 Arthur Wheeler, president of the Alpine Club of Canada, decided to implement a walking tour from Banff to Mount Assiniboine.[10] He felt that a circular tour would work well and chose to follow the Spray River to Goat Creek, travel up the creek to the Upper and Lower Spray Lakes, follow their western shores to a camp (Trail Centre Camp) that he had set up at the mouth of Bryant Creek then proceed along Bryant Creek and over Assiniboine Pass to Permanent Camp at Lake Magog.[11] To return, those following the walking tour normally crossed Citadel Pass then hiked through Sunshine Meadows and along Healy Creek to Banff. Several camps were set up along the route for lunch breaks and overnight

The Bryant Creek Warden Cabin is a prominent landmark along the Bryant Creek trail, which was part of Wheeler's walking tour. It is approximately halfway between Trail Centre Camp and Assiniboine Pass.

stops, and Trail Centre Camp had a log cabin that served as dining room, kitchen and drying room. Overnight accommodation was provided in tents until five rustic cabins were built at Permanent Camp in 1925. Ironically, the initially successful tours had disappeared by 1926, but the cabins (Naiset Cabins) are still in use, with BC Parks operating them as overnight shelter cabins.

Above: In 1920 Arthur Wheeler, best known as one of the driving forces in establishing the Alpine Club of Canada, initiated a circular walking tour from Banff along Bryant Creek to Mount Assiniboine. The successful tour inexplicably disappeared six years later.

Below: Despite a stormy and frigid first visit to the Mount Assiniboine area, artist A.C. Leighton returned many times to paint.

ALL IN A DAY'S WORK

Artist A.C. Leighton first travelled to Mount Assiniboine during a snowstorm in early October 1927. After following the trail along Brewster Creek and over Assiniboine Pass, his "outside clothing which was covered with snow had turned to ice, like a suit of armor and tin hat."[12] Darkness had already descended;

the party's provisions were frozen. The following day's attempts to paint fared little better; Leighton's watercolours froze, forcing him to switch to pastels. His diary notes: "Have just returned from making a sketch. I walked out to find a subject and thought I could sit out for a short while so did a quick pastel taking about 20 min. After that I began to get cold. It was snowing most of the time but one can blow it off quite easily like dust and it does not bother much."[13] Even though the weather was cold, he completed a dozen sketches during his 11-day stay at the lake and was impressed enough with Mount Assiniboine that he returned often to paint the lofty peak.

Mountaineering at Palliser Pass

Though Walter Wilcox found the route rather dull, he had pioneered a straightforward route by which mountaineers and other adventurers could return from Mount Assiniboine to Banff. Those wishing to explore further – most often to ascend a few peaks – could first detour south along the Spray River to Palliser Pass. Wilcox himself first undertook this exploration in 1901. He and fellow mountaineer Henry Bryant followed his 1899 route in reverse, heading south from Canmore over Whiteman's Gap and along the Spray Lakes to set up a permanent camp at the junction of Bryant Creek and the Spray River.[14] After a second unsuccessful attempt to climb Mount Assiniboine, they proceeded south along the upper Spray River.

Based on their copy of Dawson's map, they believed that the Kananaskis Lakes were just south of the Spray Lakes and expected to soon arrive on their shores. Little did they know, the lakes were actually on the other side of the Divide. They ended up crossing Palliser Pass at the headwaters of the Spray River and entering the Palliser River valley, where they became utterly lost. Fortunately, they managed to cross a pass somewhere to the south that put them into the Elk River Valley and were eventually able to cross Elk Pass and reach the Kananaskis Lakes.[15]

Eighteen years later, two major climbing expeditions intentionally set out for Palliser Pass. On August 2, 1919, Potts Outfitting of Morley supplied Val Fynn and his wife and another couple, the Eddys, with

Captain John Palliser (1817–1887)

John Palliser was born in Dublin, Ireland, on January 29, 1817, the eldest son of wealthy Irish nobleman Wray Palliser and Anne Gledstanes. Young Palliser studied in several European countries, becoming fluent in four foreign languages. He was, however, a mediocre student, and dropped out of Dublin's Trinity College after two years. He served time as captain of the Waterford Artillery Militia, and though he never served on active duty, he had some prospect of succeeding his father as colonel of the regiment. He also served a year as high sheriff of County Waterford and justice of the peace. His main interests, however, appear to have been travelling and hunting big game.

An 1847 hunting expedition took Palliser across the Atlantic to North America. He trekked up the Mississippi River from New Orleans, then up the Missouri into the western wilderness, far beyond the western limits of settlement. After many strange and dangerous adventures, he returned to Ireland in 1849. The story of his adventures, *Solitary Rambles and Adventures of a Hunter in the Prairies*, was enthusiastically received on publication in 1853.

By 1856 Palliser had started advocating for an exploratory trip across North America to investigate the British holdings north of the 49th parallel. Though he intended to pay his own way, he tried to interest the Royal Geographical Society (which had elected him a fellow in 1856) in the scheme. Because of American interests in the area that is now western Canada, the society was immediately interested and suggested a more ambitious scheme, using scientific assistants. The expanded trip led to a request for government sponsorship, which led to further expansion of the objectives, as the government wanted information on a route to the western plains entirely through British territory, including

The Palliser River, along with the lake from which it flows and the nearby pass, is named after Captain John Palliser, leader of the Palliser Expedition. The Captain explored the region around North Kananaskis Pass in 1857, in search of a transportation corridor through the mountains.

reports on the geology, climate, flora, fauna, resources and capacity for agriculture. The British treasury eventually agreed to finance the expedition to the amount of 5,000 pounds sterling, although the final bill came to two and a half times that amount.

The explorations lasted from 1857 to 1860, with Palliser publishing reports in 1859, 1860 and 1863, with a final map in 1865. Their most memorable content consists of Palliser's identification of a large tract of semi-arid land in southern Alberta and Saskatchewan considered to be unsuitable for agriculture, which has become known as the Palliser Triangle. In 1859 the Royal Geographical Society awarded Palliser the gold Patron's Medal for his travels in western Canada, and in 1877 his Canadian explorations were further recognized when he was named a Companion of the Order of St. Michael and St. George.

Palliser never married and continued to travel and explore extensively in places as remote as the West Indies and Russia after inheriting his family's Irish estates in 1862. He spent his final years on the estate, caring for several family members who had made their home with the dearly beloved bachelor. He died at home in 1877 and is buried in the graveyard of Comeragh Church, Waterford County, Ireland.

Palliser's ambitious travels seem to have taken a toll on the family fortune, most of which had been lost by the time of his death. His niece, Caroline Fairholme, declared many years later that "his days spent among the Rocky Mountains and hunting and traveling in Canada were amongst the very happiest, if not the happiest of his life."[16] Through the Palliser Range, the Palliser River and Palliser Pass, his name lives on in the Rocky Mountains of Canada. In addition to the now-famous Palliser Triangle, the Canadian prairies also boast streets, hotels and schools named in his honour.

three men and 16 horses for a two-and-a-half week outing. Waddy Potts was chief guide and cook, with Robert Baptie and Jack Fuller as wranglers. The party, which also included Swiss guide Rudolf Aemmer, used the Spray River–Goat Creek–Spray Lakes route to reach Bryant Creek. The party of eight followed the Spray River south from Banff for a few miles, crossed the river on a recently built bridge then left the river to follow Goat Creek and the shores of the Spray Lakes until they joined the Spray River again south of the lakes. They continued beyond Bryant Creek, where the trail became very rough and gave them some trouble with the pack horses. Inadequate maps led them to accidentally continue along White Man Creek toward White Man Pass at the junction where Currie Creek and White Man Creek flow into the Spray River. Once they realized their mistake, they decided to simply bushwhack east until they intercepted the trail along the Spray River. They then continued along the upper Spray River to set up camp at the base of Palliser Pass on August 5.

After some exploration of the surrounding environs, the party decided to set up permanent camp just east of Belgium Lake, near its southern end and just north of the pass. From this vantage point, they could cross Palliser Pass and follow the Palliser River past Leroy Creek and Tipperary Lake, where they were able to attempt the unclimbed Royal Group. Just over a week later, they broke camp, returned to Bryant Creek and headed up the creek to Marvel Lake. They crossed Assiniboine Pass on August 15 and set up camp at Lake Magog, from where Fynn, Eddy and Aemmer succeeded in climbing Mount Assiniboine. Having completed their climbing for the trip, they followed Wilson's route through the Valley of the Rocks, over Citadel Pass and down Healy Creek to Banff, where they arrived on August 19.[17]

Meanwhile, mountaineers J.W.A. Hickson and A.C. Stead were also camped near Palliser Pass with Swiss guide Edouard Feuz and two packers. They had chosen the route through Canmore; from Whiteman's Gap the pack train followed Wilcox's path along the Spray Lakes and River to Palliser Pass. Hickson's outfitters, the Brewsters, were likely none too impressed with Hickson's comments on this mode of travel:

> Not withstanding the opening up of motor roads in the Canadian Rockies, which enable one to be whirled in a day from Banff to Windermere or from Lake Louise to Golden and return, with hours to spare, the only means of approaching new peaks, and indeed some of the outstanding old ones, are still the use of one's legs or the tediously slow moving and expensive pack train.[18]

Having discovered that the Fynn party was still camped at the top of the pass, Hickson's party set up camp at the base of the pass. After some climbing in that vicinity, on August 12 they walked to the top of the pass, where they met with the Eddys and Mrs. Fynn. Fynn and Aemmer were out climbing.

The next day, the Hickson party and their 11 horses, who were heading south toward Leroy Creek, briefly met up with the Fynn party and their 16 horses headed north toward Bryant Creek. Fortunately the top of the pass, where the meeting took place, is relatively open and would lead to less confusion than a meeting on a narrow trail. Hickson found the pass charming but declared that the descent on the south side

> is exceedingly steep and the trail was in atrocious condition. To make a mile an hour here was not bad going. Fallen logs were a great impediment, and many burnt trees were waiting to fall, and some did actually come down with the boisterous wind which kept up most of the day. This was the worst and only really bad day on the whole trip, and we were well wet before reaching the floor of the main valley where we turned to the left and went up by a stream, Le Roy [Leroy] Creek, which runs down the valley leading from the North Kananaskis Pass. Up here the travelling was still worse, there being no trail whatever.[19]

The soaked and rather disgruntled party set up camp on Leroy Creek at the base of North Kananaskis Pass. They climbed a few more peaks before crossing the steep North Kananaskis Pass on August 15. After camping a few days on Upper Kananaskis Lake, they followed Smith-Dorrien Creek back to Bryant Creek and proceeded up Bryant Creek and over Assiniboine Pass to camp at Lake Magog, where they noted a tree recording Fynn and Eddy's recent ascent of Mount Assiniboine. The Hickson party crossed Simpson Pass to arrive back in Banff on August 25.

Nine years later, Hickson and Feuz returned to the area with trail guide Scottie Wright, two helpers and 12 horses. This time they continued over Palliser Pass and past the entrance to North Kananaskis Pass, continuing down the Palliser River Valley to Joffre Creek and Sylvan Pass.

Palliser Pass's popularity among mountaineers is reflected in the use of Hickson's campsite by another party in 1921. Henry Hall and his friend Marcus Morton, Jr. started out from Banff along Wheeler's walking tour route. They followed a gravel logging road along the Spray River to the Eau Claire Camp and Goat Creek to the Moose Lodge at Canmore (Whiteman's) Gap, then continued past the Spray Lakes to the Trail Centre Camp. There they waited for Swiss guide Edouard Feuz and trail guide Ralph Rink to arrive with the pack train. The entire party then moved up the Spray River through a scenic park-like meadow bordered by alternating virgin timber and burnt forest to Hickson's campsite below Palliser Pass. They proceeded to Hickson's campsite on Leroy Creek before crossing North Kananaskis Pass, then they established a base camp near Turbine Canyon. After doing some climbing, they followed Hickson's route to the Kananaskis Lakes and along Smith-Dorrien Creek to rejoin the Wheeler walking tour trail at Bryant Creek.[20] When the Alpine Club of Canada held its annual camp at Belgium Lake near the base of Palliser Pass the following summer, the 107 adventurers followed Hall and Morton's route to get to camp.[21]

J.W.A. Hickson was one of the few Canadians who climbed extensively in the Canadian Rockies in the early twentieth century. He is seen here sitting with three unidentified climbing companions standing above.

The Trail Today

Though most early travellers used the route over Assiniboine Pass and along Bryant Creek to exit the Mount Assiniboine area, for the convenience of modern-day hikers, we have described the route in reverse. We begin by describing the trail from the Mount Shark parking area to the Trail Centre Junction then continue with the three options: one to Assiniboine Pass, another north to Banff along the Spray Lakes and a final path south along the Spray River and over Palliser Pass.

The trail from the Mount Shark parking area to Trail Centre Junction is a convenient starting point for a large variety of hikes south of Bryant Creek. There are six passes across the Continental Divide within easy reach, as well as a number of lakes, Marvel Lake being the largest. The trail is a wide road, heavily used by both hikers and cross-country skiers. We encourage those in the area to also consider a side trip to the shore of Watridge Lake and on to the Karst Springs. The subterranean source of these springs causes them to bubble vigorously from the side of the mountain.

The trail from Trail Centre Junction to Assiniboine Pass climbs gently uphill along the southwest side of the Sundance Range until the trail splits beyond Allenby Campground. It is a pleasant valley hike with four easily accessible campgrounds and a cabin with bunk beds (no mattresses), picnic tables and a stove – a very pleasant spot to spend the night, especially in winter or during inclement weather.

At the trail juncture, there is an obvious break in the mountains to the north, with trails leading to Allenby, Og and Assiniboine passes. The horse trail to the left is shorter than the hiking trail, but it goes through some wet spots and unbridged stream crossings. This is likely the original trail to Assiniboine Pass and can be easily used in dry weather or by hikers who don't mind shallow stream fords. The newer hiking trail, which branches to the left from the Og Pass trail, climbs high on the side of Cave Mountain and is quite spectacular but not difficult, although it does involve some fairly steep climbs. Its high points provide good views over the surrounding mountains and valleys. The Bryant Creek trail is the most heavily used route to the accommodation around Lake Magog. Both variations are good trails with lots of water, no route-finding difficulties, plenty of campgrounds and a large number of opportunities to explore other areas. The trip can be done in one day by those wishing to push straight through to Lake Magog.

Once historic travellers reached the south end of the Spray Lakes, they had two main options for returning to Banff and the railroad. The most common route was to follow the Spray River to Bow Falls, where it joins the Bow and leads into Banff. Unfortunately, the portion of the route between the Spray Lakes Reservoir and the junction with Goat Creek is currently closed between April 15 and November 15. Though skiers can still use the route, it has been decommissioned and campground facilities removed.

The alternate route to Banff from the south end of the Spray Lakes Reservoir is to follow the west shore of the reservoir then continue on to Goat Creek. This trail, which is described in Route I above (McGillivray's Route), will mainly be of interest to cyclists. For hikers wishing to take the route, the first campground is Spray Lakes West Campground, approximately 20 kilometres from the Trail Centre Junction and accessible by car from the north end. The trail from Goat Creek trail to Banff is heavily used by cyclists during the summer and skiers in the winter. Its only campground is approximately 14 kilometres from the Goat Creek parking lot – less than 6 kilometres from the Banff trailhead. It is primarily used by hikers taking a short overnight trip from Banff.

The Mount Shark parking area can also be used as a starting point from which to explore the upper Spray and Palliser river valleys. The trail along the Spray passes through an open meadow and features good views of the surrounding mountains. For those not wishing to proceed all the way to Palliser Pass, the trail can be used to access White Man Pass, Burstall Pass or Spray Pass.[22] With many possible side trips to mountain lakes and passes, this is an interesting area to explore. There are two campgrounds in the 20 kilometres between the Mount Shark parking area and Palliser Pass. Once over the pass, the trail along the Palliser River is used mainly as an access route to North Kananaskis Pass.[23] Between Palliser and North Kananaskis passes, the trail cuts through Height of the Rockies Provincial Park in British Columbia, where there are no designated campgrounds. The trail is heavily used – primarily by equestrians – and generally easy to follow, though some route-finding skills are required near the junction with Leroy Creek.

Trail Guide

Distances are adapted from existing trail guides: Patton and Robinson, Potter, Beers, and Eastcott, and from Gem-Trek maps. Distances intermediate from those given in the sources are estimated from topographical maps and from hiking times. All distances are given in kilometres.

Mount Shark Parking Area to Trail Centre Junction

Maps 82 J/14 Spray Lakes Reservoir
Gem-Trek Banff and Mount Assiniboine

There is very little elevation change on this route.

Trailhead

Cross the Bow River in Canmore. As the road begins to climb, turn right (west) onto the Spray Lakes Road. Follow this road 38 km to the turn-off for Mount Engadine Lodge and the Mount Shark parking area. Turn right (west) and continue 5.3 km to the end of the road at the Mount Shark parking area. Do not turn into the entrance to the lodge or the heli-pad. The trailhead is near the northwest corner of the parking lot.

0.0 Mount Shark parking area. From the large trailhead signboards, proceed southwest along a gravel road through a clear-cut that now has many ski trails. Stay on the main trail and follow the numerous signs for Watridge Lake and Banff National Park. Cross a bridge over a major creek and enter a mature forest.

3.7 The short trail to Watridge Lake goes to the left. Keep ahead. The trail drops downhill then levels out again.

5.9 Spray River bridge.

6.0 Trail junction. The trail to Palliser Pass and White Man Pass goes to the left. Keep to the right (north) for Bryant Creek. The trail narrows.

6.7 Trail Centre Junction. The trail to the right goes to Canyon Dam. Keep left for Bryant Creek. The warden cabin is just ahead on the left.

Trail Centre Junction to Mount Assiniboine Lodge over Assiniboine Pass

Maps 82 J/13 Mount Assiniboine

82 J/14 Spray Lakes Reservoir

Gem-Trek Banff and Mount Assiniboine

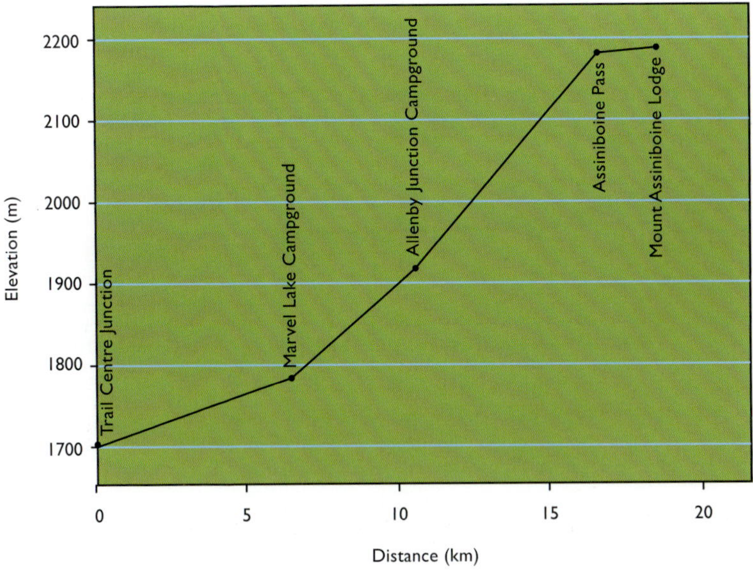

Trailhead

The trailhead is Trail Centre Junction, km 6.7 of the Mount Shark Parking Lot to Trail Centre Junction trail above.

0.0 Continue northwest on a well-used trail through the forest. The sheer rock face of Mount Turner is visible through the trees on the left. Cross a bridge over Bryant Creek.

2.9 Big Springs Campground. The trail continues through a narrow valley with mountains now visible on both sides.

5.3 Trail junction. The trail to the left (southwest) goes to Owl Lake. Continue ahead to the northwest. A large rockslide on the right provides a good vista of the mountains.

6.3 Trail junction. The Marvel Lake trail goes to the left (west). Keep moving forward. The trail climbs over a rocky ridge to a small meadow.

6.9 The Bryant Creek shelter is in the meadow, 200 m to the left.

7.5 Trail junction. The trail to Marvel Lake and Wonder Pass goes to the left. Just ahead is the Bryant Creek Warden Cabin, situated in a meadow with great views of Gibraltar Rock and Cascade Rock rising steeply along the Continental Divide. Another trail to the left leads to a horse camp and a tepee camp. The trail to the pass continues northwest through a brush-covered meadow, crossing streams on bridges.

10.6 Trail junction. Allenby Junction Campground is on the left. Continue ahead.

10.8 Trail junction. The horse trail to Assiniboine Pass goes to the left. This trail is shorter but goes through some wet areas with unbridged stream crossings. The hiking trail goes to the right (north), then west, staying high on the side of Cave Mountain to avoid wet areas down below.

11.3 The trail to Og Pass and Allenby Pass go to the right. Turn left (northwest) and start to climb on a good single-track trail to the head of a valley. Swing to the southwest along the base of sheer cliffs and continue to climb more steeply over a rock wall that has switchbacks until the trail levels out.

15.7 Trail junction. Rejoin the horse trail and continue to climb through trees.

16.3 Top of Assiniboine Pass, entering Mount Assiniboine Provincial Park. The trail proceeds downhill through open forest and meadows with a full view of the towering Mount Assiniboine to the left (south).

18.1 Trail junction. The trail to Og Lake and Pass and Citadel Pass goes to the right. Keep left (southeast) for Mount Assiniboine Lodge.

18.6 Mount Assiniboine Lodge.

Trail Centre Junction to Banff along the Spray Lakes, Goat Creek and the Spray River

Maps 82 J/14 Spray Lakes Reservoir

82 O/3 Canmore

82 O/4 Banff

Gem-Trek Banff and Mount Assiniboine

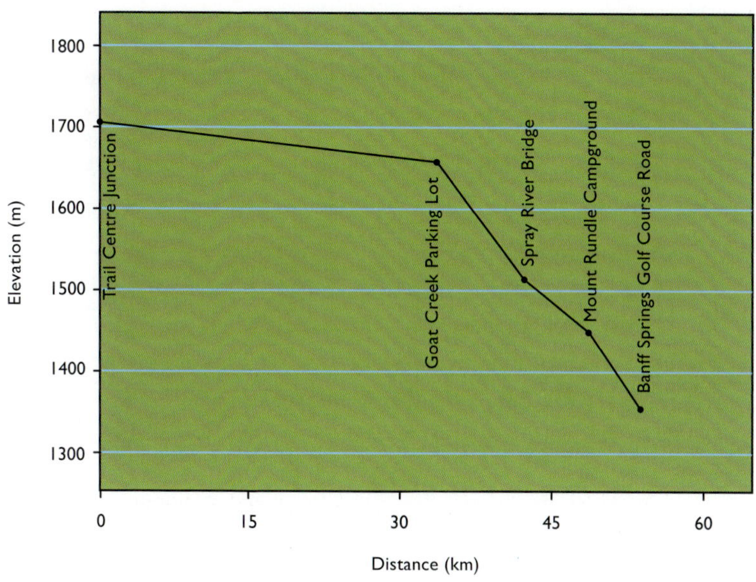

Trailhead

The trailhead is Trail Centre Junction, km 6.7 of the Mount Shark Parking Area to Trail Centre Junction trail above.

0.0 The trail from Trail Centre Junction to Goat Creek along the west shore of the Spray Lakes Reservoir is described in Route I above, km 41.4 to km 8.6, in the reverse direction (Old Bow Fort to the Cross River along the Spray Lakes and over White Man Pass trail). Km 41.4 of Route I is considered to be km 0.0 of this route. (The route along the Spray River, used by Wilcox and others, is now closed from April 15 to November 15 and is not available as a hiking trail. The alternate route along the Spray Lakes Reservoir is described here.)

33.8 (Km 8.6 of the route above.) Goat Creek trail junction, Banff National Park boundary and national park trailhead sign. The trail to the right reaches the Goat Creek parking lot on the Spray Lakes Road in 1 km. Keep to the left (west) along the Goat Creek trail, which is the old Spray River Fire Road. The trail goes gently downhill across three bridged streams then turns northwest, with frequent breaks in the trees providing views of the mountains on the left (south). The old road does a sharp hairpin turn down a steep hill as it approaches Goat Creek.

40.0 Goat Creek bridge. The old road climbs out of the Goat Creek valley and soon drops again, this time into the Spray River valley.

41.8 Spray River bridge. The trail climbs out of the Spray River valley.

42.1 Trail junction. The historic route along the Spray River, which is now closed from April 15 to November 15, goes to the left (southwest). Stay to the right on the old fire road, which is now a hard-packed gravel road that proceeds gradually downhill to the northwest along the Spray River. This is quite a scenic route. Come to an open area with picnic tables.

46.2 Trail junction. The trail straight ahead goes down the west side of the Spray River to the Banff Springs Hotel. Keep to the right (east), cross the river on a bridge and proceed down the east side of the river on a good trail.

47.1 Mount Rundle Campground.

50.8 Viewpoint with a good view of the Banff Springs Hotel.

51.3 Trail junction. The trail up Mount Rundle branches to the right. Keep ahead for Banff Springs Golf Course Road. When the trail reaches the golf course fairway, keep left (west) along the edge of the fairway to the Spray River, then turn right (north) along the river to the road, always keeping watch for golfers on the tee west of the river or on the fairway.

52.2 Banff Springs Golf Course Road and a road bridge across the Spray River.

Trail Centre Junction to Leroy Creek along the Spray River and over Palliser Pass

Maps 82 J/14 Spray Lakes Reservoir

82 J/11 Kananaskis Lakes

Gem-Trek Banff and Mount Assiniboine

Gem-Trek Kananaskis Lakes

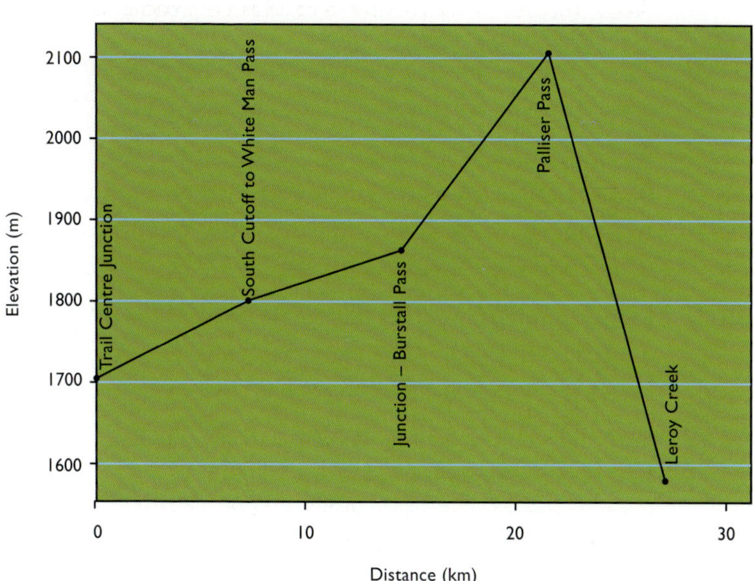

Trailhead

The trailhead is Trail Centre Junction, km 6.7 of the Mount Shark Parking Lot to Trail Centre Junction trail above. For those coming from Mount Assiniboine along Bryant Creek, proceed straight ahead at the trail junction (km 0.0 below). The trail to the left (north) goes to Canyon Dam. For those coming from the Mount Shark Parking Lot, turn left (south) at km 0.7 below.

0.0 Proceed southeast along the trail, which skirts the west end of the Spray Lakes Reservoir.

0.7 Trail junction. The trail to the Mount Shark Parking Lot goes to the left (east). Keep to the right (south) on the Palliser Pass trail, which follows the west bank of the Spray River. The trail passes through the forest to an old outfitter's camp with a fire warning sign from the 1920s, then it enters an extensive meadow.

3.9 Trail junction. The trail to White Man Pass goes to the right (southwest). Continue south across a bridge through a broad meadow and cross two bridged streams as the trail moves primarily into the forest.

7.5 Trail junction. The southern trail to White Man Pass goes to the right. Continue ahead to the southeast, following the bank of the Spray River through the forest then the edge of a meadow on a heavily used horse trail.

9.9 Birdwood Campground (US15). Come to an old outfitter's camp followed by a fence across the trail (with a gate) and a bridge across Birdwood Creek.

10.5 Palliser Warden Cabin. The trail continues along the right side of a meadow to avoid a large pond then switches to the left side, enters the woods and re-emerges onto the meadow.

14.5 Trail junction. The trail to Burstall Pass goes to the left (east). Keep going forward (south).

14.7 Trail junction. Burstall Campground is 300 m to the right on the trail to Leman Lake and Spray Pass. Continue ahead (south) along the west side of the meadow and sometimes in the trees along the side of the meadow as you pass through this very beautiful valley.

19.3 Begin the steep climb toward the pass on a good horse trail along the east side of Spray River ravine.

20.6 Pass between two lakes, the largest of which (to the west) is Belgium Lake.

21.4 Palliser Pass, with signs and markers for the Continental Divide and the Alberta–British Columbia border. This is the end of Banff National Park. The trail drops downhill to the south, crosses a meadow with several small ponds then arrives at the north shore of a pretty lake. The trail climbs a short distance above the lake then drops steeply to a small meadow with a good camping spot before again dropping very steeply along the left bank of the Palliser River. The well-used and easy-to-follow horse trail proceeds down the valley past several avalanche paths that provide great views of the surrounding mountains. The Leroy Creek valley becomes visible on the left (east) before the trail reaches a small meadow where the trail is a bit faint.

27.1 Leroy Creek and trail junction. The trail to the left proceeds northeast up Leroy Creek and over North Kananaskis Pass. The trail ahead continues south down the Palliser River. This trail junction is km 105.4 of the Old Bow Fort to the Palliser River over North Kananaskis Pass trail, described in Route III above.

Redearth Creek Route to Ball Pass, Redearth Pass and Gibbon Pass

ROUTE VII

Talc Trail: Redearth Creek Route to Ball Pass, Redearth Pass and Gibbon Pass

Heavy rain poured from the skies as six teenagers and I set up camp at the Hawk Creek gravel pit. We were in the midst of a 13-day trek along the Continental Divide. Four hikers had just left the core group of three teenagers and myself at the Floe Lake Parking Lot, and three more had joined us to pass through the Egypt Lakes valley, past Mount Assiniboine and on to the Kananaskis Lakes. Much to our chagrin, the heavy rain had not let up by morning. We used our one large tent as a shelter in which to pack up everything else we had brought, then we quickly dismantled the big tent and fly sheet and apologetically passed the soggy mass to the hikers designated to carry them.

As we started up toward Ball Pass, we silently noted the snow adorning the packs of hikers descending from the pass. By the time we reached treeline, there were 10–15 centimetres of snow on the ground. The trail proceeded through a rocky barren area marked by small cairns. It became increasingly difficult to follow as we approached the pass and could only be discerned by a slight depression in the snow cover. The cairns, each looking more and more like all the other snow-covered rocks, tested my route-finding skills to the limit. It did not help that the six young people behind me had complete faith in my ability to find the trail and lead them through this storm over the pass and into the relative safety of the Egypt Lakes valley.

As we proceeded, I carefully brushed off each snow-covered protrusion that looked anything like a cairn, with an immediate cheer arising from the group if it proved to be the lifeline. We were still on the trail! Slowly but surely we ascended the pass and managed to reach a campground at the junction of the Whistling Valley trail. Although nobody felt much like stopping for lunch in the midst of a snowstorm, I insisted that we all needed nourishment.

Once we had stopped, I realized that one of the girls, who had been instructed to bring a waterproof jacket and pants, had not tested her borrowed jacket. The heavy rain and wet snow on the approach to Ball Pass had soaked her to the skin, and she was starting to show early signs of hypothermia. It was the nature of these hardy youngsters not to complain and to soldier on, regardless of conditions.

Weather in the mountains is unpredictable at the best of times, and late August snowstorms are common. Here a party attempts to eat lunch during a late-August hike over Ball Pass.

Nevertheless, something had to be done immediately. Pooling our resources, we compiled a suit of dry clothes and ushered her into an outhouse to change. I was relieved to find that we had grasped the situation in time, and she soon warmed up. As we ate our lunch, a cow moose wandered through the campsite, bringing a modicum of cheer to the party – most of whom were wishing we had mother moose's style of clothing.

After finishing our lunch, such as it was, we proceeded on our way. Although we had managed to cross the pass, the going had been slow, and the campsite at Egypt Lake was still a long way off. By now, all were starting to feel the effects of the wet day. Everyone had wet feet, and our clothing was starting to feel damp from body moisture under raingear, if nothing else. Fatigue was also becoming a factor. I took some consolation in knowing that there was a cabin near the Egypt Lakes Campground where we could stay if it was not fully occupied, but I did not mention it to the young travellers as I did not want to get their hopes up. Once smoke rising from the cabin chimney was visible though, I had to explain its source.

As we drew nearer, we could see the silhouettes of people moving around inside the cabin but could not discern the number of occupants. It was nearly dark when, chilled and exhausted, we reached its threshold. We threw off our packs and trooped into the cabin. The lone young American couple we found inside were no doubt hoping to have a peaceful night to themselves. Instead, they retreated to the sleeping quarters at one end of the cabin and began to fix some supper. Asked to comment on his opinion of the day, one of the teenage boys immediately spluttered, "This has been the worst day of my life." But by morning, everything had dried out and the sun had ushered in a warm and beautiful late-August day. We packed up and moved on, spirits fully restored, with the trials of the previous day put behind us.

One feature of late summer snowstorms in the mountains is that they are often over in a day. This image shows the authors (on the right) with their hiking group on the top of Healy Pass with Egypt Lakes in the background, a day after a heavy snowstorm. Summer weather has returned, and everyone is ready to continue with the trek.

Chronology

1895 Colonel Robert O'Hara embarks upon the first recorded exploration in the area north and west of Simpson Pass. Two of Tom Wilson's men take him from Vermilion Pass to Simpson Pass. He later writes Tom Wilson about the soapy talc he saw near Redearth Pass.

1913 The Parks Department builds a trail along Redearth Creek and Pharaoh Creek as far as Simpson's Summit. It may have been cut in conjunction with a survey taking place that year.

A.O. Wheeler visits the Egypt Lake area as part of the Alberta–British Columbia boundary survey. He names the five lakes and is very impressed with the area.

1915 Banff outfitter Jim Brewster, Parks Commissioner J.B. Harkin and two CPR officials ride up Healy Creek to Sunshine Village then head northwest to Simpson Pass, Healy Pass, Egypt Lake, Whistling Pass and Shadow Lake. The feasibility of having a trail running approximately parallel to the Bow River from Banff to Lake Louise, high on the southwest side of the valley (The Highline Trail), is confirmed.

1917 Bill Peyto, who has spent a lot of time prospecting in the Simpson Pass area, stakes a claim at Redearth Pass.

1920 The route from Sunshine Meadows to Vermilion Pass is hiked by a honeymooning couple, A.S. Sibbald and his wife. This was the first-recorded long backpacking trip in the Rockies, and it was an experiment to see if the pony could be dispensed with on long trips through the mountains.

1921 Mountaineer-artist Belmore Browne visits Shadow Lake by taking the trail up Redearth Creek to its junction with Pharaoh Creek, then following Redearth Creek to the lake.

1928 The National Talc Company builds a bridge across the Bow River and a rough road up Redearth Creek and Pharaoh Creek over Redearth Pass to Talc Lake.

CPR publicist John Murray Gibbon, Jim Brewster and a CPR photographer follow a series of blazed trees to a high ridge west of Shadow Lake (Gibbon Pass) and continue on to Twin Lakes, Arnica Lake and Altrude Creek near Vermilion Pass.

1929 The Trail Riders of the Canadian Rockies ride the southern part of the High Line Trail for the first time. They ride up Healy Creek to Sunshine Meadows and across the Simpson Pass trail to the pass, then on to Shadow Lake before continuing over the ridge (Gibbon Pass) to Twin Lakes and Castle Mountain.

The CPR builds a substantial rest cabin near Shadow Lake. It is sold to the Brewster Transportation Company in 1938. In 1991 the original cabin is remodelled into a lodge and renamed Shadow Lake Lodge. Six additional cabins are added.

1930 The Parks Department cuts a trail up Redearth Creek past Shadow Lake and on to Ball Pass. The Trail Riders of the Canadian Rockies take the new trail to Ball Pass.

1933 The Crosby family from Minneapolis camp at Shadow Lake. Various members of the family take trips to Ball Pass, Whistling Lake and Egypt Lake, returning along Pharaoh Creek.

1934 The Fraser family from Ottawa takes a pack-train trip to Shadow Lake then proceeds over Ball Pass and down Hawk Creek to the Vermilion River.

History

Scouting out the Area

The first recorded exploration in the area north and west of Simpson Pass took place in 1895, when two of Tom Wilson's men escorted Colonel Robert O'Hara from Vermilion Pass to Simpson Pass. Little is known of the trip, except that the anonymous guides refused to participate in later trips with the irascible O'Hara, who ran his camps on a strict military basis, and that O'Hara observed soapy talc near Redearth Pass.

If O'Hara enjoyed the area, he must have kept his enthusiasm to himself, as there are no records of anyone else travelling in the area until 1913, when the Parks Department built a trail along Redearth Creek and Pharaoh Creek as far as Simpson's Summit, presumably to facilitate patrolling the area. A survey party was also in the area that summer; the trail may have been cut in conjunction with their work. Austrian mountain guide Conrad Kain, who was assisting with the survey, sat by the side of Shadow Lake on August 30 and wrote:

> I am sitting here under a larch tree, on the shore of a lovely, deep blue lake, between two rocky peaks. At the end of the lake there is a waterfall, which comes from another lake further on, above which is a third lake higher up. The background is snow and ice, an indescribable picture when one adds the fine tone of the bells worn by the horses. I see some goats on the grass slopes above timber. It is one of the most beautiful places I have ever seen.[1]

Despite Kain's opinion about the beauty of the lake, the only recorded visitor to the Shadow Lake area between 1913 and the late 1920s was mountaineer-artist Belmore Browne. The trip started at Jimmy Simpson's camp near Massif, 12 miles west of Banff, on September 2, 1921. The party consisted of Browne, his wife, Agnes, their children, George and Evelyn, a woman named Christine and two wranglers. Earlier, Simpson had offered

The Redearth Creek area was first visited in 1895, and the first description of Shadow Lake, shown here, was recorded in 1913. Despite the area's beauty, it did not become popular with travellers until much later.

to lend some of his horses and men to transport the family and their duffle to Shadow Lake. They started out with two pack horses, one horse for the two children, and one horse each for the adults. In Agnes's words, as they started to climb the steep trail:

> It was beautiful beyond words as well as rough and hard: fallen timber to jump, streams to ford, and rough boulders to cross, but as mountaineers know, the greater the effort the greater was our reward.... Our trail led us up a deep gash in the southern wall of the Bow Valley.... Our journey proved to be a hard nine miles instead of an easy six.... At last a beautiful green open, cut by a clear stream halted us. And we dismounted by a stand of old teepee poles.... A teepee is a splendid wilderness home, the product of unknown centuries of struggle with the forces of nature by the Indians who travelled these very mountains.[2]

Artist Belmore Browne was one of few visitors to Shadow Lake during the 1920s. He spent five days in the vicinity with his family and friends.

The family stayed at Shadow Lake until September 7, when they moved on to a cabin at Simpson Pass, probably via Whistling Pass. On September 9, they returned to Redearth Creek, probably via Pharaoh Creek, then on to the Bow River.

Seeds of a Trail

The inspiration for the trail that was to increase the region's popularity had begun back in 1913, when A.O. Wheeler, co-founder of the Alpine Club of Canada, visited the Egypt Lake area as part of the Alberta–British Columbia boundary survey. Declaring that "after thirty years of exploration, surveys and mapping of the main ranges of the Canadian Rockies, the writer can safely say that outstanding among them for scenic charm and interest may be classed the group of peaks, lakes and alpine meadows of the Egypt Lake area,"[3] he named the five lakes Egypt, Mummy, Scarab, Pharaoh and Sphinx. "Because of the shrill, resounding whistles of a number of hoary marmots who greeted me when I first entered the valley,"[4] Wheeler also chose the name Whistling for the valley and pass along the trail leading to Haiduk Lake. The name Haiduk he selected as "a Polish term for a lively young woman, a hoiden. First seen from a height with sunshine and shadow dancing on the surface of the lake the name seemed as suitable as any other and has an impressive sound."[5]

Two years later, Banff outfitter Jim Brewster, Parks Commissioner J.B. Harkin and two CPR officials rode up Healy Creek to Sunshine Village and headed northwest to Simpson Pass, Healy Pass, Egypt Lake, Whistling Pass and Shadow Lake. Duly impressed with the spectacular views, the officials needed no further convincing that a trail running approximately parallel to the Bow River from Banff to Lake Louise, high on the southwest side of the valley, should be built.[6]

It was some time, however, before this idea came to fruition. In the meantime, a couple of innovative newlyweds passed though the area as part of the first-recorded, long, backpacking trip in the Canadian Rockies. Curious to see whether the pony could be dispensed with on long trips through the Rockies, A.S. Sibbald and his wife began their 1920 trip at Lake Louise, travelling through Paradise Valley, over Sentinel Pass to Moraine Lake and past Taylor Lakes to Vermilion Pass. Believing that by the time they had reached Vermilion Pass they would have established the practicability of travelling without pack horses, they established a food cache near Twin Lakes on Vermilion Pass before setting out on their adventure:

Above: Jim Brewster was involved in transportation in the Rocky Mountains, beginning with pack and saddle horses and progressing to wheeled transport. He was instrumental in the early planning for a trail from Banff to Lake Louise on the southwest side of the Bow Valley.

Right: Parks Commissioner J.B. Harkin rode part of the trail from Healy Creek to Redearth Creek with Jim Brewster and others. He needed no further convincing of the desirability of building a trail from Lake Louise to Banff high on the southwest side of the Bow Valley.

Early on the 13th the route from Vermilion Pass was continued to the right of the Little Vermilion down into the very dense vegetation of the deep-lying valley which drains Vista Lake. This and other streams on the trip, half a dozen or more in number, were waded barefoot in order to keep our single pairs of boots reasonably dry from day to day. The crossing of the creek was followed by a somewhat steep climb out of the valley through a fine forest which later gave way to two miles or more of burnt over timber land ... The going was slow amongst the fallen timber but conditions were by no means as bad as often exist on burnt over lands. By eleven o'clock the edge of the standing forest was again reached and we lunched in the shade by the bank

> of an opportune steam. Two hours travel in the afternoon brought us through a beautifully treed country to the stream which drains Twin Lakes. It was reached at a point almost identical with the location of the cache. The latter was found to be quite undisturbed. With new supplies there followed a luxurious camp meal and we set up the tent a little way below the precipices of Storm Mountain at peace with all the world and joyous in our undertaking.[7]

On July 14, they followed the shore of Twin Lakes and continued on to Shadow Lake and Haiduk Lake, where they camped.[8] Two days later they travelled through Whistling Valley, down to Egypt Lake and on to Simpson Pass, where they expected to find an ACC camp. Not finding one (the camp was actually at Sunshine Meadows) and having run out of food, they decided to head down Healy Creek to Banff. En route, however, they met an outfitter who informed them of the camp's location, and so they continued on to Sunshine Meadows and the ACC Camp the following day.

A.S. Sibbald was the first adventurer to plan an extensive trip through the mountains without the aid of pack horses. He is shown here in front of the tent he and his wife used on their 1920 honeymoon backpacking trip from Lake Louise to Sunshine Meadows.

In the summer of 1928, Jim Brewster returned to the area with a new duo of CPR staff: publicist John Murray Gibbon and a photographer. Their main intention was to investigate some mining prospects near Shadow Lake. After reaching the lake, Brewster was tempted to follow some tree blazes (likely carved by a trapper) that led past an old Aboriginal campsite to a high ridge west of Shadow Lake. From the ridge, which Brewster later named Gibbon Pass in his honour, Gibbon spied the roof of a bungalow camp off to the northwest.

Entertainment was always an important part of the trips taken by the Trail Riders of the Canadian Rockies, and a professional singer was often taken along. Wilf Carter is shown here performing for an attentive audience.

CPR publicist John Murray Gibbon was instrumental in founding the Trail Riders of the Canadian Rockies. The organization kept records of members' rides and awarded buttons for various combined lengths. Here, Gibbon is presenting a 100-mile (161-kilometre) pin to five-year-old Michael Smith.

Although there was no trail marked on their maps, Gibbon suggested they head toward the camp. He led the party to Twin Lakes then on to Arnica Lake and Altrude Creek, which they followed to the bungalow camp.[9]

As a result of this trip, Gibbon and Brewster recommended the route for the 1928 Trail Riders of the Canadian Rockies excursion. The Trail Riders of the Canadian Rockies had arisen out of John Murray Gibbon's 1923 suggestion that a trail-riding organization might do for horse travel in the Rockies what the Alpine Club had done for mountaineering in the area. Membership was open to anyone, and most years two or three trail rides were organized, each concluding with a powwow. Musicians have always been an important part of the trail rides, with Wilf Carter being one of the best known. Gibbon's and Brewster's Shadow Lake recommendation came too late to arrange for that season, but the following summer, the Trail Riders rode the southern part of the long-wished-for High Line Trail.

The official description of their 1929 ride proposed following Healy Creek to Sunshine Meadows and across the Simpson Pass trail to the pass, where the first camp would be set up. The second camp would be on the shores of Shadow Lake, followed by an easy ride over the ridge (Gibbon Pass) to Twin Lakes. On the final day, participants would travel to the ride's concluding powwow at the Castle Mountain bungalow camp on the Banff–Windermere highway.[10]

The Cutting Begins

Ironically, it was not until the late 1920s – when the Great Depression and Second World War were about to dramatically alter the nature of alpine travel – that Redearth Creek saw widespread use. Bill Peyto, who spent a lot of time prospecting in the Simpson Pass area, had staked a claim at Redearth Pass in 1917.[11] He pursued the development as time permitted until 1927, when he sold it to the National Talc Company (NTC). The company built a bridge across the Bow River and a rough road up Redearth Creek and Pharaoh Creek over Redearth Pass to Talc Lake (now called Natalko Lake), but it did not begin mining before going bankrupt in 1929. At that time, Peyto sold his claim to Western Talc Holdings, but they allowed the claim to lapse after doing very little work.[12]

In 1930 the Parks Department extended the National Talc Company trail up Redearth Creek by cutting a trail beyond Pharaoh Creek, past Shadow Lake, where the CPR had built a substantial rest cabin, and on to Ball Pass.[13] That very year, the Trail Riders took advantage of the new trail, riding over Ball Pass and down Hawk Creek to the Vermilion River.[14] Three years later, another large party travelled the trail to Shadow Lake. Nine members of the Crosby family from Minneapolis – Mr. Crosby; his daughter, Margaret; and sons, Albert and Henry; and their wives and children – set out with Rudolph Aemmer as head guide, Ken Jones as packer, Mike Wassil as cook, Harry Smith as wrangler and a pack train of 30 horses.[15] They followed Redearth Creek to Shadow Lake, where they set up camp. Over the course of their stay, various members of the family took trips to Ball Pass, Whistling Lake and Egypt Lake, returning along Pharaoh Creek. They then moved up Pharaoh Creek to Simpson Pass, Citadel Pass and Mount Assiniboine.[16] The following year, essentially the same outfit took the Fraser family from Ottawa and about 15 horses along Redearth Creek to Shadow Lake. After their sojourn at the lake, the family proceeded over Ball Pass and down Hawk Creek to the Vermilion River, and then on into the Rockwall area.

Right: The rest cabin the CPR built in 1929 at Shadow Lake was remodelled after being sold to the Brewsters in 1938 and transformed into Shadow Lake Lodge. The structure shown here is currently the lounge and dining area. Six cabins provide sleeping accommodation.

Below: When a large group on horseback is on the move, the riders often get widely separated on the trail. This image of the Trail Riders on top of Gibbon Pass gives an indication of just how long the string can be.

Ken Jones (1910–2004)

Ken Jones was born in Golden, British Columbia, on November 1, 1910, to Welsh immigrants William Jones and Sarah Jane Huxley. In 1912 the family moved to a homestead a short distance from Golden. That year, Sarah Jones returned to Britain to show off her new baby and tried to book their return on the Titanic. Fortunately, the ship was fully booked, and they returned on an older slower vessel.

Growing up on the homestead, Jones developed a love of the outdoors. He learned to ski at age nine, when the father of some Swedish schoolmates made a pair of skis for him. At about this time, he started climbing in the hills and mountains around his home; this love of climbing continued into his teen years. At age 16 he started going out on hunting trips with outfitters and guides, mainly Bill Harrison and Conrad Kain. He claimed that his mother was part gypsy and that he had inherited his love of travel from her.

His main interest at the time was, however, hockey: Jones entertained thoughts of becoming a professional hockey player. His first year after high school was spent with the Kimberley Dynamiters in the Western Senior League, but the many injuries and bruises he sustained helped his mother convince him to give up hockey in favour of studying medicine at McGill University in Montreal.

Jones headed off to McGill in the fall of 1929, the year the Great Depression hit. His inability to pay medical school fees brought his studies to an end after the fall semester of 1931. He returned home to pick up odd jobs and study engineering by correspondence from the University of British Columbia. After earning his degree in civil engineering in 1934, he turned his efforts toward a degree in biology and recreational studies in photography.

In the summer of 1933, Swiss guide Walter Feuz, who lived in Golden, asked Jones to be a packer for the famous climber,

Katie Gardner. This was the beginning of Jones's love of the mountains and the first step toward becoming the first full-time Canadian mountain guide.

Four years later, Jones began work for Consolidated Mining and Smelting, surveying and exploring claims in northern British Columbia and Yukon. This outdoor job – his first as an engineer – suited him perfectly, but after being transferred to Vancouver in 1940, he quit in favour of enlisting in the Air Force. He learned to fly but spent most of the war years in the mountains, training troops in the art of mountain warfare.

By the war's end, Jones was fully committed to life in the mountains. He had attended his first Alpine Club of Canada camp at Mount Assiniboine in 1935 and participated in virtually every winter and summer camp for the next 30 years, doing every job that was required. He guided climbing, hunting, fishing and skiing parties and worked at Skoki and Mount Assiniboine lodges. From 1967 to 1974 he served as the first park ranger at Mount Assiniboine Provincial Park. From his retirement until his final days, he continued to work at the lodges doing odd jobs, guiding guests and entertaining them with his stories.

Little has been written about Jones's family life. He had a daughter, Susan, from an early marriage and later in life made his family home outside the mountains in Nanton, Alberta, with his wife, Bridget, and their two children: son Pat and daughter Jennifer.

Much of Jones's success during his long life was due to his cheerful and generous disposition and his willingness to work hard and diligently at any job that came his way. Up until his death at age 94 in 2004, he was regarded as a living legend by the Alpine Club of Canada and the Association of Canadian Mountain Guides, and he had a standing invitation to attend their functions. During his final years, he was able to spend a few weeks each summer and winter hauling water and chopping wood at the lodges and enjoying the mountains, which he considered his true home. He has been honoured by the naming of Jones Peak, a glacier-draped mountain in the Mummery Icefield area.[17]

Ken Jones was studying to become a physician when the Great Depression interrupted his studies. He later became an engineer but spent most of his life working a variety of jobs in his beloved Canadian Rockies.

The Trail Today

The easy and uninspiring trail up Redearth Creek to its junction with Pharaoh Creek proceeds gradually uphill along an old forested road. Beyond the junction, the trail climbs very steeply for a short distance, with the beautiful Shadow Lake area rewarding those who persevere. This makes a good day hike for those able to hike approximately 30 kilometres in one day, or a great camping spot for hikers wishing to explore the lake, Gibbon and Ball passes and Haiduk Lake. The trail up Redearth Creek is also a favourite cross-country ski outing, with many going only as far as Lost Horse Creek Campground.

For backpackers proceeding over Ball Pass, the trail leading to the Continental Divide is both rewarding and demanding. The trail up Redearth Creek and over Ball Pass is an easy trail to follow that does not require trail-finding skills. It passes through meadows, along creeks, beside sheer rock walls and across old rockslides, with great views of the surrounding mountains. After the summit, the trail drops steadily through a very pretty, narrow valley with scenic views. It then reaches an area that was totally burned in 2003, which reveals to hikers how plants regenerate after a forest fire. What is visible will depend on the number of years after the fire, but grasses and other plants begin the regeneration, with pine trees usually being the first tree growth to appear. The dead trees from the aftermath of the fire will be visible for many years. The Ball Pass–Hawk Creek portion of the trail is suitable for any backpacker who is reasonably physically fit.

Redearth Creek can also be used to access Egypt Lake, either via Pharaoh Creek or Whistling Pass. When I hiked through Whistling Pass in 2003, there was a grizzly bear in the small valley just east of the pass. When I entered the valley, the bear was on the trail, feeding on plant growth, and pretended it did not know I was there. I proceeded slowly and the bear gradually wandered off the trail, still feeding and ignoring me. I stayed in the valley for more than half an hour observing and photographing the bear, all the while giving the bruin lots of space. I gradually exited the valley over Whistling Pass, with the bear still feeding and ignoring me. This is fairly typical behaviour for bears that are used to having a lot of people around, and this trail is a busy one in the summer months. The bear is not wild in the sense that it tolerates and ignores people, given a chance. But it is still very much a wild animal if people invade its space or try and chase it or otherwise anger it. The consequence of such rash behaviour is usually unpredictable and can be disastrous.

Although the Redearth Creek trail is the main entrance to the Shadow Lake area and the trails leading from there, those wishing to hike the Highline Trail from Healy Creek to near the top of Vermilion Pass will likely want to start at Healy Creek. This is a long and demanding hike but very rewarding throughout its length. The Healy Pass area is spectacular in spring and summer for its display of wildflowers and in the fall for the beautiful golds of the larches and other plant growth. This area is a favourite day hike from Banff. The Egypt Lake area is very busy in summer, as it can be accessed by backpackers in a single day, and the seven or more lakes in the area provide scenic beauty for day trips from the campground and shelter.

Following the Highline Trail from Shadow Lake to Highway 93 is more demanding, with the steep Gibbon Pass followed by other steep climbs and drops. The hiker is rewarded with views of the mountains along the Continental Divide on the left and the Bow Valley on the right, with four major lakes adding to the beauty. The final drop from Arnica Lake to Vista Lake will test most backpackers' knees; many will wish they had left that nice-to-have but unnecessary item at home.

When I was last hiking over Gibbon Pass, my exhausting climb from Shadow Lake Lodge to the pass was interrupted by the sound of someone descending the trail in a very big hurry. My first thought was that someone had been injured on the trail and a companion was going for help. As soon as the rushing traveller came into view, I stopped and stepped to the side of the trail, fully prepared to help in any way that I could. But what I saw running down the trail was not a hiker but a young woman in running gear. When she saw me she stopped to chat and told me that she worked at the lodge and regularly ran to the top

Above: Grizzly bears can be seen anywhere in the Canadian Rockies, at any time. Often they become accustomed to having people around and will ignore anyone who keeps their distance from them. This one, in Whistling Valley, pretended that it did not know I was around, while I observed it from a safe distance for more than half an hour.

Right: Peyto's talc mines can be seen above the tailings scree high above Natalko Lake. A road leading up to the mine openings can be seen on the left of the image. The footings of old buildings and blocks of talc that can be seen on the shore of the lake are not apparent in this photo.

of the pass as part of her weekly workouts. She was obviously very fit, as the trail was extremely steep. She was apologetic for having startled me, but the pleasantness of our encounter more than compensated for my undue alarm.

When I embark on long hikes, such as this one, my wife, Cheryl, drops me off at the beginning and picks me up at the end, usually several days later. The pickup times are based on me hiking approximately 30 kilometres per day, depending on the location of campgrounds. Normally all is well, but the entire hike from Shadow Lake was more demanding than I had expected and the final drop from Arnica Lake did me in. I reached the area at the end of a long day, and the steepness of the trail and length of the downhill section slowed my pace. I arrived at our meeting spot at the Vista Lake viewpoint more than two hours late. As dusk fell, I climbed the last bit of trail to the highway and emerged from behind the trail signboard. Meanwhile, Cheryl was approaching the signboard from the other direction with a note in her hand to be posted on the board telling me that she had waited and was now going for help. Fortunately, our last-minute chance meeting avoided what could have been the start of a rather expensive search by the Warden Service. Searches for lost or injured hikers are provided by the wardens as part of their duties, but I was always conscious of not wanting to initiate an unnecessary search because fatigue had kept me from reaching my destination in time. Over six years of solo backcountry hiking to obtain trail information for the *Life of the Trail* series, this was as close as I came to having the search parties called out.

The Highline Trail crosses the old wagon road to the talc mines in the Egypt Lake area but does not follow it. This old road up Pharaoh Creek is mainly of interest to those wishing to use it to access the Egypt Lakes area or to explore the historically significant road and mine at Natalko Lake. The old road is often but not always visible. Strewn along its route are artefacts such as corrugated galvanized steel culverts, steel pipes and sections of corduroy roads. After the shelter at Egypt Lake, signs of the old road disappear until Natalko Lake. There hikers will find traces of old roads, as well as concrete foundations, lumber and many pieces of talc from the mines. Mine entrances are clearly visible high on the side of the mountain south of the lake. An old road curves around the mountain to the south, leading to yet more mine shafts. I knew that the eccentric and reclusive Bill Peyto, who had discovered the mines and worked them for many years, had a cabin several kilometres away at Simpson Pass, but I wondered if he might have another nearer the mine. The available timber in the area west of the lake made it a likely spot, but sadly a thorough search did not turn up any signs of either a cabin or cut trees.

Trail Guide

Distances are adapted from existing trail guides: Patton and Robinson, Potter, Beers, and Eastcott, and from Gem-Trek maps. Distances intermediate from those given in the sources are estimated from topographical maps and from hiking times. All distances are given in kilometres.

Bow River to Vermilion River up Redearth Creek and over Ball Pass

Maps 82 O/4 Banff

82 N/1 Mount Goodsir

Gem-Trek Kootenay National Park

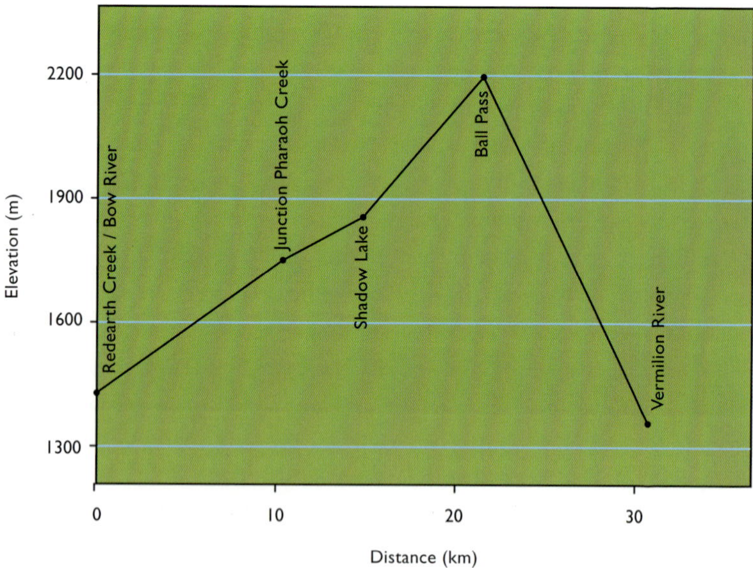

Trailhead

The Redearth Creek parking lot is located on the south side of the Trans-Canada Highway, 20 km northwest of Banff (there is a left turn lane and crossing road), or 10 km southeast of Castle Junction. The trailhead is at a gate in the animal control fence on the southwest side of the parking lot.

The trailhead at the Vermilion River end of the route (described here as the end of the hike) is on the east side of Highway 93, across the road from the Floe Lake–Hawk Creek Parking Lot. This parking area is 22.5 km south of Vermilion Pass and 8.3 km north of the Vermilion Crossing Visitor Centre.

0.0 Animal control fence and gate. The trail climbs to the top of a bank, soon joining an old flat bulldozed road that continues gently uphill to the southwest along Redearth Creek. The trail is largely in the forest. The creek can be heard below on the right and frequent breaks in the trees allow views of the surrounding mountains.

6.9 Bridge over Redearth Creek and Lost Horse Creek Campground (Re6). The trail continues to follow the old road along the creek, which is now on the left.

10.5 Trail junction. The trail up Pharaoh Creek proceeds ahead to the left (south). Keep to the right (west) and start climbing a steep, rough, rocky trail that soon levels out. The trail remains in the forest, with limited views and a lot of boardwalks over wet areas. The trail comes to a small meadow area.

12.7 Shadow Lake Campground (Re14). Immediately ahead is Shadow Lake Lodge. Keep to the right around the lodge cabins.

13.0 Trail junction. The trail to Gibbon Pass goes to the right (northwest). Keep ahead toward the lake. At the lake, a trail leads along the shore to the right. Keep left.

14.0 Cross the lake's outlet on a long bridge. The trail initially follows the south shore of the lake then veers to the left (south) through the forest and starts climbing along Haiduk Creek toward the pass. As the trail climbs it passes small meadows and steep rock walls and crosses bridged streams.

18.3 Trail junction and Ball Pass Junction Campground (Re21). The trail to Haiduk Lake and Whistling Pass goes to the left (southeast). Keep ahead, continuing to climb toward the southwest. You will cross a rocky ridge then steep switchbacks over a rockslide.

21.0 Ball Pass. A Parks Canada signpost marks the Continental Divide at the top of the pass. The trail drops steeply through a narrow valley on the south side of the pass, with Hawk Creek at the bottom to the left (south).

26.0 Enter an area that was completely devoid of vegetation in 2003 as the result of a recent forest fire. There were many dead trees left standing. Continue through the burned-out area on a good trail, generally beside the creek, and steadily drop toward the highway, passing the Hawk Creek gravel pit and camping area.

31.1 Highway 93, just east of the Flow Lake–Hawk Creek parking area and east of the Vermilion River.

Healy Creek to Highway 93 over Healy, Whistling and Gibbon Passes

Maps 82 O/4 Banff

82 N/1 Mount Goodsir

Gem-Trek Kootenay National Park

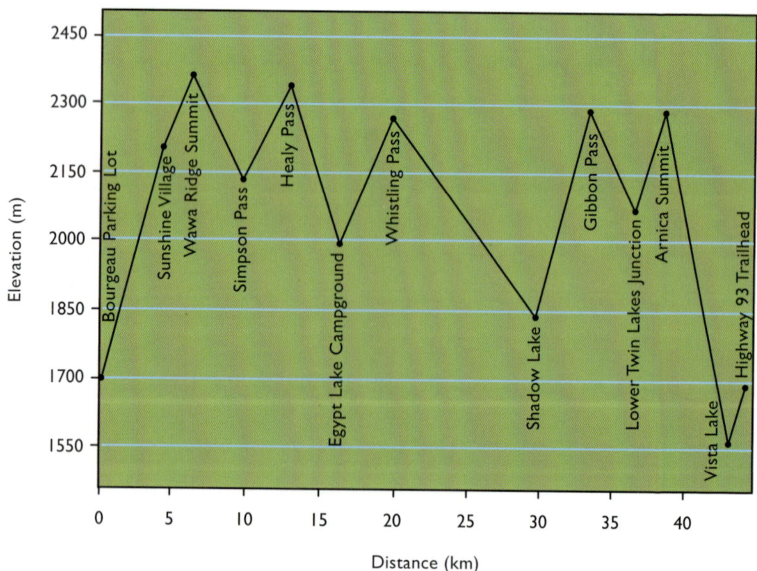

Trailhead

To drive to the Bourgeau Parking Lot (Sunshine gondola station), proceed west of Banff for 9 km on the Trans-Canada Highway and exit at the Sunshine Village interchange. Drive the Sunshine Village Road 9 km southwest to the Bourgeau Parking Lot. The trailhead signboard is just beyond the gondola station terminal building, on the west side of Healy Creek. At the other end of the route, the trailhead on Highway 93 is 8 km west of the Castle Junction interchange and 2 km northeast of the Continental Divide at Vermilion Pass, at the Vista Lake viewpoint and trailhead.

0.0 Healy Pass trailhead. Cross Healy Creek on a bridge and head uphill (south) on a broad gravel road.

0.9 Trail junction. The trail to Healy Pass branches to the right. Continue straight ahead (south) on an old road parallel to the current ski hill access road. The old road soon diverges from the current road and becomes more like a trail. It follows Sunshine Creek, crossing it several times, generally on rocks, and continues climbing. After a rocky uphill section, the trail rejoins the old road then follows a dry creek bed to a steep-walled canyon. The trail continues steeply uphill along the left side of the canyon then follows the creek bed. After passing the Wolverine Express Chair, the trail proceeds under a power line, which it follows to Sunshine Village.

4.2 Gondola station at Sunshine Village. The trail curves around to the right (north) and heads uphill. The well-made trail climbs the ski run. As it reaches the top of Wawa Ridge, the surrounding countryside becomes very open, rocky and barren. The top of the Wawa chairlift is to the left.

5.8 Trail Junction. The trail to the left (south) goes to Rock Isle Lake. Continue ahead on a smooth gravel trail for Simpson Pass.

6.1 Wawa Ridge summit.

6.5 Monarch Viewpoint. Look out over broad meadows and towering mountains. The trail starts to drop steeply then proceeds along the top of a high ridge parallel to the Healy Creek valley. The terrain is open, rugged and undulating, with rocky cliffs on the left. The trail continues along the cliffs, enters the forest and continues to drop until it reaches a small meadow.

9.8 Simpson Pass and trail junction, marked with interprovincial boundary markers and a Parks Canada sign. The trail to the right leads to the Healy Pass trail and Healy Creek Campground (E5). Continue ahead (west) along a stream up a steep hill and continue to climb, mainly in the forest.

10.2 Trail junction. The trail to Eohippus Lake goes to the left (south). Continue ahead (west). The trail climbs a short distance to open meadows with small lakes. It skirts around the south end of a large lake then continues along the meadow past another two small lakes.

11.8 Trail junction. The trail joins the Healy Pass trail. Turn left and proceed west on a good trail that climbs steadily through the open larch-covered meadow.

13.3 Healy Pass. Start downhill through a larch-covered open area. The trail gradually enters the forest then continues downhill into mature forest until it reaches a meadow at the bottom of the valley.

16.5 Trail junction. The trail to Redearth Pass goes to the left (south). The warden cabin is to the right on the edge of the meadow. Continue ahead across a bridged stream and up a small ridge to the shelter and Egypt Lake Campground (E13). The Pharaoh Creek trail goes to the right (north) from the shelter. Continue left (southwest) toward Whistling Pass.

17.0 Trail junction. The trail to Egypt Lake branches to the left (south). Continue straight ahead as the trail climbs the side of a steep old avalanche path, including a very rugged and scenic section with switchbacks. The trail eventually reaches a flat open valley, with the Pharaoh Peaks very visible on the right, then it crosses a ridge and drops into a narrow valley.

18.4 Trail junction. The trail to Scarab–Mummy Lakes goes to the left (south). Continue ahead (west) across the small meadow and begin climbing toward Whistling Pass. Near the top of the pass, the trail becomes very open, offering spectacular views of the lake and mountains behind. The trail passes a small lake on the left (southwest) then crosses an open meadow.

19.8 Whistling Pass. The trail drops through an open meadow then enters a steep rocky area before crossing another meadow and dropping steeply through a mature forest.

22.0 Haiduk Lake. The trail skirts around the right (northeast) shore of the lake along the edge of a wetland meadow. As it passes a sheer cliff on the left, a cleft in the mountains (Ball Pass) becomes visible straight ahead. The trail drops steeply to a broad flat meadow. Keep left along this meadow and follow a creek upstream, then cross it on a bridge.

25.2 Trail junction and Ball Pass Junction Campground. The trail to Ball Pass goes to the left (south). Turn right (north) for Shadow Lake. The trail continues along the edge of a wetland meadow with good views of the mountains. It crosses several bridged streams then veers to the right (east) into the forest.

29.5 Shadow Lake. Take the bridge across the outlet stream (Redearth Creek) and follow a heavily used path into the woods at the end of the lake. The trail follows the edge of the meadow in which Shadow Lake Lodge is situated, passing just behind some of the cabins.

30.5 Trail junction. The Redearth Creek trail continues ahead (northeast). Turn left (north) toward Gibbon Pass. The trail starts climbing steadily toward the pass. At first it is extremely steep with the occasional switchback, but it soon levels out and climbs more gently through an open larch forest before reaching a broad flat plateau marked with a cairn. This is not the top of the pass. Continue the gentle climb through a beautiful alpine meadow covered with larch trees.

33.6 Gibbon Pass. The trail begins to drop along a meadow then enters a narrow rocky valley with a view of Lower Twin Lake. The trail continues to drop through the forest then crosses the lake's outlet stream on a bridge.

36.5 Trail junction. The trail leading to the Trans-Canada Highway leads to the right (northeast). A trail to the left goes to Lower Twin Lake. Continue ahead (northwest) for Upper Twin Lake. The trail climbs through the woods to the top of a ridge then levels out.

37.3 Twin Lakes Campground (Tw7) and upper lake. The trail begins climbing through the trees, becoming more open with good views as the elevation increases. It passes through a small meadow.

38.7 Arnica summit. The trail descends steeply toward a small lake nestled against sheer cliffs.

39.5 Arnica Lake. In the distance, Highway 93 is visible across a very large valley that was burned in a 1968 fire. The trail drops steadily and at times steeply, with switchbacks, through a young pine forest to a long wooden bridge, which marks the end of this long and punishing downhill.

43.1 Vista Lake. The trail skirts the north side of the lake then climbs steadily along the mountainside to the highway.

44.5 Trailhead and Highway 93 viewpoint.

Redearth Creek to Natalko Lake along Pharaoh Creek

Maps 82 O/4 Banff

Gem-Trek Kootenay National Park

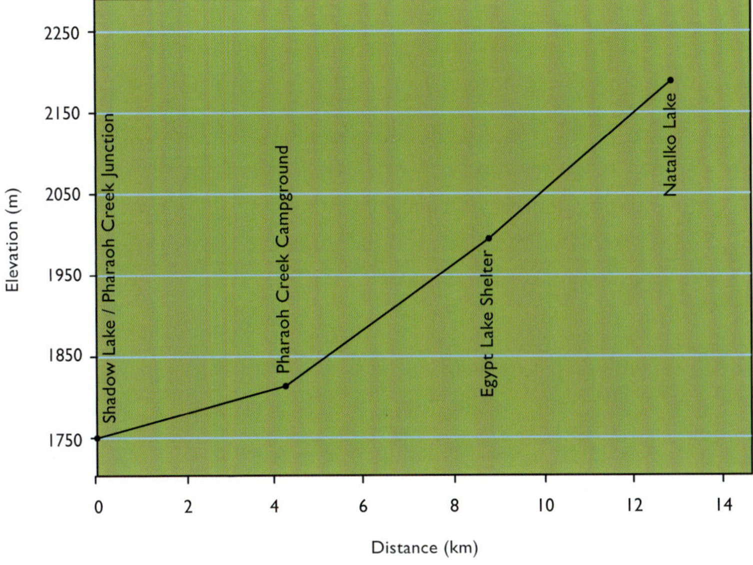

Trailhead

The trailhead is km 10.5 of the Bow River to Vermilion River up Redearth Creek and over Ball Pass trail, described above.

0.0 Trail junction. The trail to Shadow Lake goes ahead (west). Take the trail up Pharaoh Creek to the left (south). The trail was once a road but is now merely a single track.

0.2 Redearth Creek Warden Cabin, at the junction of Pharaoh and Redearth creeks. Cross the bridge in front of the cabin and continue south upstream along Pharaoh Creek. The trail, which sometimes follows the old road, proceeds through a heavily forested area, crossing back and forth across the rocky turbulent creek on bridges. It then passes through a fairly narrow valley.

4.2 Pharaoh Creek Campground (Re16). The trail is now high above the creek, mainly in the forest. Many artefacts from the old road are strewn along its path. It proceeds along a meadow, quite close to the mountains on the right, before crossing a bridge over a major creek coming in from the left (east).

8.2 Trail junction. The trail to Pharaoh Lake goes to the right (west). Continue ahead (south) across an open meadow toward Egypt Lake and the warden cabin, which is visible in the distance.

8.7 Egypt Lake Campground (E13) and shelter. Take the trail to the left toward the warden cabin, cross Pharaoh Creek on a bridge, then immediately turn right (south) on the Redearth Pass trail. The trail is rather faint in places but follows the creek closely, generally in a narrow valley.

11.3 Trail junction. The trail straight ahead (south) follows the creek gently uphill to Redearth Pass and the national park boundary in 500 m. Turn right (west) for Natalko Lake. The trail crosses a small meadow then climbs steadily up a wooded ridge and across a rockslide.

12.7 Natalko Lake. The outline of concrete footings and other artefacts are still visible, as are the mine shafts high above the lake on the side of the mountain to the south.

The foundations of an old mine building on the shore of Natalko Lake are still very evident today, as are blocks of stone from the talc mining days and other artefacts. The mine shafts, which are high on the side of the mountain behind the lake, cannot be seen in this image.

Notes

Introduction

1 F.O. (Pat) Brewster, *They Came West: Pat's Tales of the Early Days* (Banff: no publisher given, 1979), quote from dedication, no page number.

2 A.S. Sibbald, "On Foot in the Rockies," *Ever Upward: A Century of Canadian Alpine Journals* (*Canadian Alpine Journal* digital edition), 7 (1921–22), 104.

Route I

1 For a description of this trip, see Emerson Sanford and Janice Sanford Beck, *Life of the Trail 3: The Historic Route from Old Bow Fort to Jasper* (Calgary: Rocky Mountain Books, 2009), 28–29.

2 Eleanor G. Luxton, *Banff: Canada's First National Park* (Banff: Summerthought, 1975), 49.

3 Unfortunately, there is no written report of this trip, but the details have been worked out by historian A.S. Morton. See Arthur S. Morton, *The Canadian West to 1870-71*, 2nd edition, Lewis G. Thomas, ed. (Toronto: University of Toronto Press, 1973), 467. There is documentation that McGillivray and Thompson actually took a trip across the mountains, but there are no details as to where they went. Their route is largely assumed from the names on Thompson's map. In the early 1800s, natural features, such as lakes, rivers and mountains, were not normally named after important figures but rather after the first person to travel across the mountain, down the river or on the lake in question. Because Thompson named the mountains near White Man Pass "Duncan's Mountains," today's Kootenay River "M'Gillivray's River" and today's Kootenay Lake "M'Gillivray's Lake," and because Thompson put these areas on his map without having travelled in some of these areas at any other time, Morton has assumed that they travelled in those areas. He considers one of the most telling features to be today's Canal Flats. This is a low uninspiring piece of land about three kilometres long between Columbia Lake and the Columbia River, and the Kootenay River drainage that Thompson named Duncan's Portage. Morton explains that to name this feature after one's superior unless that person had been the first to cross it would have been more of an insult than an honour.

4 For details of this trip, see Emerson Sanford and Janice Sanford Beck, *Life of the Trail 2: Historic Hikes in Northern Yoho National Park* (Calgary: Rocky Mountain Books, 2008), 24–32.

5 D. Geneva Lent, *West of the Mountains: James Sinclair and the HBC* (Seattle: University of Washington Press, 1963), 108.

6 Irene Spry, "Routes through the Rockies," *The Beaver* 43:2 (Autumn 1963): 36.

7 James White, "Place Names in Vicinity of Yellowhead Pass," *Ever Upward: A Century of Canadian Alpine Journals* (*Canadian Alpine Journal* digital edition) 6 (1914–15), 107.

8 A.O. Wheeler, "Passes of the Great Divide," *Ever Upward: A Century of Canadian Alpine Journals* (*Canadian Alpine Journal* digital edition), 16 (1926–27), 125.

9 Bill Round, quoted in Peter Ross, "The Fate of Father De Smet's Cross," *Mountain Heritage Magazine* 3:2 (2000): 19. Ross cites a tale told by Bill Round to a Catholic Priest, Father O'Byrne, on a 1963 oral history tape at the Whyte Museum of the Canadian Rockies. As Wilson was reported to be prospecting at the time, his encounter with the cross would have occurred in the 1880s.

10 H.J. Warre, *Overland to Oregon* in 1845, organized by the Public Archives of Canada (Ottawa: Information Canada, 1976), 46.

11 E.J. Hart, *The Place of Bows: Exploring the Heritage of the Banff–Bow Valley, Part I, to 1930* (Banff: EJH Literary Enterprises, 1999), 95.

12 Pierre Berton, *The Last Spike: The Great Railway 1881–1885* (Toronto: McClelland and Stewart, 1971), 148.

13 Aphrodite Karamitsanis, *Place Names of Alberta Volume I: Mountains, Mountain Parks and Foothills* (Calgary: University of Calgary Press, 1991), 267.

14 For more information on the naming of White Man Pass, see page 27.

15 For more information on Father de Smet's cross, see pages 32–37.

16 Don Beers, *Banff-Assiniboine: A Beautiful World* (Calgary: Highline Publishing, 1993), 67.

17 Walter D. Wilcox, "An Early Attempt to Climb Mt. Assiniboine," *Ever Upward: A Century of Canadian Alpine Journals* 2:1 (*Canadian Alpine Journal* digital edition) (1909), 18.

18 Ibid, 20.

19 Ibid.

20 David W. Peyto, ed. *Banff Town Warden* (Calgary: Peyto Lake Books, 2002), 21–22.

21 Sid Marty, "The Silvertip," *Sound Heritage* 5:3 (1976), 26. Revised by Sid Marty, 2009. Reproduced with permission.

22 For details on the history of this route, see *Life of the Trail 3*, page 77.

23 Lawrence Christmas, *Canmore Miners Coal Miner Portraits and Stories* (Calgary: Cambria Publishing, 2002), 27.

24 For information about the history of Old Bow Fort, see *Life of the Trail 3*, pages 30–33.

Route II

1 In *Indians in the Rockies* (Banff: Altitude, 1985), Jon Whyte indicates that Piché, also known as Peechee or Peche, was a Métis who had been raised by the Cree. He became chief of the Mountain Cree, making his home near Lake Minnewanka.

2 George Simpson, "Simpson's Pass," *Tales from the Canadian Rockies,* ed. Brian Patton (Edmonton: Hurtig, 1984), 24.

3 Ibid, 26.

4 Ibid, 27.

5 F.O. (Pat) Brewster, *Weathered Wood: Anecdotes and History of the Banff–Sunshine Area* (Banff: F.O. Brewster, 1977), 22.

6 Walter Wilcox, *The Rockies of Canada* (Surrey, BC: Rocky Mountain Books, 2008), 91–92.

7 For a brief biography of William Twin, see Emerson Sanford and Janice Sanford Beck, *Life of the Trail 1: Historic Hikes in Eastern Banff National Park* (Calgary: Rocky Mountain Books, 2008), 132–33.

8 Jim Deegan, "Prospector of Talc Mountain," in *Timberland Tales*, Jim Deegan and John Porter (Banff: The Peter Whyte Foundation, 1977). Reprinted with permission.

9 "Report of the Healy Creek Camp," *Ever Upward: A Century of Canadian Alpine Journals* (*Canadian Alpine Jounral* digital edition) 8 (1917), 118.

10 Simpson, 24.

11 Aphrodite Karamitsanis, *Place Names of Alberta Volume I: Mountains, Mountain Parks and Foothills* (Calgary: University of Calgary Press, 1991), 166.

12 Barbara Huck and Doug Whiteway, *In Search of Ancient Alberta* (Winnipeg: Heartland Publications, 1998), 110.

13 R.W. Sandford, *Lake Minnewanka, The Spirit and the Waters: A Banff History* (Banff: Lake Minnewanka Boat Tours, 1999), 11. For a brief biography of the Rev. Rundle, see Emerson Sanford and Janice Sanford Beck, *Life of the Trail 3: The Historic Route from Old Bow Fort to Jasper* (Calgary: Rocky Mountain Books, 2009), 39–41.

14 William Vaux, Notes from CPR trip, 1894, June 28 to August 4, Vaux fonds, Whyte Museum of the Canadian Rockies, M107, 16.

15 Walter Wilcox, *The Rockies of Canada* (Surrey, BC: Rocky Mountain Books, 2008), 5–6.

16 Ellis L. Yochelson, *Smithsonian Institution Secretary: Charles Doolittle Walcott* (Kent, Ohio: Kent State University Press, 2001), 270.

17 Sandford, 29–37.

18 For a brief biography of Bill Peyto, see Emerson Sanford and Janice Sanford Beck, *Life of the Trail 2: Historic Hikes in Northern Yoho National Park* (Calgary: Rocky Mountain Books, 2008), 46–48.

19 Nicky Brink and Stephen R. Bown, *Forgotten Highways: Wilderness Journeys Down the Historic Trails of the Canadian Rockies* (Victoria: Brindle & Glass Publishing, 2007), 105–109.

Route III

1 See Route I on pages 30–32 for details of this trip.

2 Geneva D. Lent, *West of the Mountains: James Sinclair and the HBC* (Seattle: University of Washington Press, 1963), 234.

3 Irene Spry, *The Palliser Expedition: The Dramatic Story of Western Canadian Exploration 1857–1860* (Calgary: Fifth House, 1995), 140.

4 Irene Spry, ed., *The Papers of the Palliser Expedition: 1857–1860* (Toronto: The Champlain Society, 1968), 24.

5 Although most evidence indicates that Palliser crossed North Kananaskis Pass, historian J.N. Wallace explains that it is possible that he crossed South Kananaskis Pass. J.N. Wallace collection, Bruce Peel Special Collections Library, University of Alberta. Others believe that he actually crossed Elk Pass just south of the Upper Kananaskis Lake. See Ernie Lakusta, *Canmore and Kananaskis History Explorer* (Canmore: Altitude, 2002), 51.

According to Wallace, Palliser named the pass after a legendary Aboriginal man who recovered from a near-fatal blow with an axe. The river flowing through its gorge also bears his name. It is unclear whether Palliser named both the river and the pass, or merely extended the Aboriginal name for the river to the pass. Wallace feels that the former is the more likely, as Aboriginal people did not normally name features after people.

6 Spry, 1968, 24.

7 Richard Thomas Wright, *Overlanders: 1858 Gold* (Saskatoon: Western Producer Prairie Books, 1985,) 45.

8 Ibid, 111.

9 For more information on Southesk's journey, see Emerson Sanford and Janice Sanford Beck, *Life of the Trail 4: Historic Hikes in Eastern Jasper National Park* (Calgary: Rocky Mountain Books, 2009), 54–64.

10 Eleanor G. Luxton, *Banff: Canada's First National Park* (Banff: Summerthought, 1975), 50.

11 For details of this portion of their journey, see Route VI on page 173.

12 Ruth Oltmann, *My Valley: The Kananaskis* (Calgary: Rocky Mountain Books, 1997), 25–26.

13 Lillian Gest fonds, Whyte Museum of the Canadian Rockies, M67:41.

14 For the story of Old Bow Fort, see Emerson Sanford and Janice Sanford Beck, *Life of the Trail 3: The Historic Route from Old Bow Fort to Jasper* (Calgary: Rocky Mountain Books, 2009), 30–33.

Route IV

1 Quoted in Esther Fraser, *The Canadian Rockies: Early Travels and Explorations* (Edmonton: Hurtig, 1969), 42.

2 By travelling along the spine of the Continental Divide east of the White Man Pass trail then scrambling approximately one-third the way up a small unnamed mountain, the view of Mount Assiniboine in the image shown in the text can be seen. Only the very top of the mountain can be seen from this vantage point, and it does not look imposing, except that it did have a considerable amount of snow on it in mid-August 2009. It is also possible that Mount Assiniboine could be viewed by climbing a high ridge to the west of the trail. Either way, it is unlikely that Father de Smet would go to these efforts and not mention it in his notes of the trip. Father de Smet was a portly man not taken to mountain climbing.

3 Lillian Gest, *History of Mount Assiniboine* (Lillian Gest, 1979), 11.

4 E.J. Hart, *Diamond Hitch: The Early Outfitters and Guides of Banff and Jasper* (Banff: Summerthought, 1979), 16.

5 Gest, 12.

6 Quoted in Gest, 12.

7 For details of this trip, see Emerson Sanford and Janice Sanford Beck, *Life of the Trail 2: Historic Hikes in Northern Yoho National Park* (Calgary: Rocky Mountain Books, 2008), 94.

8 Gest, 13.

9 Hart, 24–25.

10 Walter Wilcox, *The Rockies of Canada* (Surrey, BC: Rocky Mountain Books, 2008), 49.

11 Ibid, 51.

12 Ibid, 52–53.

13 Ibid, 55.

14 Tom Longstaff, *This is My Voyage* (London: John Murray, 1950), 221.

15 For information on this route, see Route VI below, pages 182–85.

16 For information on this route, see Route V below, pages 159–61.

17 Ruth Oltmann, *Lizzie Rummel: Baroness of the Rockies* (Calgary: Rocky Mountain Books, 1983), 58–74.

Route V

1 Walter Wilcox, *The Rockies of Canada* (Surrey, BC: Rocky Mountain Books, 2008), 68.

2 Ibid, 71.

3 For details of this portion of the trip see Route VI below, pages 167–168.

4 For more information on their travels, see Emerson Sanford and Janice Sanford Beck, *Life of the Trail 2: Historic Hikes in Northern Yoho National Park* (Calgary: Rocky Mountain Books, 2008), 101–107.

5 James Outram, *In the Heart of the Canadian Rockies* (Surrey, BC: Rocky Mountain Books, 2007), 29–30.

6 Ibid, 32–33.

7 Ibid, 41.

8 Ibid, 43.

9 Ibid, 44.

10 Gertrude, E. Benham, "The Ascent of Mount Assiniboine," *Ever Upward: A Century of Canadian Alpine Journals* (*Canadian Alpine Journal* digital edition) 1:1 (1907), 71–73.

11 Jimmy Simpson, "Days Remembered," *American Alpine Journal* 19 (1974): 48.

12 For more information on their travels, see Sanford and Sanford Beck, *Life of the Trail 2*, 101–107.

13 "Report of the Assiniboine Camp, 1920," *Ever Upward: A Century of Canadian Alpine Journals* (*Canadian Alpine Journal* digital edition) 8 (1921–22), 154–57.

14 For a brief biography of Charles Walcott, see Sanford and Sanford Beck, *Life of the Trail 2*, 120–22.

15 Ellis L. Yochelson, *Smithsonian Institution Secretary: Charles Doolittle Walcott* (Kent, Ohio: Kent State University Press, 2001), 190.

16 *Trail Riders of the Canadian Rockies Bulletin* 13 (March 1927): 1. For more information on the Trail Riders of the Canadian Rockies, see Sanford and Sanford Beck, *Life of the Trail 2*, 132–33.

17 Lorne Tetarenko and Kim Tetarenko, *Ken Jones: Mountain Man* (Calgary: Rocky Mountain Books, 1996), 54.

18 For more information on this route, see Route VII below, page 199.

19 Tetarenko, 57.

20 For more information on this route, see Route VI below, pages 173–79.

21 Cliff Kopas, *Packhorses to the Pacific: A Wilderness Honeymoon* (Victoria, BC: TouchWood Editions, 2004), 23–33. For more of the Kopas story, see Sanford and Sanford Beck, *Life of the Trail 2*, 172; Ibid, *Life of the Trail 3: The Historic Route from Old Bow Fort to Jasper* (Calgary: Rocky Mountain Books, 2009), 75–76, 131 and 179–81; and Ibid, *Life of the Trail 4: Historic Hikes in Eastern Jasper National Park* (Calgary: Rocky Mountain Books, 2009), 40–41 and 131.

22 See the trail guide for the Healy Creek to Highway 93 section, pages 216–20 below.

23 This photo can be found in E.J. Hart, *Diamond Hitch: The Early Outfitters and Guides of Banff and Jasper* (Banff: Summerthought, 1979), 69; and Emerson Sanford and Janice Sanford Beck, *Life of the Trail 1: Historic Hikes in Eastern Banff National Park* (Calgary: Rocky Mountain Books), 135.

24 For a brief biography of Bill Peyto, see Sanford and Sanford Beck, *Life of the Trail 2*, 46–48.

Route VI

1 This is Duncan McGillivray's route. See Route I above.

2 This route consists of an extension of Route VI, followed by James Sinclair's route. See Route III above.

3 See Route V above for details of this trip.

4 Walter Wilcox, *The Rockies of Canada* (Surrey, BC: Rocky Mountain Books, 2008), 74–75.

5 E.J. Hart, *Jimmy Simpson: Legend of the Rockies* (Canmore: Altitude, 1991), 28.

6 Quoted in Don Beers, *Banff-Assiniboine: A Beautiful World* (Calgary: Highline, 1993), 142.

7 Elizabeth Brown Robbins, "Ten New York Girls on Horseback Through the Canadian Rockies," *Illustrated Canadian Forest and Outdoors* 20:7 (July 1924): 435.

8 Hart, 115.

9 For details on the North Kananaskis Pass portion of the trip, see Route III above, page 102.

10 Beers, 38.

11 The Goat Creek to Spray Lakes portion of the tour is part of Wilcox's Route (Route VI). The Spray Lakes to Bryant Creek portion of the tour is described in Route I above, McGillivray's Route, pages 49–50.

12 A.C. Leighton fonds, Whyte Museum of the Canadian Rockies, M214/V727.

13 Ibid.

14 For details of this trip. see Route I above on pages 47–51.

15 Ruth Oltmann, *My Valley: The Kananaskis* (Calgary: Rocky Mountain Books, 1997), 24. See Route III above, page 101, for details of this portion of the journey.

16 Irene Spry, *The Palliser Expedition: The Dramatic Story of Western Canadian Exploration 1857–1860* (Calgary: Fifth House, 1995), 297–98.

17 Val A. Fynn, "First Ascent of Mt. King George," *Ever Upward: A Century of Canadian Alpine Journals* (*Canadian Alpine Journal* digital edition) 11 (1920), 29–45.

18 J.W.A. Hickson, "The British and French Military Groups Revisited, 1928," *Ever Upward: A Century of Canadian Alpine Journals* (*Canadian Alpine Journal* digital edition) 17 (1928), 39.

19 Ibid, "A Mountaineering Trip to the British and French Military and Assiniboine Groups, 1919," *Ever Upward: A Century of Canadian*

Alpine Journals (*Canadian Alpine Journal* digital edition) 11 (1920), 20.

20 Henry S. Hall, Jr., "The First Ascent of Mt. French," *Ever Upward: A Century of Canadian Alpine Journals* (*Canadian Alpine Journal* digital edition) 12 (1921–22), 35–46.

21 "Report of the Palliser Pass Camp, 1922," *Ever Upward: A Century of Canadian Alpine Journals* (*Canadian Alpine Journal* digital edition) 13 (1923), 192.

22 For information on White Man Pass, see Route I on pages 27–43.

23 For information on North Kananaskis Pass, see Route III on pages 92–102.

Route VII

1 Conrad Kain, *Where the Clouds Can Go*, original forewords by J. Monroe Thorington & Hans Gmoser, new foreword by Pat Morrow, Edited, with additional chapters, by J. Monroe Thorington (Calgary: Rocky Mountain Books, 2009), 365.

2 Browne family fonds, Whyte Museum of the Canadian Rockies, M473/V39/2.

3 Quoted in Brian Patton and Bart Robinson, *The Canadian Rockies Trail Guide*, Seventh Edition Revised (Banff: Summerthought, 2000), 64.

4 Don Beers, *Banff–Assiniboine: A Beautiful World* (Calgary: Highline Publishing, 1993), 99.

5 Ibid.

6 Patton and Robinson, 76.

7 A.S. Sibbald, "On Foot in the Rockies," *Ever Upward: A Century of Canadian Alpine Journals* (*Canadian Alpine Journal* digital edition) 12 (1921–22), 99.

8 The Twin Lakes were first visited by geologist George M. Dawson in 1884.

9 Gary Bret Kines, *Chief Man-of-Many-Sides: John Murray Gibbon and his Contributions to the Development of Tourism and the Arts in Canada* (Ottawa: UMI Dissertation Services, Carlton University, 1988), 90.

10 *Trail Riders of the Canadian Rockies Bulletin* 19 (February 1929): 1.

11 For more information on Bill Peyto's prospecting activity, see Route II above on pages 68–71.

12 Beers, 87.

13 In 1929 the CPR decided to build a substantial rest cabin near Shadow Lake. The cabin was sold to Brewster Transportation in 1938. The original cabin was remodelled into a lodge and, with the addition of six new cabins in 1991, became Shadow Lake Lodge.

14 *Trail Riders of the Canadian Rockies Bulletin* 23 (May 1930): 1.

15 For more details of this trip, see Route V on pages 152–53.

16 Lorne Tetarenko and Kim Tetarenko, *Ken Jones: Mountain Man* (Calgary: Rocky Mountain Books, 1996), 54–59.

17 Ibid, throughout.

Image Credits

Page 28 David Thompson and Duncan McGillivray are considered by some scholars to be the first white men to have crossed the Continental Divide over White Man Pass. They made the trek in 1801, and the name of the pass likely refers to them. This is an artist's depiction of what Thompson may have looked like, since no image exists. (Compliments of Algonquin Park Visitor Centre)

Page 29 This portion of David Thompson's great map of the Northwest shows Duncan's Mountains and M'Gillivray's River. The names are both taken as evidence that McGillivray and Thompson crossed White Man Pass. (Take from Arthur S. Morton, "The Last of Fort George and Duncan M'Gillivray," in *The Journal of Duncan M'Gillivray of the North West Company at Fort George on the Saskatchewan, 1794–5* [Toronto: Macmillan, 1929], 13.)

Page 35 Father Pierre Jean de Smet was a Jesuit priest from the Oregon Territory who crossed White Man Pass on a mission of peace to the Blackfoot peoples. He failed to find the Blackfoot and today is best known in the region for the cross he erected near the top of the pass. (Whyte Museum of the Canadian Rockies, V701/LC-218)

Page 38 Major A.B. Rogers, well-known for his picturesque profanity, traversed wild untravelled country through the Brisco Range to cross White Man Pass and meet up with his men on the Bow River. (Glenbow Museum and Archives, NA-1949-1)

Page 40 Colonel Robert O'Hara (left), whose name is immortalized in one of the most beautiful areas of the Rockies, was a loner who passed through Whiteman's Gap in an attempt to reach Mount Assiniboine from the east. He is seen here with Tom Wilson, the man purported to have burned Father de Smet's cross near White Man Pass. (Whyte Museum of the Canadian Rockies, V701/LC-105)

Page 63 Governor George Simpson of the Hudson's Bay Company was the first European to pass through Devil's Gap to the Ghost Lakes and Lake Minnewanka. As well, he went on to become the first European to pass through the present-day Banff area. (Library and Archives Canada, C-044702)

Page 67 At the top of Simpson Pass, George Simpson and John Rowand stopped to carve their initials and the year on a tree. The fallen tree containing the inscription was found 63 years later. The register now resides in the Banff Park Museum. (Whyte Museum and Archives, V90-278)

Page 69 Brothers Joshua (l) and William Twin were prominent figures in late-nineteenth- and early-twentieth-century Banff. William was a great tracker who managed to follow the path of a lost prospector for two days until his whereabouts were determined. (Glenbow Museum and Archives, NA-714-38)

Page 69 Bill Peyto was an eccentric but very competent guide and later park warden who built a cabin near Simpson Pass. He spent much of his life there as a recluse, prospecting and working his talc mine. (Whyte Museum and Archives, NA-66-465)

Page 75 Reverend Robert Rundle was a Methodist minister who spent eight years working with Aboriginal peoples on the plains south of Edmonton. He ventured into the mountains twice, and on one trip spent several days camped on the shores of Lake Minnewanka. (Glenbow Museum and Archives, NA-589-3)

Page 77 This dam, built on Devil's Creek in 1895, was intended to moderate the water level at the wharf at Minnewanka Landing. The original village on Lake Minnewanka was flooded by later dams. (Whyte Museum and Archives, 03.6 H38 page 72)

Page 78 Predators take advantage of the fact that the shore of Lake Minnewanka is often visited by bighorn sheep. Tourists in a small boat were able to capture this remarkable image of a cougar taking down a bighorn sheep on the lakeshore. (Courtesy Shawn Geniole, Tahni Phillips, Kayla Pronger, Paige Baker and Chris Phillips)

Page 95 James Sinclair was a Métis born north of Fort Garry and educated in Scotland. He led two large groups of Red River settlers across the mountains to the Oregon Territory. The second trip involved a very difficult crossing of North Kananaskis Pass. (Royal British Columbia Museum and BC Archives, A-01741)

Page 101 Henry G. Bryant explored with his friend Walter Wilcox in the Mount Assiniboine and Kananaskis Lakes region. The stream leading from Assiniboine Pass to the Spray River was named Bryant Creek in his honour. (Whyte Museum and Archives, AAJ, Vol. 5, 1943-5, p. 168–69)

Page 101 Walter Wilcox explored extensively in the Rocky Mountains, pioneering the route east from Mount Assiniboine along Bryant Creek to the Spray River. He later explored the Kananaskis Lakes region to the south, making it as far as the top of North Kananaskis Pass. (Whyte Museum and Archives, AAJ, Vol. 5, 1943-5, p. 168–69)

Page 102 Lillian Gest spent most summers of her adult life in the Canadian Rockies, often accompanying her friend Caroline Hinman on her Off the Beaten Track tours. Gest enjoyed hunting and fishing and is seen here with the spoils of one of her fishing adventures. (Whyte Museum of the Canadian Rockies, V-225/PD-6, p. 68)

Page 102 In the first two decades of the twentieth century, Caroline Hinman led her Off the Beaten Track tours throughout the Canadian Rocky Mountains. Her 1926 tour took a group from the Kananaskis Lakes over North Kananaskis Pass to the Palliser River. (Whyte Museum of the Canadian Rockies, V-225/PD-8)

Page 119 George Dawson was a brilliant scholar and skilled surveyor. Few could match his physical endurance despite the fact that a childhood illness left him with a hunchback and the stature of a young boy. This image of him (standing, centre) with fellow surveyors and helpers gives an indication of his size but not his ability. (Glenbow Museum and Archives, NA-302-7)

Page 121 Tom Wilson did not leave any records of his travels, but his route over Ferro Pass likely resulted from having been in the vicinity with surveyors. His knowledge of the mountains, which was second to none during the late 1880s, was a boon to his successful outfitting business. (Whyte Museum of the Canada Rockies, V-701/LC-107)

Page 122 Colonel Robert O'Hara explored the Vermilion Pass area and recommended it over Simpson Pass as the best way to access the Simpson River. In spite of its greater length, the Vermilion Pass route continues to be used to reach Ferro Pass. (Whyte Museum of the Canadian Rockies, V-701/LC-3)

Page 124 Samuel Allen conducted most of his explorations in the Rockies in the Lake Louise–Lake O'Hara areas but made two trips to Mount Assiniboine, one over Vermilion Pass and the other over Simpson Pass. (Whyte Museum of the Canadian Rockies, M-88/309)

Page 147 Reverend James Outram (centre) and climbing guides Christian Häsler (left) and Christian Bohren, ready for an outing with their climbing paraphernalia ready. The three were the first to climb Mount Assiniboine. (Whyte Museum of the Canadian Rockies, AAJ, V-4,1940-42, p. 190)

Page 149 Charles Walcott, a workaholic who spent almost every summer of the last 20 years of his life studying geology and searching for fossils throughout the Canadian Rockies, is shown here pursuing a rare leisure activity. (Smithsonian Institution Archives, 90-16682)

Page 150 Mary Vaux first came to the Canadian Rockies in 1887 and returned seven years later. For the next 40 years, she spent nearly every summer in her favourite playground. In 1914 she married Charles Walcott and they travelled together, with Mary pursuing her main interest of painting and photographing wildflowers. (Smithsonian Institution Archives, 89-6346)

Page 150 Early Trail Riders of the Canadian Rockies outings tended to be very well attended. A large party, similar to this one photographed at the Lake of Hanging Glaciers, travelled to Mount Assiniboine in 1927. (Whyte Museum of the Canadian Rockies, NA- 66-2402)

Page 151 Arthur Brown, long-time servant of the Walcott family, was treated like a family member. Reputed to be the best camp manager and cook in the Canadian Rockies, he sometimes caused a bit of a stir among locals as there were very few black people in the Rockies at the time. (Smithsonian Institution Archives, 31656)

Page 152 Ken Jones, the first Canadian to become a licensed mountain guide, spent most of his life in the mountains, guiding on both mountaineer exploits and outfitted trips. He is shown here when he worked as a climbing guide at a 1936 Mount Assiniboine camp. (Whyte Museum of the Canadian Rockies, V-157/accn. 7937 (unprocessed) Ken Jones fonds)

Page 169 Following his somewhat audacious start at the age of eight, Pat Brewster went on to become a well-known trail guide and citizen of Banff. This member of the famous Brewster family recorded many of his early exploits in three small books. (Whyte Museum of the Canadian Rockies, V-500/A3-137-1)

Page 172 In 1920 Arthur Wheeler, best known as one of the driving forces in establishing the Alpine Club of Canada, initiated a circular walking tour from Banff along Bryant Creek to Mount Assiniboine. The successful tour inexplicably disappeared six years later. (Whyte Museum of the Canadian Rockies, V-225/PD-9)

Page 172 Despite a stormy and frigid first visit to the Mount Assiniboine area, artist A.C. Leighton returned many times to paint. (Whyte Museum of the Canadian Rockies, NA-66-2220)

Page 175 The Palliser River, along with the lake from which it flows and the nearby pass, is named after Captain John Palliser, leader of the Palliser Expedition. The Captain explored the region around North Kananaskis Pass in 1857, in search of a transportation corridor through the mountains. (Glenbow Museum and Archives, NB-29-1)

Page 179 J.W.A. Hickson was one of the few Canadians who climbed extensively in the Canadian Rockies in the early twentieth century. He is seen here sitting with three unidentified climbing companions standing above. (Whyte Museum of the Canadian Rockies, V-14/ACC 55P/33(15))

Page 198 Artist Belmore Browne was one of few visitors to Shadow Lake during the 1920s. He spent five days in the vicinity with his family and friends. (Whyte Museum of the Canadian Rockies, v-39-1)

Page 200 Jim Brewster was involved in transportation in the Rocky Mountains, beginning with pack and saddle horses and progressing to wheeled transport. He was instrumental in the early planning for a trail from Banff to Lake Louise on the southwest side of the Bow Valley. (Whyte Museum of the Canadian Rockies, NA-66-58/V-439)

Page 200 Parks Commissioner J.B. Harkin rode part of the trail from Healy Creek to Redearth Creek with Jim Brewster and others. He needed no further convincing of the desirability of building a trail from Lake Louise to Banff high on the southwest side of the Bow Valley. (Whyte Museum of the Canadian Rockies, Harkin (1946) v-84/accn. 7743 (unprocessed), Photo by Yousef Karsh, J.B. Harkin fonds)

Page 202 A.S. Sibbald was the first adventurer to plan an extensive trip through the mountains without the aid of pack horses. He is shown here in front of the tent he and his wife used on their 1920 honeymoon backpacking trip from Lake Louise to Sunshine Meadows. (Whyte Museum of the Canadian Rockies, CAJ 1922, p. 116 opposite)

Page 203 Entertainment was always an important part of the trips taken by the Trail Riders of the Canadian Rockies, and a professional singer was often taken along. Wilf Carter is shown here performing for an attentive audience. (Whyte Museum of the Canadian Rockies, NA-66-2036)

Page 204 CPR publicist John Murray Gibbon was instrumental in founding the Trail Riders of the Canadian Rockies. The organization kept records of members' rides and awarded buttons for various combined lengths. Here, Gibbon is presenting a 100-mile (161-kilometre) pin to five-year-old Michael Smith. (Whyte Museum of the Canadian Rockies, NA66-2328)

Page 206 When a large group on horseback is on the move, the riders often get widely separated on the trail. This image of the Trail Riders on top of Gibbon Pass gives an indication of just how long the string can be. (Whyte Museum of the Canadian Rockies, NA 66-2409)

Page 209 Ken Jones was studying to become a physician when the Great Depression interrupted his studies. He later became an engineer but spent most of his life working a variety of jobs in his beloved Canadian Rockies. (Whyte Museum of the Canadian Rockies, ken, 1950 v-157/ACCN. 7937 (unprocessed) Ken Jones fonds)

All other photographs: Emerson Sanford

Bibliography

A.C. Leighton fonds. Whyte Museum of the Canadian Rockies. Banff, Alberta. M214/V727.

Beers, Don. *Banff–Assiniboine: A Beautiful World.* Calgary: Highline, 1993.

Benham, Gertrude, E. "The Ascent of Mount Assiniboine." *Ever Upward: A Century of Canadian Alpine Journals* (*Canadian Alpine Journal* digital edition) 1:1 (1907): 71–73.

Brewster, F.O. (Pat). *They Came West: Pat's Tales of the Early Days.* Banff: F.O. Brewster, 1979.

F.O. (Pat) Brewster. *Weathered Wood: Anecdotes and History of the Banff–Sunshine Area.* Banff: F. O. Brewster, 1977.

Brink, Nicky and Stephen R. Bown. *Forgotten Highways: Wilderness Journeys Down the Historic Trails of the Canadian Rockies.* Victoria: Brindle & Glass Publishing, 2007.

Browne family fonds. Whyte Museum of the Canadian Rockies. Banff, Alberta. M473/V39/2.

Christensen, Lisa. *A Hiker's Guide to the Art of the Canadian Rockies.* Calgary: Glenbow Museum, 1996.

Christmas, Lawrence. *Canmore Miners: Coal Miner Portraits and Stories.* Calgary: Cambria Publishing, 2002.

Deegan, Jim and John Porter. *Timberland Tales.* Banff: The Peter Whyte Foundation, 1977.

Eastcott, Doug. *Backcountry Biking in the Canadian Rockies.* Calgary: Rocky Mountain Books, 1999.

Fraser, Esther. *The Canadian Rockies: Early Travels and Explorations.* Edmonton: M.G. Hurtig, 1969.

Fynn, Val A. "First Ascent of Mt. King George." *Ever Upward: A Century of Canadian Alpine Journals* (*Canadian Alpine Journal* digital edition) 11 (1920): 29–45.

Gest, Lillian. *History of Mount Assiniboine.* Lillian Gest, 1979.

Hall, Henry S. "The First Ascent of Mt. French." *Ever Upward: A Century of Canadian Alpine Journals* (*Canadian Alpine Journal* digital edition). XII (1922): 34–46.

Hickson, J.W.A. "The British and French Military Groups Revisited, 1928." *Ever Upward: A Century of Canadian Alpine Journals* (*Canadian Alpine Journal* digital edition) 17 (1928): 39–47.

Hickson, J.W.A. "A Mountaineering Trip to the British and French Military and Assiniboine Groups, 1919." *Ever Upward: A Century of Canadian Alpine Journals* (*Canadan Alpine Journal* digital edition) XI (1920): 15–29.

Hart, E.J. *Diamond Hitch: The Early Outfitters and Guides of Banff and Jasper.* Banff: Summerthought, 1979.

Hart, E. J. *Jimmy Simpson: Legend of the Rockies.* Canmore: Altitude, 1991.

Hart, E.J. *The Place of Bows: Exploring the Heritage of the Banff–Bow Valley, Part I, to 1930.* Banff: EJH Literary Enterprises, 1999.

Huck, Barbara and Doug Whiteway. *In Search of Ancient Alberta.* Winnipeg: Heartland, 1998.

J.N. Wallace collection. Bruce Peel Special Collections Library, University of Alberta. Edmonton, Alberta.

Kain, Conrad. *Where the Clouds Can Go*, original forewords by J. Monroe Thorington & Hans Gmoser, new foreword by Pat Morrow, Edited, with additional chapters, by J. Monroe Thorington. Calgary: Rocky Mountain Books, 2009.

Karamitsanis, Aphrodite. *Place Names of Alberta, Volume I: Mountains, Mountain Parks and Foothills.* Calgary: University of Calgary Press, 1991.

Kines, Gary Bret. *Chief Man-of-Many-Sides: John Murray Gibbon and his Contributions to the Development of Tourism and the Arts in Canada.* Ottawa: UMI Dissertation Services, Carlton University, 1988.

Kopas, Cliff. *Packhorses to the Pacific: A Wilderness Honeymoon.* Victoria, BC: TouchWood Editions, 2004.

Lakusta, Ernie. *Canmore and Kananaskis History Explorer.* Canmore: Altitude, 2002.

Lent, D. Geneva. *West of the Mountains: James Sinclair and the HBC.* Seattle: University of Washington Press, 1963.

Lillian Gest fonds. Whyte Museum of the Canadian Rockies. Banff, Alberta. M67:41.

Longstaff, Tom. *This is My Voyage.* London: John Murray, 1950.

Luxton, Eleanor G. *Banff: Canada's First National Park.* Banff: Summerthought, 1975.

Marty, Sid. "The Silvertip." Sound Heritage 5:3 (1976): 26.

Morton, Arthur S. "The Last of Fort George and Duncan M'Gillivray." In *The Journal of Duncan M'Gillivray of the North West Company at Fort George on the Saskatchewan, 1794–5, With Introduction, Notes and Appendix by Arthur S. Morton.* Toronto: Macmillan, 1929.

Morton, Arthur S. *The Canadian West to 1870–71*, 2nd edition. Ed., Lewis G. Thomas. Toronto: University of Toronto Press, 1973 (1st edition, 1939).

Oltmann, Ruth. *My Valley: The Kananaskis.* Calgary: Rocky Mountain Books, 1997.

Outram, James. *In the Heart of the Canadian Rockies.* Surrey, BC: Rocky Mountain Books, 2007.

Patton, Brian, ed. *Tales from the Canadian Rockies.* Edmonton: Hurtig, 1984.

Patton, Brian and Bart Robinson. *The Canadian Rockies Trail Guide*, 7th edition, revised. Banff: Summerthought, 2000.

Peyto, David W. ed. *Banff Town Warden.* Calgary: Peyto Lake Books, 2002.

"Report of the Assiniboine Camp, 1920." *Ever Upward: A Century of Canadian Alpine Journals* (*Canadian Alpine Journal* digital edition) 12 (1921–22): 154–57.

"Report of the Healy Creek Camp." *Ever Upward: A Century of Canadian Alpine Journals* (*Canadian Alpine Journal* digital edition) 8 (1917): 118.

"Report of the Palliser Pass Camp, 1922." *Ever Upward: A Century of Canadian Alpine Journals* (*Canadian Alpine Journal* digital edition) 8 (1923): 192–24.

Robbins, Elizabeth Brown. "Ten New York Girls on Horseback through the Canadian Rockies." *Illustrated Canadian Forest and Outdoors* 20:7 (July 1924): 435–37, 473.

Ross, Peter. "The Fate of Father De Smet's Cross." *Mountain Heritage Magazine* 3:2 (2000): 19.

Sandford, R.W. *Lake Minnewanka The Spirit and the Waters: A Banff History.* Banff: Lake Minnewanka Boat Tours, 1999.

Sibbald, A.S. "On Foot in the Rockies." *Ever Upward: A Century of Canadian Alpine Journals* (*Canadian Alpine Journal* digital edition) 7 (1921–22): 93–104.

Simpson, Jimmy. "Days Remembered." *American Alpine Journal* 19 (1974): 42–54.

Spry, Irene. *The Palliser Expedition: The Dramatic Story of Western Canadian Exploration 1857–1860.* Calgary: Fifth House, 1995.

Spry, Irene, ed. *The Papers of the Palliser Expedition, 1857–1860.* Toronto: The Champlain Society, 1968.

Spry, Irene. "Routes through the Rockies." *The Beaver* 43:2 (Autumn 1963): 26–39.

Tetarenko, Lorne and Kim Tetarenko. *Ken Jones: Mountain Man.* Calgary: Rocky Mountain Books, 1996.

Trail Riders of the Canadian Rockies Bulletin 13 (March 1927).

Trail Riders of the Canadian Rockies Bulletin 19 (February 1929).

Trail Riders of the Canadian Rockies Bulletin 23 (May 1930).

Vaux family fonds. Whyte Museum of the Canadian Rockies. Banff, Alberta. M107.

Warre, H.J. *Overland to Oregon in 1845.* Organized by the Public Archives of Canada. Ottawa: Information Canada, 1976.

Wheeler, A.O. "Passes of the Great Divide." *Ever Upward: A Century of Canadian Alpine Journals* (*Canadian Alpine Journal* digital edition) 16 (1926–27): 117–35.

White, James. "Places Names in Vicinity of Yellowhead Pass." *Ever Upward: A Century of Canadian Alpine Journals* (*Canadian Alpine Journal* digital edition) 6 (1914–15): 107–14.

Whyte, Jon. *Indians in the Rockies.* Banff: Altitude, 1985.

Wilcox, Walter D. "An Early Attempt to Climb Mt. Assiniboine." *Ever Upward: A Century of Canadian Alpine Journals* (*Canadian Alpine Journal* digital edition) 2:1 (1909): 17–29.

Wilcox, Walter. *The Rockies of Canada.* Surrey, BC: Rocky Mountain Books, 2008.

Wright, Richard Thomas. *Overlanders: 1858 Gold.* Saskatoon: Western Producer Prairie Books, 1985.

Yochelson, Ellis L. *Smithsonian Institution Secretary: Charles Doolittle Walcott.* Kent, Ohio: Kent State University Press, 2001.

Index

Aemmer, Rudolf 130, 152, 177, 178, 206
Allenby Campground 180, 184
Allenby Pass 152, 184
Allen, Samuel 115, 122–25, 127, 130
Alpine Club of Canada 11, 36, 60, 72, 139, 148, 166, 171, 172, 179, 199, 205, 208
Altrude Creek 17, 195, 205
Arnica Lake 195, 205, 211, 213, 220
Assiniboine Pass 130, 141, 149, 152, 153, 165, 166, 167, 168, 170–72, 177, 179, 180, 183–85
Athabasca Pass 12, 14, 25, 30, 37, 97
Ball Pass 18, 191, 192, 195, 206, 210, 214, 215, 216, 219, 221
Baptie, Robert 177
Barrett, Ed 36
Barrett, Robert L. 114, 115, 120, 127, 130, 131
Belgium Lake 166, 177, 179, 189
Bella Coola 153
Benham, Gertrude E. 139, 145
Blackfoot 25, 29, 32, 34, 35, 37
Black, Reverend William 68
Blakiston, Thomas 99
Bohren, Christian 143, 147
Bourgeau Parking Lot 79, 84, 134, 154, 159, 217
Bow River 17, 25, 27, 29, 30, 37, 39, 44–45, 48, 59, 61, 67, 68, 72, 76, 79, 83, 84, 91, 92, 97, 101, 102, 103, 107, 122, 127, 148, 167, 182, 194, 195, 199, 205, 214, 221
Bow Valley Provincial Park 103, 107
Bow Valley Trail 48
Boyce, Jim 42, 60, 72, 102, 170
Brewster Creek 59, 66, 72, 84, 152, 172
Brewster, Fred 17
Brewster, Jim 194, 195, 199, 200, 202, 205
Brewster, Lade 66
Brewster, Pat 131, 165, 169, 170
Brierly, James 130
Brisco Range 25, 38, 39
Brooks, Max 170
Brown, Arthur 149, 151
Browne, Belmore 194, 196, 198
Bryant Creek 26, 41, 50, 101, 120, 130, 153, 165–68, 170, 171, 172, 173, 177–80, 183, 184, 188
Bryant, Henry 26, 40, 91, 101, 139–140, 165, 167, 173
Burgess Shale 149
Burstall Pass 181, 188
Calgary Power 60, 75, 76
Campbell, Bob 140
Campbell, Colin 94
Campbell, Mary 94
Canadian Pacific Railway (CPR) 25, 36, 39, 59, 60, 67, 72, 73, 91, 101, 130, 147, 152, 158, 194, 195, 199, 202, 204, 206
Canmore 25–27, 30, 39–41, 44, 45, 48, 51, 52, 54, 82, 165–68, 173, 177, 182
Canyon Dam 49, 50, 183, 188
Carrot Creek Summit 23, 30, 31, 44, 51, 53, 55, 82
Carryer, Yule 115, 122
Cascade Mountain 59, 61, 74, 79, 146
Cascade Pond 79, 83
Cascade River 73, 79
Cascade Valley Trail 83
Castle Mountain 195, 205
Cave and Basin 84
Cave Mountain 180, 184
Cerulean Lake 122, 128, 129, 132, 134, 135
Citadel Pass 85, 120, 130, 131, 137, 139, 140, 142, 148, 149, 152–56, 159–61, 167, 171, 177, 185, 206
Clarke, Charles 168
Clovis people 73
Columbia River 25, 32, 37, 68, 80, 94, 96, 99, 100, 104, 111
Continental Divide 28, 32, 34, 37, 59, 66, 67, 72, 79, 85, 89, 90, 98, 104, 116, 128, 139, 140, 144, 148, 149, 152, 155, 160, 161, 163, 180, 184, 189, 191, 210, 211, 216, 217
Copper Mountain 115, 116

Crosby family 139, 152, 195, 206
Cross River 25, 26, 27, 29, 30, 32, 39, 41, 46, 47, 54, 186
Curry Creek 50
Dawson, George 25, 27, 32, 36, 39, 115, 116, 117–19
Deegan, Howard 170
Deegan, Jim 68
de Smet, Father Jean 25, 32, 33–35, 37, 39, 115, 116
Devil's Creek 59, 75, 77
Devil's Gap 24, 30, 31, 44, 51, 52, 57, 59, 61, 63, 73, 74, 76, 78, 79, 81, 82, 92, 134, 159
Devil's Head Lake 73, 74
Drewry, W.S. 120
Duncan's Mountains 27, 29
Eau Claire Camp 179
Eddys, Mr. and Mrs. 165, 173, 178
Edwards, Ralph 127, 130
Egypt Lake 17, 19, 85, 152, 191–95, 199, 202, 206, 210, 211, 213, 218, 222
Elk Pass 101, 102, 173
Elk River Valley 173
Faribault men 99
Farrell (artist) 165, 168
Fatigue Pass 161
Fear, George 120
Ferro Pass 85, 113, 115, 120–22, 126–28, 130–35, 157
Feuz, Edouard 40, 168, 177, 179
Feuz, Walter 207
Floe Lake Parking Lot 191, 215
Fort Edmonton 30, 37, 92, 99, 100
Fort Ellis 96
Fort Garry 30, 37, 91, 92, 94, 95, 100
Fraser River 98, 99
Frissell, Louis 125
Fuller, Jack 177
Fynn, Val 165, 173, 177–79
Gest, Lillian 102, 122
Ghost Lakes 23, 24, 31, 44, 52, 59, 61, 63, 78, 82
Ghost River 23, 44, 52, 59, 60, 74, 75, 76
Gibbon, John Murray 152, 195, 202, 204, 205
Gibbon Pass 191, 195, 202, 205, 206, 210, 211, 215, 219, 220
Goat Creek 49, 165–67, 171, 177, 179, 181, 185, 186
Golden Valley 140, 144, 148, 156, 157, 161
Goodrich–Hastings party 99, 100
Grassi Lakes 26, 45, 46, 49
Haiduk Lake 199, 202, 210, 215, 219
Hall, Henry 166, 179
Harkin, J.B. 194, 199, 200
Harrison, George 152, 153
Häsler, Christian 143, 147
Hawk Creek 191, 195, 206, 210, 215, 216
Healy Creek 39, 59, 66–68, 72, 79, 84, 114, 115, 120, 122, 130, 140, 143, 145, 148, 149, 152, 159, 160, 171, 177, 194, 195, 199, 200, 202, 205, 211, 216–18
Healy, Joe 25, 39
Healy Meadows 79
Healy Pass 39, 72, 79, 84, 85, 114, 153, 154, 193, 194, 199, 211, 216–18
Hector, James 59, 66, 67, 99, 100
Height of the Rockies Provincial Park 17, 181
Henderson, Yandell 125
Hickson, J.W.A. 166, 177, 178, 179
Highline Trail 194, 211, 213
Highway 1A 16, 44, 48, 52, 107
Highwood Pass 102
Hinman, Caroline 91, 102, 165, 166, 170, 171
Hoodoos Viewpoint 83
Howard Douglas Lake 137, 142, 156, 160
Hudson's Bay Company (HBC) 25, 30, 37, 59, 61–66, 93, 95
Invincible Creek 104, 109
Jones, Ken 152, 153, 206, 207–209
Kain, Conrad 196, 207
Kalispell Lake 37
Kananaskis Lakes 89, 91, 92, 97, 101, 102, 103, 106, 163, 173, 179, 187, 191
Kananaskis River 39, 92, 97, 100, 102, 103, 107, 109
Kananaskis Village 47, 103, 104, 105, 106

Karst Springs 180
Kaufmann, Christian and Hans 145
Kootenay Lake 27, 223
Kootenay National Park 81, 85, 214, 216, 220
Kootenay people 26, 27, 32, 92
Kootenay River 23, 27, 29, 30, 32, 36, 57, 66, 80, 86, 87, 89, 96, 98, 104, 107, 111
Kopas, Cliff and Ruth 139, 153
LaCasse, Ulysses 170
Lac Ste. Anne 99
Lake Louise Club 125
Lake Magog 85, 128, 131, 133–135, 139, 144, 148, 149, 152, 155, 157–59, 161, 166, 167, 170, 171, 177, 179, 180, 181
Lake Minnewanka 23, 30, 31, 44, 51, 52, 57–61, 63, 73–79, 81–83
Lang, Harry 127
Lawson Lake 91, 101, 110
Leighton, A.C. 166, 172, 173
Leman Lake 189
Leroy Creek 89–91, 102, 104, 110, 111, 166, 177–79, 181, 187, 189
Longstaff, Katherine 115, 130
Longstaff, Tom 115, 130
Lovgren, Oscar 26, 41–43
Lusk, Tom 41, 101
Marty, Sid 42
Marvel Lake 153, 171, 177, 180, 184
Maskapetoon, Chief 25, 30, 39, 91, 92
Maude Lake 90, 91, 98, 101, 104, 110
McDougall, David 73, 100
McGillivray, Duncan 17, 18, 23, 25, 27–29, 39, 44, 45, 48, 181
McMillan, Donald 59, 67
Métis immigrants 18, 25, 30, 92, 93, 94, 96
M'Gillivray's Lake 27
M'Gillivray's River 27, 29
Michel, Friedrich 40
Minnewanka Landing 59, 75, 77
Mitchell River 115, 120, 127, 130
Mitton, Alex 149
Monarch, the 73
Moose Lodge 179
Moraine Lake 125, 199
Morton, Marcus Jr. 166, 179
Mount Assiniboine Lodge 131, 135, 156–58, 183, 185, 208
Mount Bourgeau 72
Mount Engadine Lodge 182
Mount Inglismaldie 74, 82
Mount Leroy 163
Mount Shark 131, 156, 157
Mount Shark parking area 46, 50, 180–83, 186, 188
Mummy Lake 199, 219
Musgrove, Harry 45
Naiset Cabins 131, 135, 157, 158, 172
Nakiska 103, 108
Natalko Lake 205, 213, 220, 222
National Talc Company 195, 205, 206
New Brunswick party 100
North Kananaskis Pass 89–92, 95–04, 106, 109–11, 163, 166, 167, 171, 175, 178, 179, 181, 189
North Kootenay Pass 98, 99
North West Company (NWC, Nor'Westers) 27, 30, 62
Off the Beaten Track tours 91, 102, 165, 166, 170, 171
Ogden, Peter Skene 37
Og Lake 137, 138, 140, 141, 148, 155, 156, 157, 161, 185
O'Hara, Colonel Robert 26, 40, 115, 122, 194, 196
Old Bow Fort 44, 47, 48, 54, 89, 91, 92, 97–100, 103, 106, 107, 186, 189
Old Fort Creek 44, 48, 107
Oregon Territory 18, 25, 30, 32, 34, 35, 37, 39, 92–95, 100
Outram, Reverend James 18, 139, 143–48
Overlanders 17, 91, 98–100, 103
Padmore 39
Palliser, Captain John 91, 96–99, 103, 174, 175
Palliser Expedition 14, 66, 97–99, 175
Palliser Pass 40, 50, 102, 153, 163-167, 171, 173, 176, 177, 179–81, 183, 187, 189
Palliser Range 78, 176

Palliser River 89, 91, 92, 96, 102, 104, 106, 107, 110, 111, 163, 164, 166, 167, 173, 175–77, 179, 181, 189
Paradise Valley 125, 199
Permanent Camp 41, 171–73, 177
Peyto, Bill 59, 68, 70, 71, 73, 80, 127, 128, 130, 139, 143–45, 147, 154, 155, 194, 205, 212, 213
Pharaoh Creek 194–96, 198, 205, 206, 210, 213, 215, 218, 220–22
Piché, Alexis 61, 73
Police Meadows 156, 161
Porcupine Camp 85, 153, 161
Porcupine Creek 102
Porter, J.F. 115, 127
Potts Outfitting 173
Potts, Waddy 177
Redearth Creek 115, 116, 152, 153, 191, 194–98, 200, 205, 206, 210, 211, 214, 215, 219–21
Redearth Pass 191, 194, 195, 196, 205, 218, 222
Rink, Ralph 179
Robbins, Elizabeth Brown 170
Rockwall area 12, 206
Rocky Mountain House 27, 29, 37
Rogers, Major A.B. 25, 38, 39
Ross, Peter 36
Rowand, John 66, 67
Rummel, Lizzie 131, 132
Rundle, Reverend Robert Terrill 59, 73, 75
Scarab Lake 199, 219
Sentinel Pass 199
Shadow Lake 194–99, 202, 205, 206, 210, 211, 213, 219, 221, 227
Shadow Lake Lodge 195, 206, 215, 219, 227
Shuswap Pass 59, 66, 67
Shuswap people 66
Sibbald, A.S. 202
Sibbald, A.S. and wife 19, 194, 199
Simpson, Frances 64
Simpson, George 24, 25, 30, 32, 37, 39, 57, 59, 61–67, 72–74, 78, 79, 84, 85, 87, 92, 93–95, 120
Simpson, Jimmy 130, 146, 168, 170, 196
Simpson Pass 30, 59, 60, 66–68, 72, 79–81, 84, 85, 98, 115, 116, 120, 122, 127, 128, 130, 133–34, 139, 140, 143, 144, 148, 149, 152–53, 154–55, 159, 179, 194, 195-96, 198, 199, 202, 205, 206, 213, 216–18
Simpson Register 66
Simpson River 59, 66, 68, 80, 82, 85, 113, 115, 120, 122, 126–28, 131–34, 141, 144, 149, 153, 154, 156, 161
Sinclair Canyon 30, 32
Sinclair, Jack 143
Sinclair, James 23–25, 30, 31, 39, 44, 45, 53, 55, 89, 91–98, 102, 103
Sinclair Pass 32, 80
Smith-Dorrien Creek 179
Smith, Dr. Howard 115, 125, 127, 130
Smith, Harry 152, 153, 206
Smith (prospector) 59, 67, 68
Southesk, Earl of 100
Sphinx Lake 199
Spray Lakes 18, 26–30, 37, 40, 41, 45–49, 54, 106, 116, 165–68, 170, 171, 173, 177, 179–82, 185, 186, 188
Spray Lakes West Campground 181
Spray Pass 181, 189
Spray River 25–27, 30, 39–41, 46, 49, 50, 101, 116, 130, 141, 163, 165–68, 170, 171, 173, 177, 179–82, 185–89
Stead, A.C. 166, 177
Steele, L.J. 139, 140, 165, 167
Stewart Canyon 73, 83
Stewart, George 74
Stoney Indian Reserve 48, 107
Stoney language 73, 122, 123, 125
Stoney people 27, 61, 66, 100, 107
Sunburst Lake 129, 131, 132, 135
Sundance Range 180
Sunshine Meadows 79, 85, 131, 139, 140, 142, 144, 148, 152, 171, 194, 195, 202, 205
Surprise Creek 80, 85, 120, 122, 131, 133, 134
Talc Lake 195, 205
Taylor Lakes 199
Temple (prospector) 59, 67, 68
Thompson, David 25, 27–29

Tipperary Cabin 111, 163, 164
Tipperary Creek 111
Trail Riders of the Canadian Rockies 139, 150, 152, 195, 203–206
Trot, Jesse 145
Tunnel Mountain Road 79, 83
Turbine Canyon 102, 104, 110, 179
Turbulent Creek 50
Twin, Joshua 68
Twin Lakes 195, 199, 202, 205, 220
Twin, William 68
Valley of the Rocks 137, 139–42, 144, 145, 148, 152, 155–57, 161, 167, 177
Vaux, William 74
Vavasour, Mervin 18, 25, 37
Verdant Creek 85
Vermilion Lakes 79, 148
Vermilion Pass 60, 72, 115, 120, 122, 124, 126, 130, 194–96, 199, 200, 211, 215, 217
Vermilion River 59, 66–68, 80–82, 85, 86, 120, 126, 131, 134, 159, 195, 206, 214–216, 221
Vista Lake 200, 211, 213, 217, 220
Walcott, Dr. Charles 60, 76, 139, 149, 150, 151
Walcott, Mary Vaux 76, 139, 149, 150
Walling, Willoughby and English 165, 168, 170
Warden Service 12, 15, 60, 72, 165, 170, 213
Warre, Henry James 18, 25, 37
Warrington, George 125
Wassil, Mike 152, 206
Watridge Lake 18, 180, 182
Wawa Ridge 141, 154, 160, 217
Western Talc Holdings 205
Wheeler, Arthur 36, 72, 157, 166, 171, 172, 194, 199
Wheeler's walking tour 166, 171, 172, 179
Whistling Lake 195, 199, 206
Whistling Pass 194, 198, 199, 210, 215, 216, 218, 219
Whistling Valley trail 192, 202, 212
White, James 36
White Man Creek 50, 177
White Man Pass 23, 25–30, 32, 34–41, 44, 46, 47, 50, 51, 54, 59, 92, 98, 116, 120, 168, 177, 181, 183, 186, 188
Whiteman's Gap 26–28, 30, 37, 40, 41, 45, 46, 48, 49, 165–68, 170, 173, 177
Whymper party 143, 147
Wilcox, Walter 26, 40, 41, 59, 74, 91, 101, 115, 123, 127, 130, 139–42, 163, 165, 167, 173
Wilson, Tom 36, 40, 41, 101, 113–15, 120, 121, 127, 131, 133, 137, 139, 140, 146, 154, 168, 194, 196
Wonder Pass 102, 149, 153, 171, 184
Wood, Jim 41, 101
Woodworth, Ben 41, 101
Wright, Scottie 179
Yellowhead Pass 99
Zurfluh, Henry 168

About the Authors

Emerson Sanford, originally from Nova Scotia, first visited the mountains of western Canada in the summer of 1961. Eleven years later, he moved to Alberta and has been hiking ever since. After beginning to backpack seriously with his teenaged daughters in 1990, he began to wonder who cut the trails and how their routing had been determined. Since then, not only has he delved through printed material about the trails, he has also solo hiked every historic route and most long trails between Mount Robson and the Kananaskis Lakes – over 3000 kilometres over five years! Emerson now lives in Canmore with his wife, Cheryl.

Janice Sanford Beck is the author of the best-selling *No Ordinary Woman: the Story of Mary Schäffer Warren* (Rocky Mountain Books, 2001). She has also written the introduction to the latest edition of Mary T.S. Schäffer's *Old Indian Trails of the Canadian Rockies* (Rocky Mountain Books, 2007) and, with Cheryl Sanford, researched the Mary Schäffer Warren portion of the Glenbow Museum's new permanent exhibit, *Mavericks*. Janice is presently masquerading as a flatlander, making her home in Saskatoon with her partner, Shawn, and their three children.

Other Titles in This Series

ISBN 978-1-894765-99-2 | $26.95 | Softcover

ISBN 978-1-897522-00-4 | $26.95 | Softcover

ISBN 978-1-897522-41-7 | $26.95 | Softcover

ISBN 978-1-897522-42-2 | $26.95 | Softcover